Once Upon a Time in Goa

⤬

Once Upon a Time in Goa

❧

An Odyssey to India, Nepal & the Far East

❧

Terry Tarnoff

AVIAN PRESS

San Francisco

An earlier version of this book was published under the title, *The Reflectionist*. This edition has been revised, expanded, retuned and retitled.

Front cover photo from the collection of Yael Aviv. Photographer unknown.

Back cover photo by Andrew Rogers.

ISBN 978-0-9888585-7-2

www.terrytarnoff.com

*For Robert, whose many years of friendship
and support helped make this book possible*

Once Upon a Time in Goa

Row, row, row your boat,
Gently down the stream.
Merrily, merrily, merrily, merrily,
Life is but a dream.

—Christy Minstrels
New York, 1852

"I did what I wanted to do."

—Eight Finger Eddie
Kathmandu, 1975

Chapter 1
The Reflectionist

Tobias Parker is alive again. He died many years ago from a fatal allergic reaction to a glass of red wine, but now he's back because there's unfinished business that needs attending to. This makes absolutely no sense, of course, since Tobias was a fictional character in a book, *The Thousand Year Journey of Tobias Parker,* and bringing him back to life breaks just about every rule of responsible storytelling. But this is a new world we're living in, a world that's gone upside-down, and the old rules simply don't apply. So forget the burial, the eulogies and the wasted tears. Forget the autopsy, the Green Street Mortuary Marching Band and the heavenly klieg lights. None of it matters anymore. Tobias Parker is back from the dead.

This strange turn of events will be explained in due time, but for now there are more important issues to be addressed. Like the fact that the world might be ending. Or that the atmosphere is poisoned. Or that humanity has lost its collective mind. Tobias has important commentary on it all that's been bottled up for decades, but in the interest of proper plotting and character development he's agreed to let things unfold at their own pace. That's part of a bargain he's made with the author. Tobias will have all the space he needs to make his case, while the author will reserve editorial rights to insure that things don't completely fly off the rails.

And who exactly is the author who has agreed to these conditions? Well, me, of course, the idiot who killed off Tobias in the first place, thereby alienating my readers and turning the entire publishing world against me. It was a mistake of historic proportions, a mistake born of hubris and every writer's natural instinct to do irreparable harm to himself whenever possible. In due time I was chastened to the edge of despair—a painter who'd painted himself into a corner, a reporter with nothing left to report, a stoolie without a stool. Then something happened. It occurred to me one day that rather than endlessly bemoan the fact that I'd eliminated my most beloved character, I could simply bring him back to life. After all, who was going to stop me? Some editor at a fancy New York publishing house? Hah! They'd all abandoned me long ago. No, I could do whatever I wanted. Where exactly does it say I can't resurrect my hero on nothing more than a whim? Doesn't the Bible, the most popular book of all time depend exactly on such an unlikely turn of events?

There's a greater purpose to all of this, of course. As I look back upon an eight-year journey I embarked upon many years ago, events get confused, names get lost, and dates get jumbled to such a degree that certain memories have disappeared altogether. I wrote about some of those events in *The Bone Man of Benares,* but half the story remains untold. That's where Tobias comes in. He's my alter ego from an earlier time, the fanciful character I created to help tell my story. Doesn't it make sense, then, that if I were to bring him back from the previous century, Tobias could be relied upon to recount those adventures with much greater detail than I could ever hope to retrieve from this diminished memory of mine? Of course it does. He's me, after all, stripped of all millennial baggage and unencumbered by events of the intervening years.

I head for Golden Gate Park with renewed vision and an ambitious plan. It's time to take the past into my own hands and throw logic out the window. What is logic, anyway? Logic is nothing but an artificial construct designed to assure us that things make sense. But things don't make sense. They never did and they never will. They're not supposed to make sense. That's the beauty of it. We're senseless beings in a senseless universe. The only thing we can count on is our own imagination, and we can't count on that at all.

I park outside the gates of the Botanical Garden and quickly make my way through the Old World Cloud Forest and the California Natives to the Succulent Garden, an unprepossessing patch of dirt that most people pass without noticing. Hidden in the shadows of the arboretum's giant redwoods, a hearty group of succulents sprouts through the cracks and crevices of a barely tended plot of land. The succulents might seem like an afterthought to the grandeur of the trees, but hidden within those puffy leaves and squat stems is a magical ability to store water, change color, and seamlessly blend in with their surroundings.

I glance around to make sure no one's looking and quickly get to work. I start by pulling a withered six-foot stalk from a long-dead century plant and lay its prickly spine along the edge of the pathway. It looks suitable, just about Tobias's height and strong enough to hold some additional weight. Next I spot a plump echeveria, big as a cabbage and misshapen as a mangled brain, and nudge it to the upper end of the century plant. I gather some aeonium for the ears, a clump of crassula for the eyes, and a big gasping sempervivum for the mouth. Then, moving down the stalk, I arrange bits of haworthia and kalanchoe for the arms and legs, delosperma for the reproductive organs, and assorted sedum and portulacaria for the eyelashes and earlobes.

I step back to admire my jumble of foliage. Like any fine piece of art, it leaves much to the imagination and even suggests multiple levels of interpretation. Is it a bleak commentary on death and destruction? An ironic vision of market capitalism and economic collapse? A psychological study of alienation and dissociation? It might be all of those things to the untrained eye but what I see is not a garbage dump of dead twigs and leaves, but rather the veritable promise of life reborn. Of resurrection. Of redemption. Of repatriation.

I walk clockwise around the succulents three times, the way Tibetan Buddhists do when circling a prayer wheel. Not that there's anything particularly Buddhist about my offering, but it's the closest thing to something holy that I remember, so around I go, once, twice, three times, doing various incantations, eyeball shazaams and impromptu hand jives in an attempt to give the moment a kind of heightened significance. It's not much, really, just an amateur's attempt to inject a bit of magic into a world gone cold and digital, but my hocus-pocus falls predictably flat. The foliage just lies there, an inert pile of refuse ready to scatter to the winds.

With my bag of tricks exposed and exhausted I am, alas, left with nothing but a simple command: "Arise!" I call out. It's a bit pathetic, really, just a plaintive cry into the wilderness, but what I lack in methodology I more than make up for in conviction. My plea echoes through the forest with the urgency of a revival preacher beseeching his minions.

Nothing much happens. A squirrel glances up from an acorn it's been nibbling. The branches of a eucalyptus tree shudder slightly. A blue jay flaps off towards the Pacific. But then something happens that would cause me to shout to the heavens were I not left so utterly speechless: Tobias Parker opens his eyes.

It's not much at first. A flickering of the crassula. A fluttering of the sedum. A tiny blink. Then comes a slow pan of the eyeball, first left to right, then up and down. Next a deeper focus, a contraction of the cornea, a wide-angle view of the trees and sky. Then a darting action—left, right, left, right—followed by a squint and a raising of one eyebrow, sarcastic almost, like, *you've got to be kidding me.*

Tobias's fingers begin tapping against the ground, rhythmic at first, then clearly impatient. The forearms move reflexively, as if the muscles were independent of the brain. Within moments the whole pile of branches, stalks, arms and legs is in motion. It's a bit like a frog on a hotplate, twitching this way and that, a hundred muscles going in a hundred different directions, a quivering mass of body parts dancing a crazy calypso. It's not really Frankenstein's monster come alive; it's more like Frankenstein's garden.

And so, some thirty years after his demise, Tobias Parker is back in his body. Not the original lemon, thankfully, but some approximation of what a factory-approved model might look like. This one is long and sleek, well-appointed with a lush interior and a good undercoating. He tries out the parts to make sure they all work. The fingers are soft to the touch and indent slightly when pressed upon. The hands produce a sensation of warmth when held up to the sun. The thumbs are opposable and seem capable of complex movement. The toes are less flexible but appear to be suitable for simple digging.

There are mostly two of everything. Two arms, two legs, two hands, two feet, two eyes, two ears, two testicles, two lungs and two kidneys. Interestingly, there appears to be only one mouth, one heart, and one penis, an observation that will need to be more fully contemplated at a later date. Tobias runs through the rest of the equipment. Pushing here does this, contracting there does that, and squeezing this thing does something altogether different and should definitely be remembered for later. The turning of the head from side to side provides adequate peripheral vision, if not the owl-like range he'd prefer. The eyesight is impressive, the hearing less so, the taste and touch stuff pretty much as expected. On a scale of physiological adaptation, it would rate about a B-minus.

Tobias stretches his arms above his head and checks out the range of motion. It's not bad, especially the way the arms rotate in the shoulder sockets and move independently of each other. He probes a bit further, raising his arms like propellers, but nothing much happens. It's as he suspected. He's earthbound. The lack of feathers was a dead giveaway. All in all, it's a pretty good package, if a little light on optional frills. If he was hoping for a Mercedes, he'd have to make due with a Volkswagen.

"Here," I say, handing him a bundle of clothing. It's a striped linen shirt, some cotton trousers, and an old pair of patent leather shoes.

"Is this the best you could do?" says Tobias, running his hands across the collar.

"I just grabbed whatever was handy."

Tobias slowly, begrudgingly, slips into his new duds. The shirt's a bit crummy and in need of ironing. The pants are frayed at the cuffs and too loose in the waist. Then he gets to the shoes. Ah, the shoes. The shoes are a bridge too far. "What's with the shiny leather?" he says.

"What, you don't like them?"

"Patent leather and linen? Are you kidding? What am I, an insurance salesman?"

I'm not entirely sure what to make of Tobias. More than a quarter of a century has passed, governments have come and gone, countries have been born and died, species have gone extinct, populations have doubled, languages have been lost, economies have collapsed, glaciers have melted, and he wants to talk about patent leather shoes? "So," I say, "you're back."

"There's a good reason for this, I assume?"

"As a matter of fact, there is. I need you to fill in some blanks from the old days, stuff only you'd remember."

Tobias nods knowingly. "I should've known. I'm back for two minutes and already you've got my head in a vise."

"Well, if you'd rather not be here—"

"Relax, relax," he quickly interjects, realizing his position isn't all that secure. "It's not like I was doing much of anything anyway." Tobias stretches his arms, rubs his neck, and lets out a yawn of the decades. "Truth is, I could use a little excitement. You'll fill me in on all the latest?"

"We'll see how it goes," I say, having little intention of overwhelming him with thirty years of depressing news. Where would I possibly begin? Climate change? Depletion of natural resources? The environment? It's all so impersonal and abstract—

"What's big at the movies these days?" he continues. "And music. Oh, and what about the best seller lists?"

With that, I lose it. I'm not sure if Tobias is needling me or not, but he's definitely figured out which buttons to push. "The publishing world's gone to hell in a handbasket!" I blurt out.

"You don't say."

"Nobody's reading anymore. And if they are it's on some crappy device that's also monitoring their heart rate and blood pressure."

"Uh-huh," he says, staring absent-mindedly into the sky. Tobias seems to be more interested in the cloud patterns blowing in off the Pacific than in my tales of woe, and to tell you the truth, maybe I am too.

"How about we check out the rest of the park?" I say.

"Yeah, sure," he says, the idea of exploration igniting his

curiosity. We head for the Fragrance Garden, where Tobias insists on stopping at every seedling and taking a good whiff. Then it's over to the Waterfowl Pond, where a family of swans glides aimlessly across the waters and a couple of sleepy turtles sun themselves along the banks of the lake. Tobias gazes upon a wild profusion of fuchsias with a look of longing. "Do I have a girlfriend?" he asks.

"Not that I know of."

"If I had a girlfriend I'd give her those flowers. I'd cut up the petals and sprinkle them over her bed. I'd make it rain with flowers."

I'm encouraged to see that his sense of romance is undiminished after all these years. We cross through the damp undergrowth of the Mesoamerican Cloud Forest, then head over to the Bamboo Pond, where a single water lily floats upon the surface of the water. "This is one of my favorite spots," I say.

Tobias admires the pagoda temples, ancestral monuments and stone Buddhas that surround the pond. "I like it."

We turn our gaze to the surface of the water, where the pool mirrors a fluff of clouds that brushes across the sky. Tobias is particularly drawn to a lotus flower that floats at the edge of the pond. Lotuses are shrouded in mystery, living in stagnant and murky waters yet emerging every three days in a perfectly pristine state. From out of the muck arises the purest blossom, the universal symbol of rebirth and salvation, and isn't that Tobias himself? Reborn into this alien world, seeking to make sense of his past? He loses himself in the lotus, staring at it for so long I begin to wonder if he's nodded off. I give him a little nudge. "What are you thinking about?" I say.

Tobias blinks a few times as if coming out of a reverie. "I was in the backseat of a van," he says. "We were on some country road. There was a man with a movie camera."

"What kind of van?" I say, wondering how the pond could

possibly elicit such an unusual vision.

"Does it really matter?" he says with a hint of exasperation. "I'm telling you about a man with a movie camera and you want to know what kind of van he's driving?"

"I'm just trying to make the connection," I say, feeling a bit foolish. I decide not to push it. Everything in its own time. We lean back against a thicket of bamboo and look out across the park to Lincoln Avenue and a stretch of nondescript apartment buildings. With their big bay windows, beige shades, iron verandas and squared-off doorways, they seem completely at odds with their surroundings. Even the hibiscus growing along the walls feels strangely muted and unenthusiastic. I suspect that if we were to return to this spot a few hundred years from now, the trees would be gone, the pond would be dried up, and the paths would be grown over with an encroaching jungle, but those buildings would still be there, a stark reminder of a past that was teetering on the edge of collapse.

We glance back into the bamboo pond and are immediately transported into a more welcoming world. A bearded iris floats at the water's edge and a dwarf conifer reflects a bright swatch of mustard yellow onto the surface. Even the reflection of the building from across the street becomes more interesting, especially when a ripple of water stretches its shape into a kind of shimmering tower. When seen through the water the whole structure appears tilted and out of joint. The walls tremble, the roof sways, the windows move back and forth, and the hibiscus oscillates unpredictably from side to side. What had been a stark, uninviting structure takes on a new life as the waves and currents ebb and flow. Reflected in the water, the big concrete box turns into a living, breathing plaything, like a darkened theatre flinging open its doors.

"I see a woman in the window," Tobias says, getting lost in the reflection of the building in the pond. "She's staring out onto the street, like maybe she's waiting for someone. I think it's me."

"Sure, that sounds about right."

He watches intently, studying the vision as it undulates in the currents. "Yeah, definitely. She's definitely waiting for me." Tobias continues, his voice steady and assured but strangely monotone at the same time, as if he were reciting from a trance. "Her skin is creamy, her hair's done up in a kind of swirl with a few locks falling aimlessly across her cheeks, her lips are painted the crimson red of desire, she wonders where I am, she checks herself in the mirror, glances out the window again, it's all shimmery, every-thing's in motion, it's hard to tell what's up and what's down, the windows move into one another, the roof droops and touches the garden, the fire escapes dance side to side, everything's alive, there's artwork inside, it's floating up the stairs and bursting out the windows, flowers are sprouting in the doorways, fish are swimming through the living room, birds are flying across the bedroom walls—"

I stare at Tobias in a kind of hypnotic awe. "Tell me about the man with the movie camera," I say.

"Through the water?"

"Through the way you remember him."

Tobias leans closer to the pond, getting lost in the ripples of the waves. Characters shimmer through like apparitions, some of them exaggerated by the crests of water, some made flat by the shallows. Mountains and deserts appear, expanding and contracting, some larger than life, some disappearing into the undertow. "It's a jumble of memories," he says, "things out of order, pieces that float in and out."

"Tell me what you see in the ripple of the waves," I say.

"Okay, then," he says, staring into the reflections in the pond, "I'll tell you what I remember, every bit of it. I'll tell you everything you want to know—"

Chapter 2

The Summer of Near Misses

It was 1968, the summer of near misses. I'm not sure if I was chasing events or if they were chasing me, but somehow or other I managed to stay just outside the maelstroms that were swirling everywhere and consuming everything. Martin Luther King had been assassinated only months before, Bobby Kennedy just weeks later, and the entire world felt as if it was coming apart at the seams. For me, it was the summer of my junior year in college, the summer I nearly got arrested, the summer I nearly got deported, the summer I nearly got killed, and the summer I nearly fell in love. It all began in London when I took on a grandmaster of European chess... and won. How one can win by losing was one of the many lessons I learned on my first trip abroad, and it taught me to be a bit more circumspect about the challenges that lie ahead.

The South End Park Cafe, at the edge of Hampstead Heath, was home to some of the world's finest chess players. Most of them were Eastern European refugees from World War II who were living out their final years in exile. I had no business being in the cafe but it was close to where I was staying and offered English tea and scones at a reasonable price, that price being to sit in complete silence and not interfere with the chess matches being waged at each and every table. I was also drawn to the place because some twenty years earlier it had been the site of a bookstore where George Orwell once worked. A plaque outside gave landmark status to the building and the apartment upstairs where Orwell lived and wrote *Animal Farm*. There was a certain gravity to the structure and it was in keeping with the seriousness of the surroundings that these old men would gravitate to its somber environs and engage in intellectual battles to the bitter end.

One day I had the severe misfortune of being seated across from a Hungarian grandmaster whose partner had failed to show. The old man mumbled something to me that sounded like a challenge and before I fully understood what was happening he was holding out two fists with hidden pieces for me to choose. With no way out—and with utmost trepidation—I chose the left hand. He unwrapped his fingers to expose a white pawn, and the game was on.

I liked to think of myself as being of a new generation of psychedelic chess players who made moves not by logic but by intuition. It was hard to say whether I was a good player or a bad player since I played a delusional game against delirious opponents. This, though, was something entirely different. With my palms already sweating I moved a pawn, he moved his, I brought out my knight, he countered with his bishop, I moved another pawn, he moved his, and I was completely lost. I'd been rendered insensate in three moves. My opponent was clearly performing some kind of presti-digitation that had taken me right out of my body. No matter, I played my game, the same game I always played, plodding though it might have been. I couldn't concede after three moves, after all, not in front of the world's greatest players. I continued on, making one idiotic move after another. I had no idea what was happening. He was playing chess and I was playing marbles—*oh, God, let this be over!*—and then he sacrificed his bishop for my rook, his queen for my queen, and all of the pieces began falling, his move, my move, his move, my move—*he looked at me to see if I was still breathing*—and then things began to turn, he looked puzzled, wondering how anyone could actually make such a ridiculous move, thinking maybe it was a clever ploy on my part, and then with true Orwellian paranoia, he began to read into my moves an intent I couldn't even begin to imagine, other players gathered around, mystified by the turn of events, and he began countering moves made not by me but his own dark imagination—*what was he doing?*—and moments later, in a flurry of action so far above my head it could've taken place in George Orwell's upstairs apartment, my opponent went down in defeat, not by me but by his own apprehension. For me it was a lesson well-learned: when encountering superior intellects, it's best to confound them so totally with one's own futility that they'll simply outthink themselves. I'm not sure if I won by losing or lost by winning, but I learned there are many ways to skin a cat. It was a notion that would serve me well through the rest of my travels.

❦

Kungsträdgården in Stockholm seemed like the last place in the world to be the scene of protests. Sweden was the most liberal country in Europe and the government was well-known for its opposition to war, poverty and racism. Still, when I arrived at the central square one sunny afternoon, several hundred people were milling around, erupting every few moments with slogans I couldn't understand, then fading back into silence. It wasn't clear to me what they were protesting but a scattering of Viet Cong flags indicated it was an anti-war rally. It all felt a bit halfhearted, like it was a good idea to stand up against the war but a bit odd to do so in the one country that had opposed the war from the very beginning.

Several speakers took the stage and made speeches that were received with polite applause, a bit of chanting, and more milling around. I was about to leave when I noticed a familiar face on the stage. It was Stewart, an acquaintance from college who was on his own summer excursion. I didn't expect to see anyone I knew in Sweden, of all places, and certainly not on a stage leading an antiwar rally. When he took the microphone, everyone gathered around to hear what a real, red-blooded American revolutionary had to say. "The war in Vietnam must be stopped," Stewart began, in a cool, calm voice. "Innocent people are being massacred and the world does nothing to stop it." Several people in the crowd cheered and moved closer to the stage. "Meanwhile the American war machine continues to expand its forces."

Stewart's voice rang out loud and clear over the gathering and the entire square began filling. A muffled chant arose from somewhere in the rear of the crowd and quickly spread: "Ho-Ho-Ho Chi Minh... Ho-Ho-Ho Chi Minh..."

"The people of Vietnam deserve the right to choose their own government, not have it imposed by the West," said Stewart, his voice rising over the chant. "And what can we do from here in the safety of our bourgeois Western lives?"

"What?" answered the crowd.

"We can fight the power! We can resist capitalist imperialism by standing strong, standing firm, and standing together!"

"Ho-Ho-Ho Chi Minh! Ho-Ho-Ho Chi Minh!"

I stood on the outside of the crowd, which was building in size, intensity and fervor. I agreed with every word that Stewart spoke even if I couldn't quite get over the fact that it was he who was up there on the stage. I didn't remember seeing him much at the protests back at the University of Wisconsin.

"We have to unite against the politicians and police who

try to silence our voices!" said Stewart, his voice booming over the loudspeakers. "And the police will come! We know that, don't we?"

"Yes!"

"And what will we do when they try to break up our peaceful protest?"

"Resist!"

"That's right! Resist! We have to show the police that we aren't afraid of them! Let them arrest us! We'll never back down!"

"*HO-HO-HO CHI MINH! HO-HO-HO CHI MINH!*"

"It's time to show the world what we're made of!" said Stewart, riling up the crowd further with his impassioned speech—

At that moment a dozen unmarked vans pulled up at the edge of the square. In a quick coordinated action, the doors swung open, whistles blew, and lines of riot police marched out. Stewart was one of the last to notice and one of the first to flee. And flee he did. He was gone so fast that even the little cartoon balloons containing his words seemed to vanish into thin air. Was he ever actually there? Was I imagining all of this?

The chanting gradually diminished, the crowd began milling around again, and the park slowly emptied. I walked past a line of cops who watched me with growing suspicion. I was clearly an American troublemaker who would make for an easy arrest. It was another game of chess. They moved, I retreated, they moved again, and I wisely panicked. I sacrificed my king, queen and anything else I had lying around and rushed headlong into the midnight sun. What the hell was I doing in Sweden, anyway? My shrinking shadow was last seen boarding the express to Paris, before they could deport me to the North Pole.

⤷∽⤶

I awoke to a thud that shook the walls of my hotel room, then a grinding, screeching sound that set my teeth on edge. After another thud and the clatter of heavy machinery scraping along the road, I quickly dressed and headed down the back stairs of the Hotel Monsieur le Prince, a low rent *pension* populated by travelers and bohemians. The lobby was deserted except for the day clerk who buried his head in the morning paper. "What's going on?" I yelled to him over the noise.

"*C'est ridicule!*" he shot back, clearly irritated by the activities outside his door. I glanced through the window to see a crew of workmen following a parade of machines that was pounding, tamping and paving the street. Was it possible? Were they actually paving over the cobblestone streets of Paris?

It had been only a few weeks since the Sorbonne University riots that tore the whole city apart and Paris was unusually subdued, as if still recovering from a bad hangover. I'd just missed the riots but I was there to see the aftermath. The Sorbonne was down the street in the heart of the Latin Quarter, and it had been the site of students occupying the halls of power, protesting the elitist nature of French education, and fighting the government's support of America's war. What started out with a few dozen protestors quickly grew into a mass demonstration that was joined by millions of workers, an alliance that left Charles de Gaulle barely hanging onto power. He called in the police, the national guard, and then the army before finally putting down the revolt.

What was left now were tattered protest posters flapping in the wind and the remnants of barricades still piled along the road. From behind those barricades students had thrown stones at charging police forces who were armed with staves and riot gear. It was an unfair fight, as it always is when students and the police square off, but this one was made a bit more equal by planting several Americans in the front lines. All of those years playing baseball turned out to be useful as they displayed pinpoint accuracy when throwing bricks at the cops. Those bricks had been dug up from the cobblestone streets, and now de Gaulle was letting everyone know the consequences of their actions. The cobblestones would be buried forever and with them, a part of what made Paris so special. With each centimeter of advancing machinery, a bit more of French culture was being obliterated, street by street by street.

After a week of walking through the ghostly environs of the Left Bank, I packed up my rucksack, checked out of the hotel, and headed for Gare du Nord. As I approached the train station, I heard someone calling out my name: "Hey, man, where you been?" I turned to see a tall, lanky guy hurrying from across the street. It was Stewart.

"Wherever they'll have me," I said.

"It gets a bit dicey out here in the real world, doesn't it?" he said, noticing my rucksack. "Where you headed?"

"Prague."

"Prague? You sure about that? I hear things aren't all that cool there."

"I'm sure it's fine."

"No, really, man, why don't you stay a couple more days. We can hang out."

"Hang out? No, no—"

"I just scored some Nepalese hash. How about you grab your room again and see Paris from the other end of the telescope?"

"Yeah, well, it's tempting, but—"

"It's Nepalese temple balls, man."

"Temple balls?" I said, reconsidering. "Buddhist dope?"

"Guy told me it was straight from the Dalai Lama's personal stash."

The next two days passed in a blur. Stewart and I may or may not have gone to the Louvre, the Champs Elysees, the

Jardin du Luxembourg and Versailles, where we may or may not have gazed into a mirror that once belonged to Marie Antoinette. Two mornings later I packed up my rucksack again, checked out again, and headed once more for the Gare du Nord. It was definitely time to leave Paris.

Outside the train station, newspapers from around the world were plastered on the walls and a crowd pushed closer to read the blazing headlines:

Russian Troops Invade Czechoslovakia!
Tanks in Prague!

I scanned the news and felt the blood draining from my face. Had I left as planned two days earlier, I would've arrived in Prague exactly four hours before the Russians! Where would I be right now? Hiding in a cellar? Held captive in some outdoor arena? On my way to the gulag?

The near misses were beginning to mount. Better, perhaps, to just stay in one place.

⚬❦⚬

When I checked into the Hotel Monsieur le Prince for the third time, the clerk got suspicious. He figured I was up to something, but what exactly? Trying to get fresh sheets? A new towel? I tried to explain the Czech situation but my French was so terrible we both just gave up on it. I headed for my old room under his wary gaze.

That night, while aimlessly wandering the streets, I came upon Margo, an American jazz singer in the Quarter, whose car was disabled at the side of the road. The vehicle was a Citroen Deux Chevaux, an odd contraption that looked like an upside-down eggbeater. It had two horse-power—*deux chevaux*—which put it right up there with an Alaskan dog sled and a team of wild hamsters. After toiling with it for more than an hour I somehow managed to get the thing started and a grateful Margo invited me for a drink. We shared a bottle of wine, nuzzled a little, laughed a lot, and bemoaned the fact that she was leaving in only a few hours for Geneva. She had friends in the Living Theatre, a well-known theatre group, who were heading back to America after a long exile in Europe, and wanted to help see them off. From there she was going on holiday to Spain, which was intriguing since I'd been thinking much the same thing, and within a few moments we hatched a drunken plan to hook up in Geneva and hitchhike together to Spain. It was a good plan, as plans go, if a little light on the details. Still, after my aborted journey to Prague, I decided to follow my heart rather than my head. My head, after all, hadn't been of much use these past few weeks.

Two days later I checked out of the hotel—I promised the clerk that this really, truly would be the last time he'd see me—and took the night train to Geneva. I barely slept as the train climbed the Alps, winding its way around the steep escarpments and narrow valleys. I kept thinking about Margo, how we'd wander through the quaint villages of the Midi, hike the Pyrenees and bask on the beaches of Barcelona. I arrived in Geneva around seven, two hours before our appointed rendezvous at American Express, and drifted into a park across the street. A church tower chimed every fifteen minutes, a lovely, romantic melody that had me drifting as well, there we were, just me and Margo, lying in bed, a cool breeze blowing in through a window that was left carefully ajar, holding each other so close I could almost feel our bodies meld, the bells, the breeze, the beautiful look in her eyes, more bells, eight, nine, ten, eleven—

I awoke on the park bench with a start. It was eleven o'clock! I'd slept right through the appointment! I hurried across the street to find a letter waiting for me in the mail section. *"Sorry you couldn't make it,"* it said. *"I was so looking forward to seeing you, but after waiting an hour I decided to fly to Italy instead. In case you somehow get this, thanks again for fixing my car. Margo.*"

I never saw her again.

⤫

I fell back on my plan to go to Barcelona but decided to fly since the idea of wandering through the quaint villages of the Midi all by myself seemed a bit too pathetic. If I was trying to read the tea leaves, they weren't making it easy. It was, therefore, entirely predictable that Barcelona would make me feel uncomfortable the moment I arrived. The beauty of the city was overshadowed by a sense of impending doom. Francisco Franco was still in power and the streets were crawling with Guardia Civil, a paramilitary force whose bizarre metal helmets made them look like storm troopers from the ancient future. The helmets were round in front, flared at the sides, flat on top, and completely squared off at the back to give them an even greater edge of authority. I worried that a wrong look could land me in some forgotten Spanish Civil War dungeon. It was a war that felt unfinished, especially on these very streets where the anti-fascist movement had begun. I remembered the chilling descriptions of George Orwell—formerly of South End Park Road—who wrote about the battles so passionately in *Homage to Catalonia*. The idea that Franco was still in charge and that the Guardia Civil were still his henchmen sent chills down my spine.

I took the overnight ferry to Ibiza, a beautiful Mediterranean island that had managed to adapt to the modern world without completely losing its character. Interspersed among the ancient fincas and stone houses were bars and discos that pushed the boundaries of good taste but never quite went over the line. The locals mostly looked the other way as an international community of artists, writers and musicians spread across the island.

I felt more drawn to Formentera, an island further out in the sea that had yet to embrace cars or electricity. It was a small, barren land living under the shadow of La Mola, a mountain where witches from the mainland had been exiled during the Spanish Inquisition. Rumors abounded of all sorts of strange behavior occurring on La Mola, from ghosts to cults to alien inhabitation. After a few disquieting nights of sleeping on the beach I became convinced it was all true.

Among the travelers to Formentera were several Europeans who'd just returned from India. I was utterly transfixed by their stories. Their adventures seemed straight out of *A Thousand and One Nights*. As it happens, they were planning to go back after the monsoon and invited me to join them.

—India? Are you kidding?—

It was a once in a lifetime chance to accompany a group of seasoned travelers on a journey I'd long dreamt of making. Yes! Of course! I could do it! I could travel overland and get lost in a whole new world! I could stand on the banks of the Ganges! At that very moment my conscience— the bane of my existence—stepped in with its usual bad advice. *"Are you crazy?"* it said. *"You only have one more year of college left. Are you really going to throw away your degree? Think about your parents!"*

I eventually succumbed to my greater demons and began my journey home. I boarded the boat to Ibiza, then the boat to Barcelona, and finally the train to Paris. Along the way I met two Frenchmen who were on their way to Toulouse. When we hit the arid plains of northern Spain, they pulled out a conga drum and guitar and I chimed in with harmonica. We threw open the doors and windows and played to a growing crowd of passengers. The clacking of the wheels on the tracks, the whistle of the engine, and the puffing of the turbines created a natural rhythm that pushed us to the edge of our seats and halfway out the windows. When we arrived in Toulouse, they insisted I join them for dinner.

I had planned on taking the superfast Le Capitaine, which made the trip to Paris in only six hours, but they convinced me to take the slower overnight train which would allow a four-hour layover in Toulouse, just enough time for a typically relaxed French meal. The setting couldn't have been more dramatic. The guitar player's father was the scenarist for the Toulouse Opera and his house was an ancient chateau decorated with the props and scenery from thirty years of operas. There were massive armoires, enormous tapestries and giant urns from the Middle Ages. We sat at a table that could have come from King Arthur's court and ate with wooden spoons and handmade plates. Halfway through the dinner someone appeared wearing a Japanese mask, kimono and ceremonial sword. He poured some wine, bowed, then exited stage left. Was it a servant? An actor from the Noh Theatre? The scenarist himself? I felt the ancient world calling to me again and wondered if returning to America wasn't a mistake.

The meal might well have been comprised of mastodon stew, emu omelets, and vegetables picked from the primeval forest. We played a few tunes, talked about meeting someday in India, and had a parting glass of wine. I bid adieu to the house of opera and headed back to the station.

In contrast to the gleaming new Le Capitaine, the train from Toulouse to Paris looked like something from the Orient Express. I half-expected to find conductors with waxed mustaches and engineers with monocles as we trudged along on the slow journey north. Somewhere in the middle of the night I was awakened to the sound of the train stopping in a field. We sat there a good long while as people began milling around the aisles, glancing out the windows, and eventually moving from car to car. Finally, an hour or so later, we began heading back toward Toulouse. I asked a few people what was going on but no one had a clue. Eventually we switched over to a side track and headed north again.

We arrived in Paris the next afternoon, hours late, still with no word of what had happened. I spent the evening at a jazz club in the Latin Quarter, imagining Margo on the stage, again bemoaning my bad timing. I slept fitfully that night—at the Hotel Monsieur le Prince, of course—and then early the next morning I was back on another train, this one to Brussels, where I'd catch my plane back to New York. I noticed that everyone was glued to their newspapers and glanced over to see what was so interesting. There was a big banner headline I didn't quite understand and below it the photo of a massive train wreck. It had occurred only the day before, on the route from Toulouse to Paris. It was the superfast Le Capitaine. There'd been a head-on collision that left dozens dead.

It was the train I was supposed to take. The train I would've been on if I hadn't stopped for dinner in Toulouse. It was the last in a series of near misses that seemed to follow me throughout Europe. Was it a warning to stay away? A message to buckle down, get my degree, and make something of myself? I didn't think so. If anything, my appetite was only whetted to get back on the road as soon as possible. I was done with near misses. I wanted to embrace the real thing and find out exactly where that road would take me. I'd be back—oh yes, I would—now that I was a true man of the world.

Chapter 3
Basingstoke to Cliddesden

It took longer than expected to return to Europe. After finishing college I moved to Berkeley, California, where I bathed myself in tear gas until my eyes stung so much I could barely read from my collection of the works of Henry Miller. Miller was my beacon of light, a voice reminding me of the lure of foreign lands and the chance of a new life. After two years of clawing my way through the unfolding American nightmare, I finally wiped my eyes clean and found a way out. I was so thrilled to be embarking on a new adventure, I didn't even mind it when I arrived during the winter of one of England's worst cold spells.

I immediately discovered that the British didn't really know how to deal with the cold. All those flimsy wellies and windcheaters might've been good against the fog, but their electric fires and paraffin heaters were no match for the icy winds that drifted down from the Arctic. I was lucky enough to be staying with my friend Robb in a flat that had central heating, a rarity in London, but that didn't mean the central heating actually worked. In fact, there was a note on the door from a neighbor mentioning that he smelled gas and that someone should probably call whomever one calls in such situations. Having no idea who that might be, we simply went inside and fell asleep.

Time passed. It might've been a few minutes. It might've been a day. It might've been a week. I do vaguely remember hearing a tapping sound inside my head, no, wait, it was just outside my skull, hold on, it was from across the room and was getting louder, it was more a pound than a tap, it was definitely a pounding, a violent pounding that was shaking the front door almost off its hinges. I groggily pushed myself off an armchair, staggered past Robb, who appeared to be dead on the sofa, and opened the door.

"Bloody hell! Are you fucking insane?" screamed Rodney, whose apartment it was. He rushed in, slapped Robb across the face, and finally revived him.

"What... what?" said Robb, slowing coming out of a sleep of the near dead.

Rodney pulled me down the hall to the gas heater, handed me a flashlight, then poured a couple drops of liquid soap over a seam in the pipe. Sure enough, they started bubbling like a geyser. "Right... right... just hold steady..." he said, as he reached into his pocket, pulled out some matches, and went to strike one against the side of the box.

Now, I may not have been a plumbing genius, but I was pretty sure that it was pure madness to inspect a gas leak by the light of a match. "Are you serious?" I screamed as I pulled him away.

"Hold steady!" Rodney said again, with a demonic leer that left no room for discussion. I held the flashlight, he lit the match, and I braced myself for an ignominious conclusion to my all-too-brief British holiday. Rodney, with the calmness only a true psychopath could muster at such a moment, held the match right over the gas leak and watched as it blew itself out. "Just like I thought," he said. "The leak's so bad there's not even enough oxygen to burn a match! Bloody miracle you're still alive!"

We retrieved Robb, who was still circling the sofa in a somnambulant swoon, and retreated outdoors. Rodney strolled over to the corner phone booth, called the authorities, and calmly informed them that half of London was about to blow up. Within moments, the police cordoned off the street, a half-dozen utility trucks arrived, and a crew of explosives experts descended upon the building. What did they think, that we were the IRA? A couple of cops kept their eyes on us, especially on Robb, who had the scruffy beard and nervous eyes of an Irish terrorist. An hour later, a whistle blew, the all-clear was given, and we were back inside the flat.

"Rodney," I said, cautiously approaching our madman host, "I'm curious about something. What do you think would've happened if that leak hadn't been so bad?"

"You mean if there'd been enough oxygen for the match to stay lit? We'd have been blown to smithereens."

"That's what I thought. So you knew—"

"I didn't *know* a damn thing. I *assumed*. I took one look at your mate there and figured he was a goner. I deduced it must've been one hell of a leak to knock one of you bloody Yanks right off your pedestal."

Who was this guy, Sherlock Holmes?

From that moment on, Robb and I resorted to electric fires instead. Electric fires are British space heaters capable of heating the air three inches in front of them and absolutely nothing else. Anyone unfortunate enough to use an electric fire has the option of warming his front side or his back side, but not both at once. It makes for a body at war with itself, arms fighting legs for their moment in the sun.

Robb had been in London for several months and had already picked up on the British method of winter survival, that being the endless consumption of tepid tea. He drank tea until his eyes turned yellow and then he drank some more.

Robb was a talented guy who, like most artists in England, barely had a penny to his name. He was a playwright without a stage, a painter without a canvas, a poet without paper. Undeterred, he explored every avenue into the arts, fighting the good fight, knocking on every door and returning each night to the floor of Rodney's apartment. He was there because he was friends with Sarah, Rodney's American girlfriend, and that led to Robb taking up residence in a corner of the living room and eventually to my arrival, since all Americans were destined at one time or another to sleep on Rodney's floor.

Rodney was a leftwing sociopath film director whose love of the working man was superseded only by his hatred for humanity. He took out most of his spite on Sarah, a daughter of privilege who was doing penance for her good fortune by subjugating herself to the whims of a tyrant. They made for an interesting couple—the abuser and the abused, the master and the mastered, the lord and the lorded over—and I made every attempt to steer clear of their endless bickering. One day Rodney came home with what would've been good news had he the capacity to wallow in anything but misery. He'd been hired to direct a TV commercial in the south of England for an industrial solvent, a job so clearly beneath his talents that the bloody advertiser was bloody lucky to get his bloody signature on the bloody contract. And we—useless bunch of expatriates that we were—were bloody lucky to be allowed to come along and finally earn our keep.

⁂

Several days later we were on our way to the estate of Lord Edward Montagu, some hundred miles south of London, where the filming was to take place. It was barely sunrise and the road to Beaulieu was dead quiet as we meandered through the British countryside in an old Ford van. For me everything was left to right—the road, the signs, the van itself—as we headed down the M3 past Mapledurwell, Hatch Warren and Otterbourne. Inside the van everything felt slightly left as well—the tripod wobbling in the left rear corner, the Ariflex camera nestled in foam behind the left front seat, the portable paraffin heater snuggled against the left rear door, even me lying in my sleeping bag on the floor of the van was slightly left, left of center, left of right, left for dead for all I knew. I felt a strange burning sensation, as if the whole damn van was on fire.

After skirting west of Southampton, we found ourselves approaching Netley Marsh, with Eling and Pooksgreen just ahead. Even in my half-sleep I couldn't help but wonder if we were in some kind of British fairy tale—where else would one find names like this?—but the signs kept pointing to even more fanciful towns down the road—Balmerlawn and Brockenhurst, Ashley and Bashley, Holmesley and Ossemsley—and I finally rolled over and fell asleep.

I kept fading in and out of a dream in which flames were shooting out of my feet, my ankles were burning, and my skin was melting. I finally reached down, felt something wet on my sleeping bag, and discovered that my legs had been rubbed hairless as a baby's bum. My eyes popped open to see paraffin splashing from the portable heater as the van twisted and turned along the road. The paraffin had soaked through the sleeping bag and my flesh and bone was marinating in a soup of toxicity. "Pull over!" I screamed.

"What is it back there?" growled Rodney.

"The heater! It's leaking all over me! Pull over!"

"Sorry, mate, we're late as it is."

"My legs are all chafed to hell!"

"You'll just have to buck up, won't you?"

Robb flicked on the dome light to get a better look. "Christ!" he said, recoiling from what looked like another explosive situation. "We better take a look at this, Rodney."

"It's bloody paraffin! He'll live, won't he? Who told him to lie on the floor like that?"

Sarah, who'd been completely oblivious to my predicament, finally stirred when my throbbing leg kicked against her seat. "Rodney, he's gonna break something!" she said.

Rodney suddenly realized the gravity of the situation. "Bloody hell! The tripod! The camera!" He jammed on the brakes and pulled to the side of the road. Before the van even came to a full stop, I leapt out the side door and rolled onto a wet patch of grass. My legs actually sizzled as I rubbed off the dead hair follicles and an outer layer of skin.

Rodney's voice boomed through the cold, clear night. "God, you Yanks are a useless lot!"

Sarah, like me, was an American imbecile––all Americans in England are considered imbeciles––only she really *was* an imbecile whereas I was only faking it. "What, I suppose this was *my* fault?" she whined through the icy air.

"Of course, it was your fault. It's always your fault. Bunch of bloody wankers!"

"*You're* calling *me* a bloody wanker?"

"No, I'm calling *all* of you bloody wankers!"

Robb slipped out the side door of the van and warily approached. "You okay?" he said. "You smell like a gas station."

"I'm soaked to the bone with this shit."

"What did you do, kick the thing over?"

"How should I know? I was asleep."

"Come on, you twits!" Rodney bellowed from the Ford. "Let's move along. Time is money."

I dried my legs as best I could and called back to him. "You know, Rodney, I've never really understood what time is, but I'm pretty sure it's not money."

"We'd better get going," Robb whispered. "He could just leave us out here."

"I mean, if time is money, what's gravity? Loose change?"

"Fuck off, then!" yelled Rodney as he started up the engine and began to pull away.

"Come on!" Robb yelled as we rushed for the van. We leapt in, swung the door closed, and held on for dear life as the Ford bounced along the winding road.

Lord Montagu's estate was just over the next hill.

❧

Lord Edward John Barrington Douglas Scott Montagu owned one of the last great estates of the British Empire. While the castle itself was modest by royal standards, the ten thousand acres of land that stretched from the ocean to the New Forest district of Hampshire was some of the most spectacular property in the kingdom. Lord Montagu, who'd inherited the estate at the age of two, had faced a great challenge keeping it running after the end of World War II. The extravagant manors were falling by the wayside, their upkeep too prohibitive for all but the richest of the upper class. Montagu managed to stave off foreclosure by being the first royal to open his house to tourists, an act frowned upon by the landed gentry as being in extremely bad taste. When they saw paying customers lined up outside the gates, however, some of the largest estates followed Montagu's lead and opened their more spectacular mansions as well. With the competition crippling his business, Montagu turned to his final option. As it happens, his father had been one of England's first automobile enthusiasts and had left a 1903 De Dion Bouton to Edward as part of the estate. Over the years the boy had developed his own fascination with antique vehicles and eventually amassed two-hundred-and-fifty of the rarest cars in the kingdom. Now, alas, it was time to open his collection to the paying public. Thus was born the Montagu Motor Museum on his Beaulieu estate.

The museum became a great success, but Lord Montagu's ultimate claim to fame arose from something a bit less savory: his involvement in one of Britain's great scandals of the 1950s. He'd been arrested twice and imprisoned for nearly a year for performing "gross offenses" with an RAF serviceman at his country home. It was the same offense that had put Oscar Wilde behind bars and gave rise to endless snickering among watchers of the royalty. It became fashionable to refer to suspected gays as "having a bit of the Montagu in them," but after a public outcry Parliament was forced to overturn Britain's anti-homosexuality laws. It became Lord Montagu's greatest legacy.

The first rays of the morning sun appeared over the rolling hills of New Forest when Rodney pulled up to a grove of English Oaks. In the distance was a cluster of outlying barns and sheds with the odd farm animal ambling about. Rodney immediately jumped out of the van and began setting up his camera to film a commercial for an all-purpose oil that promised to quiet creaking doors, loosen tight locks, and fix squeaky wheels. It made as much sense as anything else in this country of oddballs and eccentrics that we'd travel a hundred miles to one of the richest manors in England to do an ad aimed at manual laborers and working mums.

It was cold as hell and my hairless legs were shaking with each gust of icy wind. Rodney, of course, had no compassion at all for my situation. "You Yanks expect central heating in an outhouse, don't you?" he said. "Well, time to deal with the real world."

Yes, yes, this was the real world and time was money and we were all twits and wankers. Rodney was becoming more insufferable by the moment. While he adjusted a tripod, the rest of us huddled in the van. After a few restless moments Sarah called to him from the front seat. "Rodney? Can you put on some music? I'm bored."

"Do you see that I might be a little busy right now?" he answered from beneath the trees. "Do you see that I'm working? Do you think maybe you could be bothered to put on some music yourself?"

"You never like what I pick."

"That, my dear, is because you have a tin ear. Maybe if you'd educate yourself a little, you'd develop a modicum of taste. It embarrasses me, the drivel you listen to."

"What's wrong with Paul McCartney and Elton John? Everybody listens to them."

"We don't listen to millionaire rock stars, damn it! We're not fucking royalists, not yet we're not!"

"Then why are we sitting here on some fancy-pants Lord's estate a hundred miles from nowhere?"

"Because we are lackeys of the ruling class, and until we gain control over the means of production we'll be nothing but cogs in their machine."

"I just want to hear some music," whined Sarah.

"All right, crew, you know what to do," said Rodney, ordering us into action. Robb removed the Ariflex from its bed of foam, Sarah pulled out a Nakamichi tape recorder, and I gathered together a mound of wires, cables, and connector pins. We set up the gear beneath the trees, hooked up some battery packs, and tied off the cables so that no one would trip over the jungle of cords and render $5000 of equipment inoperable. And then we waited. And we froze. And we waited some more.

Finally, the silhouette of a large-fendered, open-aired, wire-wheeled 1914 Vauxhall A-Type touring car appeared at the top of the road. The car struggled up the hill, sputtered a little, and glided down to our little outpost in the forest. Two men were seated behind a flat panel of glass, bundled up like Eskimos on an Arctic whaler. Behind the wheel was Lord Montagu himself, tall, thin and rosy-cheeked, dressed head to toe in matching rabbit skin coat, gloves and hat. Now, me, I'm as straight as the road from Basingstoke to Cliddesden, but if I could've just cuddled into that kangaroo pouch of a coat of his, I swear he could've had his way with me right then and there. Sitting next to Montagu was Baron

Rolf Beck, a little dumpling of a man who managed to look bored, irritated and angry all at once. Beck was an old-school Austrian, the kind that wears monocles and lederhosen and yodels to ancestral mountain nymphs in the night. He was owner of Molyslip Atlantic Ltd., a chemical company that marketed the anti-corrosive properties of molybdenum disulphide, and that was the reason we were there.

The Baron and the Lord stepped out of the Vauxhall and surveyed the lay of the land. "Very nice," said Beck, "it is just as you said."

"There's nothing quite like the British countryside," said Montagu.

"*Ja*," said Beck, playfully poking Montagu's arm, "especially when you own it."

"Well, I wouldn't say I own *all* of it," said Montagu, chuckling at his own little joke.

Beck glanced around at the mound of equipment and the ragtag band of guerilla filmmakers. "Which one is the director?"

Rodney stepped forward and bowed slightly from the waist. "That would be me. I'm Rodney—"

"*Ja, ja,* as I thought," said Beck, cutting him off, "the one with the beard. You look the part."

Rodney nodded solicitously. "Thank you."

"It is not a compliment. This is not high art we are making, it is a television commercial. Do you understand?"

"Yes, of course."

Beck glanced around at the rest of us as if we were inert chemical compounds. "And this must be the rest of the crew," he said with no little sarcasm. "Do we really need so many on the set?"

"We're already staffed well below union minimums—" said Rodney.

"Union minimums? Hah!" exploded Beck. "What do I care about union minimums? You," he said, turning to

Sarah, "what is your job description?"

"I mostly cook and clean—"

Rodney whispered sharply under his breath, "—*on the set, stupid, on the set*—"

"—and fiddle with the dials."

"A dial fiddler? This is what I'm paying for?"

"She's quite irreplaceable," said Rodney, thinking how easily he could replace her.

"And the curly-headed one?" said Beck, pointing at Robb.

"Nobody," said Rodney. "He's just some day help."

Beck removed his pashmina wool gloves and handed them to me as if I were his manservant. I stood there, not quite sure what to do with them. "And you are?" he said, barely making eye contact.

"I'm Nobody's assistant," I said, turning the gloves over in my hand. I wondered if he expected me to smooth them out, lay them on a chair, or fluff them over the car heater.

Baron Beck shot me a look, not sure how to take my meaning, then turned back to face Rodney. "Now, then, I assume you have studied the script. Lord Montagu and I will be stopped on a country road. It is cold. It is snowing. The car will not start. Lord Montagu will get out and inspect the engine. I will hand him a can of Molyslip which he will spray on the carburetor. We will get back into the car, the engine will start right up, and we will drive off into the countryside. It could not be easier, am I right?"

"It's pretty straight forward," said Rodney.

"After all," said Beck, jabbing his finger into Rodney's ribs, "we are not doing Fellini, right?"

"Right," said Rodney, biting his lip. He set up the tripod near the left front fender, attached the Ariflex to the base, set up some auxiliary lighting near the passenger door, hung some umbrellas for shade, and ran a microphone boom above the car. He then adjusted the camera, focused the lens, checked his light meter, and tested the audio dials on the Nakamichi. After double and triple checking everything, he called his actors to the set. "Any time, gentlemen."

Lord Montagu hopped onto the full-grained leather seat, glanced into the rear view mirror, brushed down his eyebrows, and nodded to Rodney. "I'm ready for make-up."

"Make-up?" said Rodney, caught off-guard. "Yes, yes, of course. Sarah, see to Lord Montagu, will you?"

Sarah glanced at him in panic, then warily approached Montagu. "What can I do for you, m'lord?"

"Don't you think my nose might be a bit shiny?"

"Shiny?" she said, looking at him like an exhibit under a microscope. "No, I don't believe so. If anything it has kind of a royal sheen."

"Oh? All right, then, you're the expert," he said with completely misplaced confidence. "Baron Beck, we await..."

Beck gallumphed his way into the passenger seat and readied himself. "I'm just a little nervous," he confided in the Lord.

"An old military man like you?" chided Montagu. "This is a piece of cake."

Rodney adjusted the Ariflex, Sarah watched the dials on the Nakamichi, Robb angled the umbrella over the lighting, and I climbed up a stepladder with a big bag full of Styrofoam bits and pieces. "Scene one, take one," called out Rodney. "Ready... and... rolling... and... snow!"

I tossed out a handful of Styrofoam into the air and a synthetic snowfall descended over the car and its occupants. Right on cue, the camera whirred for a few seconds until Rodney got his shot of the two men sitting behind the windscreen of the old Vauxhall. "Excellent. We'll shoot again for backup. Everything the same as before. Places everyone. We're ready... and... rolling... and—"

"Make-up!" yelled Montagu.

Rodney lifted his head from the viewfinder, struggling to keep an even tone. "What is it?"

"I fear my forehead might be a bit damp."

"Do you realize we've only done one take?"

"I don't mean to be difficult, but—"

"Tell you what, Monty," said Beck, beginning to lose patience. "I've got some Molyslip Lubricating Oil in my bag that will buff up your whole face."

"Yes," said Montagu coolly, "I suspect it would. All right, let's just get on with it."

Rodney refocused the camera, Robb reset the lights, and the next shot went perfectly. "Print!" yelled Rodney, as if he were David Lean in the desert.

In the next scene, Lord Montagu was meant to turn the key in the ignition and wait impatiently for the engine to start up. Unfortunately, the old Vauxhall started instantly and we needed seven or eight attempts before Montagu was able to fake that the engine was dead. I think he resisted the idea that one of his cars could in any way be deficient. Finally, he got the knack of turning the key only part way, causing the engine to sputter and die. "Very good," said Rodney, as he zoomed in on Montagu's hand.

"Maybe for you, but I have the reputation of the Montagu Motor Museum to uphold. The very idea of one of my cars not starting—"

"—is the whole point of the commercial!" said Baron Beck.

"That doesn't mean I have to like it," Montagu shot back.

"Then don't take the two thousand pounds I'm paying for this little outing."

"Gentlemen," said Rodney, "can we move on?"

In the next scene, Montagu got out from behind the steering wheel, walked to the front of the car, and opened the bonnet. This took seventeen takes and more than two hours of starting, stopping, fumbling and bumbling. It amazed me that any one person could have such a problem opening a car door, stepping onto the ground, and walking three feet, but I was new to the British aristocracy.

It was time for Baron Beck's big scene and I could hardly wait. The camera panned up from the engine where Lord Montagu was hunched over the carburetor to a full shot of Baron Beck standing at the side of the road with a can of all-purpose Molyslip Lubricating Oil. "Scene Five... quiet please... places... rolling... snow... and—"

I tossed a handful of Styrofoam into the air. Beck straightened like a Prussian general and stiffly held the can of oil to the camera. "Lord Montagu!" he bellowed.

"Cut!" yelled Rodney.

"What is it?"

"Maybe you could ease into it a little bit, Baron Beck? Your line is more of an interrogatory than a demand. It's like you have a friendly suggestion for Lord Montagu."

"*Ja*, of course."

"Rolling again... Scene Five... take two... places... rolling... snow... and—"

I tossed a bigger handful of snow into the air and watched as it drifted down over Beck's beady eyes and tight lips.

"Lord Montagu!"

"Cut!"

"What's wrong?"

"You should be asking him, not telling him. Try cooing a little with your voice."

"Cooing? What do you mean? Like a bird?"

"Yes, like a bird."

"What kind of bird?"

"It doesn't really matter. Any bird."

"How about an owl? I think I could do an owl."

"Fine, do an owl."

"A barn owl or a forest owl? You must be more specific."

"Kind of like, *Lord Monnnt-aguuuu?*"

"Understood. I am ready."

"Scene Five... take three... places... rolling... snow—"

My arm was getting tired holding it high above Beck's head. When I heard my cue, I relaxed my grip a little and let the Styrofoam dribble over the Baron's forehead. It felt surprisingly good. He caught my eye and delivered his line:

"Lord Montagu!"

"Cut!"

"Good God, Becksie," screamed Lord Montagu, "you're not leading a charge to the front. Pretend you're with your mistress."

"Ach, ja, of course."

Rodney reset the camera, Robb readjusted the microphone, Sarah rechecked the dials, and I re-readied the snow. "Scene Five... take four... places... rolling... snow—"

"Hildegard, meine Liebe!"

"Damn it, man," screamed Montagu, *"what's wrong with you?"*

On and on it went. My arms hurt. My legs burned. My toes ached. I began tossing handfuls of snow straight into the Baron's face with all the force I could muster. Always it was the same result:

"Lord Montagu!... Lord Montagu!... Lord Montagu!..."

Rodney finally came around from behind his camera and looked nervously at the horizon. "Look, we're about to lose the light. Let's just nail it this time so we can all go home. It's just two words, Baron Beck, two words."

Beck narrowed his eyes and watched as Rodney checked his light meter. "One thing is very clear to me," he said, tightly pursing his lips. "You do not work well at all with actors!"

"I'm not Fellini, right?"

"That is for certain. And you call yourself a director? Hah!"

"Maybe if you tried kind of singing it," said Sarah, "you know, like Elton John."

"Ja, ja, like Elton John," said Beck, turning impatiently to

Rodney. "Why didn't *you* think of that?"

Rodney barely controlled his anger. "Yes... Elton John... all right... let's take it again... places... rolling... snow—"

I imagined myself on the mound at the World Series and this throw was for all the marbles. I wound up and gave Baron Beck everything I had. I pitched him a storm of Styrofoam that curved, dipped, spun, circled, and nearly blew off his hat.

"*Lord Mont-aa-gu!*" he gurgled.

"Close enough!" Rodney yelled out. "Cut! Print! Pack up the gear!"

"It was good?" said Baron Beck, looking pleased with himself.

"Perfect," said Rodney, putting a cap on the lens.

Beck clicked his heels together and bowed slightly. He then turned to me and said: "Did you enjoy your little pantomime?"

"Thoroughly," I said, wishing I had a few more opportunities to go for the strike-out.

Beck turned on a dime and headed back to the car. Rodney watched him and mumbled to Montagu under his breath: "We'll fix it in post-production."

"Quite."

Rodney took a quick shot of Lord Montagu spraying the oil onto the carburetor, then closed the bonnet, shoe-horned Beck back into the front seat, and filmed the two of them starting up the old roadster. The engine turned right over, the transmission slipped into gear, and the Vauxhall purred its way up some anonymous hill in the English countryside. It teetered a little in the higher altitudes, then disappeared into a glen below.

We packed up the gear, loaded up the van, and headed back on the long ride to London. Once we got on the road, Rodney blew. His artistic instincts, his political beliefs, and his social contract had all been shredded beyond repair, and there was nothing left but rage. He raged at art, he raged at film, he raged at music, he raged at national health, he raged at taxation, he raged at immigration, he raged at the father who left him and the mother who didn't, he raged at the sunset, he raged at the starry sky, he raged at the traffic delay in Bishopstoke and the pedestrian crossing in Brambridge and the construction zone in Twyford Moors, and then he raged some more. Sarah sat back and thought about turning on the radio. Robb thought about applying at the Arts Lab in London for an internship. I thought about space heaters and electric fires and wondered if the hair would ever grow back on my legs. At least Baron Beck's pashmina gloves felt good on my chafed skin. They really were soft to the touch. I wondered how long it would be before he missed them.

Chapter 4

How to Eat a Herring

Ablue-headed wagtail descended through the crepuscular Dutch sky and landed on the ledge of the top floor apartment at 184 Warmoestraat. It was a regular stop on the bird's nightly rounds. First was a diving expedition in the North Sea in search of a herring or two, a twilight snack that wasn't entirely necessary but was such easy pickings he couldn't resist. Herrings weren't the brightest bulbs in the sea and all it took was a quick flip and a flap and down the gullet they slid in one clean gulp. That's the way you do it. One clean gulp.

The wagtail was a master of deception and misdirection, kind of a Dutch Houdini, and the herrings barely merited his flair and genius. The office workers on Leidseplein were a better challenge. They were a weary bunch at day's end who could be counted on to leave their takeaway broodjes exposed for an easy snatch and grab. If he was lucky he might even reel in a zalm broodje, which he preferred to the kaas and was much better for the digestion. Then it was over to the central train station to watch the rush hour comings and goings. The whole thing was hilarious, with carts flying this way and that, windows opening, doors shutting, and steam swirling everywhere. It was a kaleidoscope of confusion in which erwtensoep was spilled, kibbeling was dropped, and stroopwafels were left unfinished. Next came quiet time, and with an hour or two to kill before the Red Light District offered its XXX diversions, it was over to the ledge and its own smorgasbord of delights.

The building on Warmoestraat dated to the sixteenth century and could've been transported straight from a Rembrandt etching. Everything tilted slightly, the roof angled every which way, and the walls leaned on each other for support. As for the interior, the doors barely closed, the turret howled in the wind, and the staircases were so narrow they were unfit for anyone but children and crabs. Still, the wagtail preferred it on the precarious ledge, hazardous as it might be, to all those soulless monstrosities going up in the suburbs. More than once he'd knocked himself silly colliding with those god-awful windows with their aluminum frames and sheer glass. No, Amsterdam was his turf, a place where the past was still respected. Whether it was art or architecture, he preferred the classic styles of Old Masters like Rembrandt and Vermeer to upstarts like Vaserely, who left him cold, or Escher, who made him dizzy.

Out on the ledge, the wagtail settled in for the evening's entertainment, a nightly show starring those crazy Dutch kids from the wrong side of town. As the lights came up Hans appeared, a look of consternation on his face, while Cecile paced nervously, waiting for anything at all to happen. Over on the sofa Jan stared skyward, as if looking for constellations in the ceiling, while Perla glumly paged through a travel magazine.

Hans was the central figure in the show, but mostly he served as a foil to the shenanigans of his pals. He was considerably older than the others—a creaky thirty-two—and as such was living out his declining years. Hans was a former Provo, the original Beats of Holland who had much to do with the new openness in Dutch society. Now he was associated with the younger hippies, thousands of whom had come to Amsterdam from all over Europe and sought refuge wherever they could find it. Hans occupied himself by sketching on cotton rag paper, portraits mostly, done with brightly colored pencils and an uncertain grip that left a distinct psychedelic sheen. The faces faded at the edges and blended organically with molecular wave fields that appeared out of nowhere and led to dimensions unknown. Still, the drawings had a kind of raw charm, enough at least for the Dutch Ministry of Culture to commission five pieces every three months. That was the deal. Hans would bring in eight drawings, the ministry would select five, and Hans would promise not to bomb the royal palace. It was an arrangement made between the city and several dozen artists. They were given a stipend that would pay for their rent, food and hashish, while the ministry added to its growing collection of never-to-be-seen art. It's hard to say how much great art was produced under this system, but street riots were a thing of the past.

Back on the ledge, the wagtail squinted to see Hans's latest portrait of Cecile, his girlfriend. Hans adored Cecile, and so did the wagtail. Everybody adored Cecile. Still, the bird wondered why Hans never drew him, a flapper of high birth who just happened to have some pretty spectacular plumage himself. Maybe not in Cecile's class, but spectacular nonetheless. Cecile had flaming hennaed hair that put the fire department on alert whenever she walked out the door. It was the perfect color for her, given that she was always the center of attention anyway, but the hair was like a big klieg light guaranteed to outshine anyone who might have the mistaken impression they could share her stage. To put an exclamation point on a klieg light, Cecile had a sidekick, a five-year-old daughter who sported matching hennaed hair and outlandish personality. The little girl was also named Cecile—what else?—Big Cecile and Little Cecile, each vying for Hans's attention, Jan's attention, and everyone else's attention. They'd come from the village of Hertogenbosch several years earlier, determined to put their mark on the big city. And put a mark they did. They were a central attraction in Amsterdam, right up there with the canals, tulips, and museums. Now they were biding their time in Hans's pad until a bigger stage came calling.

Hans presided over a kind of Beat salon, a nightly gathering of artists, musicians and writers who delved into all matters mystical, astrological and paranormal. Jan, an architect's apprentice, was especially intrigued by the secrets of the pyramids, Cheops in particular, where a vertical passageway had been unearthed after a centuries-long search. The tunnel added new layers of mystery to a structure that had drawn curious visitors from time immemorial. Now, through the use of highly arcane mathematical formulas, the pyramid could be seen as an oracle of ancient times speaking to our modern world in the only language we might understand—the language of measurements—and by transposing a system of ancient Egyptian weights and measures into their modern equivalents, one could, in fact, and with remarkable accuracy, read into its dimensions the entire predictive history of the world. The exact date of Jesus' birth in Bethlehem was there, as was the defeat of Napoleon at Waterloo and the bombing of Hiroshima. It was all there, down to the minute and hour. It was simply a matter of interpreting the angles and distances of the upper tunnel in conjunction with the tangents and parameters of the northern wall. By factoring in the shadows of the southern exposure, the mysteries unfolded like a golden lotus. The whole thing was so obvious the only miracle was that it took this long to discover it!

The wagtail turned his attention next to the sweet young

Parisian who showed up every night at sunset and stayed until Hans cleared the room. No one knew where Perla went in the wee hours of the night, though it was generally assumed she slept on the streets. In spite of her age, Perla was the most widely traveled of the bunch, which gave her special status in the bird's pantheon of admirable humans. After all, anyone out on the road needed the eyes of a hawk, the cunning of a crow, and the elusiveness of a humming-bird. And elusive she was. He followed her a few times on her late night perambulations but always she'd dart into some alleyway or disappear down a cul de sac, and he was left with nothing but a glimpse of her head and shoulders. Perla knew how to get lost in a crowd, having hitch-hiked on her own from Paris to Pakistan at the age of twelve. She'd had unimaginable experiences and had accumulated a world of experience before most girls reached puberty. Now she was nineteen going on forty, with a few teeth missing and a history of drug addiction. That's what the bird couldn't comprehend. What was the story with these kids and their drugs? Didn't they understand the consequences? No, this is where the bird took his leave. Perla would have to be someone else's problem.

The downstairs door of 184 Warmoestraat swung open and the final member of the cast clumsily edged up the stairs, his size twelve boots no match for the narrow steps. He was a tall American who slipped in and out of the apartment like a cat burglar in the night. The American, being an American, spoke not a word of Dutch, leaving everyone else to communicate in a less favored language. The wagtail was at a particular disadvantage, his English being rusty as a nail, and he had to make do with body language and gut instinct. The American was up to some-thing, the bird figured, but what? What if he had a gun? Or a flamethrower? Who knew with these Americans? They were dumb as doorknobs, loud as louts, and aggressive as sharks. The blue-headed wagtail held his breath and watched as the door to the flat creaked open and the American came in.

⌘

And that's where I come in. I'd been crashing in a tiny loft space in Hans's apartment for a couple of months now and I relished hanging out with my little coterie of European hipsters. Hans was beaucoup cool, Cecile was enchantment personified, Perla was pure delight, and Jan was a genius visionary capable of unlocking the secrets of the universe. To be accepted into the inner circles of the Dutch underground was a dream come true, a chance to finally experience a foreign culture in its natural environment. Kind of like living with Eskimos, only warmer. Life in Hans's apartment was an endless soiree fueled by hashish, cheese sandwiches, and more hashish. What more could I possibly ask for? I'd been transported to a psychedelic heaven and was dancing with the angels. I'd wake up every morning to Van Morrison on the turntable, a hash pipe in my hand, and the sound of high-heeled boots on the streets below. Amsterdam was another place in another time in another world.

And then everything changed. As they always do. That's because all good things must come to an end. It's one of the laws of the universe. Good things must come to an end, but bad things can go on forever. It's like the Eleventh Commandment.

First, Perla left for France. There were no reasons given, just a quick good-bye and a thanks-for-everything and that was that. Then Jan left for Egypt in search of the final clue to the pyramids, the measurement that would finally explain the who-what-whys of existence. I thought the answer was eighty-four centimeters but that, admittedly, was just a guess. And then Robb arrived.

Robb was my buddy from London and before that from Madison, Wisconsin, where we first met in college. Robb had an exceptional mind and was well-versed in a range of topics that spanned philosophy, literature and the arts. He also had a propensity to share his opinions on those matters with anyone at anytime regardless of appropriateness, intent or effect. He was a stream-of-consciousness narrator, unplugged and unedited, and when stoic Hans and voluble Robb met it was a match made in a dynamite factory. Everything Robb said was inflammatory, everything Hans heard was incendiary, and suddenly my idyllic living situation was in danger of blowing sky high.

Rather than confronting the situation, I avoided the whole thing by convincing Robb that we should hop into his van and head south for a few weeks. I figured that with luck Robb would calm down, Hans would chill out, and I'd move back into my penthouse loft after a proper period of self-reflection. And so, Robb and I headed back out onto the open road. We had a long history of travel by van and, despite our little misadventure with lord such-and-such and baron who-and-who, we welcomed our next excursion.

Everything went remarkably smoothly for the first hour or so. The Dutch countryside, flat as it was, held its own charms as we wound our way through the pastoral panoramas. At our very first stop, however—lunch in Eindhoven—the picture quickly changed. Eindhoven had been mostly destroyed in the bombings of World War II and what now stood in its place was a cold, alienating mass of modern architecture that had been haphazardly slapped together. While the south of the Netherlands was but a stone's throw from the north of the Netherlands, it was like entering an entirely different country. Eindhoven was not Amsterdam. Not even close. It confirmed my suspicion that the further south one goes in any country, even one small as this, the more conservative it gets. And so, before we were even halfway through our broodjes, we were accosted by the local police, who looked us up and down as if we'd just ridden in on Harleys straight out of *Easy Rider*. Oh, yes, we were troublemakers all right, that was for sure, and the next thing we knew we were being escorted fifteen miles to the Belgian border, where we were unceremoniously booted out of the country. Reason given? None whatsoever.

Admittedly, one look at Robb's van alone was reason enough to arouse suspicion. What with its dents and cracks and missing bumpers, it wasn't exactly a model of fine European craftsmanship. Then there were the two of us ourselves, a couple of scruffy characters if there ever were ones. When the Belgian border patrol saw us coming, they were certain they'd nabbed drug smugglers. Holland was the dope capital of Europe, after all, and who likelier than us to be carrying? Of course, no one in their right minds would be stupid enough to transport drugs through these borders, but the officers got to work as if they'd captured the ringleaders of an international cartel. They stripped the van right down to its tires—dashboard, gear box, glove compartment—everything was fair game. Ridiculous as it was I could see Robb sweating through the whole thing, as if the guards would go so far as to plant drugs on us. Then again, Robb had his own particular anxieties, stemming from certain activities at the University of Wisconsin that, he was convinced, had put the CIA on his tail. This wasn't entirely realistic since the CIA certainly had bigger fish to fry, but any sight of the police caused Robb's sweat glands to activate. I dabbed his forehead, worried the guards might get even more suspicious.

The dismantling of the van went on for a good two hours and I could see the frustration building in the guards. They started tossing things here and there and when they got to Robb's precious 8mm movie camera, he looked ready to faint. "Hey, easy there!" I yelled over to them, knowing that any mishandling of Robb's Kodak could lead to a complete meltdown. The guards snickered and glared at us, then sarcastically brought the camera over as if on a velvet pillow. *"Dank je wel,"* I said huffily, in the only Dutch I knew, which was fine other than the fact that we were in Belgium.

Finally, we were back on the road. "What assholes," I said, as Robb tightly gripped the steering wheel and drove the exact speed limit and not one mile more.

"Do you have any idea what you almost did?" he said through gritted teeth.

"Yeah, I saved your Kodak from the trash heap."

"The... Kodak... is... loaded... up," he said, dramatically emphasizing every word.

"So what? I'm sure nothing got exposed."

"Not with film, you idiot, with hash!"

"What? Are you crazy? Look what you did! You almost got us busted!"

"No, *you* almost got us busted!"

We went on like that, arguing, driving through Belgium and then into France, looking for the Belgian police, the French police, and the CIA. I was beginning to think they might be after us after all.

⁕

Paris wasn't much more welcoming. Even though it was nearly three years since the Sorbonne riots, the city was still strangely subdued. The police were out in full force, guarding against any possible repeat of violence. The violence, however, mostly came from the police themselves as they patrolled the streets in groups of six and eight, trying to provoke anyone into making a false step. It was 1968 all over again, only now with stricter control. Despite the dubious circumstances, we slept in the van each night, only to be awakened at dawn by the sound of police batons smashing the roof. *"Bienvenue à Paris!"* they cackled. *"Bienvenue à*

Paris!" The sound of echoing steel rang through our heads for the rest of the day.

We considered leaving but Easter weekend soon arrived and with it everything changed. The streets were suddenly and completely clear of all cops. It was only a brief show of normalcy for the influx of holiday tourists, but for the French it was a moment to exult in freedom. And exult they did. The city erupted as thousands of people spilled out onto the streets. When a full moon rose over the Notre Dame on Good Friday, I thought the entire Latin Quarter would explode.

Robb and I joined in the festivities by splurging on a bottle of Bordeaux far beyond our normal budget, which was nothing. The wine went straight to our heads as we roamed the streets with the joyous mass of celebrants. It seemed as if everyone was out—the doctors, the lawyers, even the priests. Which got me thinking. "Why do you think they call it Good Friday?" I said, as we drunkenly stumbled past a church rectory.

"Are you serious? It's the day Jesus was crucified."

"Yeah, I know... but what was so good about it?"

Robb thought it over for a moment. "Hard to say."

"I mean, it wasn't so good for Jesus, was it? In fact, it was probably the worst day of his life."

"You got a point there."

"Seems to me they should call it Good Sunday and Horrible Fucking Friday."

"Yeah, good idea. I'll take it up with the Pope."

We ambled aimlessly through the streets, turned a few corners, and wound up at Robb's van. It was early still and the streets were packed even tighter as the moon rose higher in the sky. "Let's go somewhere," I said.

"Where?"

"I don't know. Just drive."

Robb pulled onto the street and followed whoever was in

front of us, figuring wherever they were going was good enough for us, too. As we crossed Pont Neuf on the way to the Right Bank, all I could see was a panorama of lights swirling around my head. I hoped Robb wasn't as drunk as I was. If I were driving we'd be in the Seine by now.

The Right Bank was just as crazy as the Latin Quarter. The whole city had become a giant block party, all enhanced by the bright full moon. We drove a bit further, lost the car we were following, and wound up in Pigalle on the Boulevard de Clichy. I was reminded immediately of Henry Miller and *Quiet Days in Clichy,* but this was anything but quiet, no, not at all, this was the wildest spot yet. Traffic was at a standstill, car horns were blaring, and people were dancing in the streets.

"I gotta pee," I said.

"Yeah, well, good luck with that."

"No, really, man, I'll catch up with you down the street," I said, leaping out of the van.

"Wait, wait—" said Robb, but it was too late. I was already halfway across the boulevard.

I slipped into the first bar I found, but there was a line outside the john, so I hurried next door, where it was the same story, and then on to a third bar before I finally found a vacant stall. I cleared my bladder and even my head, which now felt slightly more attached to my body. When I went outside I discovered that the traffic jam had eased a bit and I hurried down the road looking for Robb. After searching for a block or two, I wondered if I was even on the right street. That's when a woman approached.

"Can you help me with this?" she said through glazed eyes and a thick tongue. She held up a bottle of wine and an opener which she couldn't quite seem to line up with the cork.

"Yeah, sure," I said, taking the bottle.

"I am just a poor tourist from Japan," she said. "I am not

good with such things."

I looked at the bottle. It was a vintage Bordeaux that must've cost a bundle. She might've been a poor tourist, but she definitely had good taste in wine. "You're in luck," I said, "I uncork with the best of them."

"I am Atsuko," she said, putting out her hand. When I looked at her under a streetlight I could see she was quite pretty, like she could've worked in some dancehall or fancy club.

I opened the bottle and we shared a drink. Then we shared another. Then I started thinking she'd walked off the pages of *Quiet Days in Clichy*. Then I started thinking I was Henry Miller. Then I forgot all about Robb's van. Then I found myself in Atsuko's hotel room. Then I really thought I *was* Henry Miller.

We finished off the bottle and fell onto the bed. The last thing I remember is a pair of stockings, a curtain blowing in the wind, and the room swirling around and around and around...

∽

I found Robb the next day at the fountain on Boulevard St. Michel. That's where all the foreigners and Parisian hippies gathered, so I figured it was a pretty good bet. "Anything I need to know?" he said.

"Not really. Everything's under control."

"I figured I'd find you either here or in the morgue."

"Is it still Good Friday?"

"Depends who you ask."

I could see a routine coming on but I was too hung over to continue. We sat at the edge of the fountain, getting lost in the waterfall, when a voice rang out. "Terry? Is it you?"

I glanced up to see a familiar face. "Perla?" I said, stunned to see her. "No way!"

"I can't believe it!" she said, as we embraced. "What are

you doing here?"

"Taking a break from Hans."

"Was it becoming too much?"

"You know how it is. How much dope can one person smoke?"

"Yes, I can still smell the hashish on your clothing. And who is this?" see said, pointing to Robb.

"This is a famous director's assistant from London."

"Pleased to meet you," said Perla as she shook Robb's hand. "You are a filmmaker?"

"Well... yeah... 8mm mostly."

"Come," she said, taking both our arms, "let me show you my town."

We walked for a bit, then drove out to the edge of the city. This was a different Paris, far from the Eiffel Tower and the Champs-Élysées. Perla took us to the poorest districts, each alive in their own way. A jumble of cars and trucks navigated the narrow streets on their way to deliver shanks of beef or bushels of potatoes. The people were earthier here, many having come from the countryside or emigrated from Algeria. The voice of Edith Piaf echoed out from one window, Umm Kulthum from another. The crowded marketplace was a hodgepodge of kosher meat markets, halal butchers, and Vietnamese noodle shops.

As we drove back to the Left Bank, Perla directed Robb to a busy intersection not far from the Notre Dame. We parked right across from a police station, where a stream of gendarmes filed in and out of the old fortress. "Terry, can you help me a moment?" she said.

I turned to the back seat to see she had a syringe in one hand and a spoon in the other. "Um, Perla, what's this?"

"Yes, I know. I'm stopping soon. Please..."

When Robb realized what was happening, he nearly leapt through the window. "Are you crazy?" he whispered. "Do you see where we are?"

"It's the best place," said Perla. "I come here all the time. The police never suspect anyone would shoot up right in front of their headquarters."

"Oh, God," groaned Robb as I held Perla's arm until she found a good vein.

"Thank you," she said as she swooned back against the seat. After a few moments, her eyes fluttered open and she leaned forward to Robb. "Can you take me back across the river?" she said. "I need to visit my mother."

"Sure, sure, anything you say," said Robb, all too eager to get as far away as possible from the police station.

We headed for the Marais district and a nondescript tenement building that arose out of the rubble. Perla slid open the squeaky side door of the van and shaded her eyes against the midday sun. "Okay, see you," she said, squeezing my arm, then half-walked and half-floated across the street. We made sure that she made it safely to the building, then watched as she disappeared into the stairwell.

"I think I've had enough," said Robb.

"Yeah, me, too," I said, staring up at the tenement walls.

We left for Amsterdam that afternoon.

❧

Robert, another friend from college, was living in the Jordaan district, just past the central canals, and I decided to pay him a visit. "I heard you were back," he said, half-annoyed to see me. Robert was always half-annoyed to see me, at the very least, but that held a certain comfort for both us. We'd been arguing ever since our freshman year in Madison and there was no good reason to stop now. "Okay, so I'm fine... you're fine... blah blah blah..." He waited for me to nod, then continued. "I want to run something by you."

"Shoot."

"I'm thinking of buying a houseboat. It's over on

Binnenkant, near the old clock tower. At least it was the other day, assuming it hasn't sunk. It's a real tub of rust. The engine doesn't work, the roof leaks, and it smells of dead cheese."

"Sounds appealing."

"Thing is, it's only five thousand gulden."

"And that's a good deal?"

"How the hell should I know? The captain said it was a real bargain and who would know better than him? He said he's retiring and he's willing to let it go for a song."

"Yeah... okay... so it's a bit of a fixer-upper?"

"More than a bit. That's the rub. I've got five thousand, but that's it. Wiped clean. So, you might ask, how do I plan to pay for everything?"

"Good question."

Robert paused for effect... "By going into business! Right on the boat!"

I couldn't for the life of me imagine what kind of business Robert could conduct from a sinking barge. Canal tours? Sea hotel? Poker parlor? Didn't seem too likely. More importantly, why business at all? Robert's greatest fear was to follow in his father's footsteps—a fear we all shared, since our fathers were obviously our mortal enemies—but Robert's case was special. His father was a wealthy industrialist and Robert stood to inherit his business. What could be more revolting for a college revolutionary than to inherit a factory full of workers? No, Robert wanted nothing to do with his father's business, or anybody else's business, for that matter. He was determined to make his own way in the world. "Okay," I said, "you got me. The suspense is killing me."

"Charter flights."

"You mean, like the ones that go up in the sky and take people places?"

"Exactly."

Robert caught me off guard with that one. Robert as a renegade travel agent? It didn't fully compute. "And you're going to do this from a houseboat?"

"That's right, give it a homey touch. I might even serve pea soup while you wait. The Dutch love that kind of thing."

"You don't think they might get nervous that you'll just sail away with their money?"

"In that old tub? I'd never make it across the canal." Robert paced the room, excitedly running the plans through his mind, but after a brief moment of reflection his mood suddenly darkened. "Wait a minute. What if one of the planes goes down?"

"Crashes? That's not going to happen—"

"Oh, yeah? What if I sell tickets to some nice Dutch family and it goes down in the Atlantic? These are real people I'm talking about, not like you and me. How could I live with myself?"

"Look, first of all, it's not your plane. It's KLM or Lufthansa or something like that. Second of all, do you know how tiny the odds are of a plane crash?"

"I don't care if it's one in a million! Mine would be the one! My dad will bring it down just to show me!"

"Yeah... I see..." I said, trying to keep a straight face. "You've got a real problem there."

Robert, of course, was never to be taken entirely seriously. He once ran for governor of Wisconsin on a lark, then voted for the Republican incumbent when he feared his write-in ballot could be used as evidence that he was a left-wing agitator. On another occasion he publicly proclaimed that the workers hated the students, which was absolutely true but not exactly the thing to bring up at a Trotskyite anti-war rally.

"You had lunch yet?" he said as the conversation took a sudden turn. Robert had a multiplicity of interests and ever since arriving in Holland, he'd been fascinated by Dutch social customs. Learning exactly how the Dutch did things was very important to him, right down to their eating habits. It was important to fit in, he insisted, and not make an absolute fool of oneself. And so, for the moment at least, charter flights were out and Dutch etiquette was in.

Robert pulled me across the street to a fish shop for instructions on how to eat raw herrings and not stick out like a sore thumb. "You eat the whole thing," he said, "the head, the tail, the bones, the insides, the outsides, the whole damn thing, you hold it by its tail, preferably smothered in onions, that's important, lots of onions, you hold it up over your mouth and you slurp it down your throat, one bite, that's all it takes, one bite and down the hatch, and then-- *are you listening?*—this is important, because after you swallow it you have to wait five seconds, ten at the most, and then you say, *aaahhhhhh, lekker,* that's the most important part—*you got that?*—you've got to be able to distinguish between a good herring and a great herring and tell them how tasty it is—*lekker, lekker*—give it some feeling. Now listen, don't embarrass me in the unlikely event we ever go out sometime. This is important stuff. Once you get the hang of it we'll talk about pickles and mayonnaise, very important in their own right, but you're not ready for that yet, maybe in a week or two—"

"Robert, you gonna buy that boat?"

"Of course."

"And start a charter flight business?"

"You got it."

"Well, then, I want to wish you all the luck in the world."

"Thanks, pal. You get ten percent off on your first flight."

❦

Hans, it turned out, had given my loft space to someone else within hours of my departure, so I needed to make new arrangements. I saw this not as bad luck, but as the universe telling me I needed to change course. That's what Jan would've said. I checked the map and found my eyes drifting north. Hmm. Scandinavia. Interesting. Now that summer was upon us, it was the perfect time to head to the Norwegian hinterlands. Why Norway? No reason, really, except that I didn't know anyone who'd ever been to Norway and that was reason enough.

And so, despite my recent poor experiences with travel by van, I decided to buy my own transportation and see where it might take me. The cheapest thing I could find was an old Dutch milk truck that had been put out to pasture. It was still painted the distinctive white-on-top, navy-blue-on-bottom of Amsterdam's dairy company, but had otherwise been stripped down to a bare shell. The only other sign of its origins were the company's *Melk* logos, which had been painted over but still showed beneath the fresh coat.

The old VW was barely roadworthy but I converted it into exotic sleeping quarters with Belgian carpets, Indian tapestries and Turkish throw pillows. By the time I was done it looked more like a harem room than a motor vehicle. A real attention getter, that's what it was. And attract attention it did. Whenever I drove down the street, people would come out and wave to me. I'd never realized just how welcoming the Dutch could be! Only later did I realize they were trying to flag me down for a bottle of milk.

On my last night in Amsterdam I went to the Kosmos, a government-subsidized hashish club, to say good-bye to my friends. Hans was there, cool as ever, as was Cecile, who was holding court with a contingent of her admirers. I was pleased to find Robb chatting with Hans like the best of friends. They'd patched up their differences and were sharing a joint. As the night wore on, I made my farewells and was about to leave when I heard the sound of a blues piano in the basement. Blues was a rarity in Amsterdam and merited a further look. I listened to several songs, totally enthralled, as a guy sang and played for a smattering of people. When it was over I introduced myself as a longtime blues fan.

"Danny Adler's the name," he said, putting out his hand to shake, "and blues is my game." Danny spoke in the gruff voice of a Mississippi bluesman even though he was a twenty-year old white kid from Cincinnati. He had quite a story, though, which unfolded over the next several minutes. Danny had just arrived from London, where he'd been playing with Charlie Watts, Ian Stewart and Jack Bruce in a band called Rocket 88. My eyes widened, duly impressed. Those guys were from the Rolling Stones and Cream! Danny explained that their bands had been on hiatus and the three of them joined together for a side gig. They needed another player and Danny was in the right place at the right time and there it was, instant celebrity! They played for a couple of months, then time came for the others to rejoin their regular bands, and Danny was gone. And now, here he was in Amsterdam, come to check out the scene. "So where's the action in this town?" he said.

"As far as blues goes, there is none. I mean, I play a bit of harmonica and I haven't found anybody to jam with since I got here."

"Bummer."

"Anyway, there's nothing much happening this time of night. I'm just saying my good-byes before I head out tomorrow."

"You know, friend, we blues cats don't go to bed at nine."

"Yeah, I dig. Listen, if you want to you can join me. I've got a couple more stops to make."

Danny roused himself off the piano stool. "I'm ready, man. Let's boogie."

We headed up the stairs, out the door, and into my van. Danny glanced around at the Scheherazade motif but didn't say anything. We drove a few blocks, turned a few corners, and rumbled along the road as a chorus of voices rang out: "*Melk! Melk!*"

Danny glanced into the rear view mirror to see a small crowd following us. "Friends of yours?"

"It's a long story."

I headed across the center of town, negotiating the narrow streets and bumpy cobblestones. When we reached the Amstel River I parked near the Oude Brug, a classic wooden bridge that had to be raised by hand whenever a large ship sailed through. This was the real Holland.

I led Danny across the street and up the gangplank of a houseboat that was docked among a flotilla of old barges that had been converted into living quarters. "Michael? Lois? You in there?" I called out as I tapped on the hatch of their houseboat. It was late at night but I could see the glow from a kerosene lantern through one of the portals and figured they must be up.

"It's open," came a voice from below.

Michael and Lois were one-half of the Eyes of Khamphalous, a light show that had toured Europe and at various times had backed up Pink Floyd, Humble Pie, and Deep Purple. Now they did the lights at Paradiso, the hippest club in Amsterdam. It was a dream gig that kept them somehow afloat, both them and the boat.

Jerry and Kathy, the other half of the light show, were sound asleep on their side of the houseboat. Kathy was pregnant and they were preparing for the challenge of bringing a baby into the world with no hot water, a heater that barely worked, and a toilet that drained straight into the canal. They were living like Dutch sailors from the nineteenth century, but Kathy was a brave soul and Jerry took it all in stride. The four of them were living out a grand adventure and breaking new ground with inventive visuals that gave the performances a whole new dimension. Michael's bold cinematic perspective, Lois's spiritual bent,

Jerry's creative genius, and Kathy's ability to hold them all together kept the whole production on a more or less even keel.

Danny and I climbed down the ladder from the deck to a comfortable space Michael and Lois had carved out of the old barge. While a bare hull was visible in places, the walls were mostly covered in a billowing quilt of old tapestries and fabric remnants. The room was wrapped in a flicker of candlelight and shadows that danced erratically through the portals. "Well, this is it," I said. "I'm leaving tomorrow."

"You sure about this?" said Michael, looking at me dubiously. "You're really going to Norway?"

"Gonna catch me a piece of the Midnight Sun."

"Wait a minute," said Danny. "You didn't tell me Norway. That's no place for a blues musician! We need fog and shadows and somewhere to be depressed."

"Have you heard of Ibsen and Strindberg?" said Lois, glancing up from a pile of Tarot cards and astrological charts. "They were as depressed as they come."

"Sure, sure," said Danny, "didn't they do those horn riffs on Freddie King's last album?"

"That's them," said Michael, playing along.

"This is Danny," I said, "a fine singer and piano player."

Lois studied his face for a moment. "Fire sign?" she said.

"*I was born under a bad sign,*" said Danny, quoting from an old blues standard. "*If I didn't have bad luck, I wouldn't have no luck at all.*"

"Let me guess. Your Mercury's in retrograde?"

"My Mercury's in hock."

She smiled. "Okay, welcome aboard. Try not to burn anything down."

Michael sat on a rickety stool, flipping through some slides. "Check out these new shots," he said, holding up several transparencies of Jesus, Buddha, and Charlie Manson to the light. He then superimposed them one over another and shuffled them around.

"Heavy," I said.

"Is it?" said Lois. "I have no idea what it means."

"It has multiple layers of meaning," said Michael. "That's the whole point. You take from it what you want. Politics, religion, murder, it's all in there, the beginning, the middle, and the end."

Lois scrunched up her nose. "Too Hollywood."

"What do you mean, *too Hollywood*. That's a crazy thing to say."

"Is it? You're just trying to appeal to a mass audience."

"What's wrong with a mass audience?"

"What's wrong is we're making art, not a Hollywood blockbuster."

"You see, you look at opportunity and you turn away from it. That's what you always do, Lois."

"Hollywood is not opportunity. Hollywood is bullshit."

"Oh, *please*—"

Michael and Lois were known for their passionate arguments, which flared up spontaneously, hit a crescendo, then were forgotten about just as quickly. They danced around each other like boxers in a ring while their houseboat rocked in the waves.

"Hey, mind if I try out that guitar?" said Danny, noticing an acoustic six-string propped against the hull.

"Please do," said Michael, anxious to change the subject.

Danny tuned up, then proceeded to play a twelve-bar blues. His fingers ran up and down the fretboard as if the strings were made of butter. "Wow," I said, "and I thought you were great on piano."

"Oh, thanks man," he said. "No, guitar's my real instrument. My axe is back in my hotel room."

"Nice, nice," said Michael as he walked to the other side of the boat, dug through a box of odds and ends, and tossed me a harmonica. "Here, try this."

"No, no," I said, fully aware I was in way over my head, but Danny wouldn't hear of it. He launched into another blues. I played so softly no one could really hear, but eventually I gained a bit of confidence and took a short solo. Danny nodded for me to take another twelve bars, then another still. The guitar and harmonica started blending together, the notes weaving inside each other. Back and forth we went, finishing each other's riffs and hitting the turnaround together. When we finished, Danny leaned back with a big smile. "Well, awright, Mr. Harmonica Man, that's awright!"

"Really? It was okay?"

"And that's the first time you guys played together?" said Michael. "You sounded great!"

I basked in my moment of glory. "It was nothing, really," I said, feigning modesty with the exaggerated sincerity of a true bluesman. "Just fooling around."

"We want more! We want more!" chanted Lois, stomping her feet on the plywood floor.

"Hey, listen man," said Danny, "here's an idea. Why don't you delay the trip for a day or two? We could try out some stuff."

"Delay the trip?" I said. "I... I... I don't know—"

"What's the worst that could happen?" said Michael. "You get to Norway a day late? The fjords aren't going to melt."

"Yeah, I suppose not," I said. "Okay, I guess it wouldn't hurt to stay another day."

Danny leaned back like an old Delta sharecropper and slapped his knee. "Awright, awright, that's what I'm talkin' 'bout!"

⁊

The next afternoon we squeezed into the back of my van with just enough room for Danny, his guitar, me, and my harmonicas. The acoustics were good, surrounded as we were on all sides by metal, and the sounds meshed nicely. We played a couple of old blues standards, then jammed on some of Danny's original songs. I was surprised how easily we shifted from one style to another. "You know, if you keep playing you could be pretty damn good," said Danny. "Pity you gotta leave."

"Yeah, well, you know how it is. Plans are plans."

"And plans were made to be broken. Seems to me, if we practiced for a couple of days I'll bet you anything we could get some gigs around town. Isn't that what you always wanted?"

"Well... yeah..."

Danny could see I was wavering. He launched into a boogie, my favorite style of blues, and shamelessly lured me in. The song went on and on, floating and soaring, rolling and tumbling, and then, as if in the blink of an eye, we were standing on a stage in a little club off Leidseplein and were playing to an audience of twenty people, then thirty, then forty...

Over the next several months Danny and I played most of the clubs in Amsterdam, some big, some small, some barely clubs at all. I got pretty good. He got better. And then, just like that, it was over. Before I knew it, the summer ended, Danny headed back to London to rejoin Rocket 88, and I was back where I had started.

It made no sense to go to Scandinavia anymore since the midnight sun was fast sinking into the sea. But then I thought it over. I was a blues musician now and we blues cats were famous for going against the grain. And so, I decided to follow my original instincts, crazy as they might now be. I would go north for the winter. North to the snow and ice. North to the darkness. North to the whale stew, lutefisk, and frozen herrings.

Chapter 5
Interlude in the Park

A patch of fog appears at the top of Twin Peaks, then majestically swoops down along the steep slope of the hills. A moment later a low-lying cloud funnels in from the ocean and moves across the park. Tobias and I watch as the wisps of cotton mist spread out like a thick blanket, billowing here and there, engulfing the redwood trees, the succulent garden and the Old World forest. From somewhere in the distant branches, a bird's warble resonates from the treetops. It begins deep in the throat, moves up into a feathery trill, then ululates into a piercing shriek that awakens the entire forest. The screech is answered by a sweet whistle from the limbs of a conifer tree that overlooks the pond. *"Peet-weet-weeto,"* trumpets a spotted sandpiper. *"Kaa-kaa-kaa,"* coos a red-throated loon. *"Tchuck-tchuck,"* rasps a hermit thrush.

A turtle stirs from its midday sleep, opens a lazy eye, and dips a toe into the pond. At the edge of the water, clusters of lilies, lilacs and azaleas cover every square inch of land fighting for their place in the sun. Even here it's survival of the fittest, although on the scale of biological conflict this is about as benign as it gets. Golden Gate Park is a pleasant respite from reality, a step back into the archeology of time where nature stretches out its arms, embraces the land, and pulls it close to its chest.

"So when do I get to see more of the city?" says Tobias.

"You don't," I say, thinking how that's just about the last thing Tobias needs right now. The battle for survival will do just fine without him getting involved.

"Well, that's not fair, is it?"

"No, it isn't," I say with a tinge of regret. Tobias is a man reborn into a world he neither knows nor understands. He's an anomaly, a man out of time, the product of a generation now gray and fading into oblivion. I'm the personification of that generation, retreating into the shadows while still trying to make sense of an earlier age. We are, of course, the same person, two aspects of a single life come to review our past, one of us with the benefit of hindsight, the other unaware of how the future would unfold. Together we pick through the corpse of history, dredging up the memories of an idealized past.

"I don't like feeling confined," he says. "It goes against my nature."

"Yeah, I know. You can go anywhere you want and do anything you like, just so long as it's within the confines of the park. That's not so bad, is it?"

"I guess."

"Well, sorry, that's the deal."

We continue our walk along the edge of the pond, Tobias spritely and clear-eyed, me a bit tired and unsure of the next step. The truth is, my stories don't compare to his. He wandered the world at a time when the possibilities were endless, whereas I now mostly wander through the nooks and crannies of my own mind. It's a solitary adventure, devoid of glamorous locales and charismatic characters, but when I think about the possibilities of quantum mechanics, string theory and multiverses, the mythologies of the ancient world seem strangely tame. I'm more comfortable now in my imagination than in some hot bus rumbling through the desert.

The fog clears just as quickly as it had blown in. It's possible to spend a day in Golden Gate Park and experience all four seasons in a single visit. The Bay Area consists of numerous climate zones, all of which have chosen to converge upon the tiny space Tobias and I have claimed as our retreat. A meteorologist would probably explain that it's the confluence of the ocean, the bay, the hills, the wind and the currents, but I think it's simply a spot where nature threw up its hands and said enough is enough. If the weather is too complicated for nature to sort out, how are we mere mortals expected to make sense of basking in the sun one minute, freezing in the fog the next, buttoning up, dressing down, and defrosting like a slab of meat in a microwave?

Tobias and I stare into the bamboo pond at the reflection of the building across the street. The woman we'd seen earlier appears in the window once again and I can see her more clearly now. She has thick black hair that reaches to her shoulders and silver filigreed earrings that dangle along her neck. A cluster of garnets catches a sliver of the sun as she leans out the window. I watch as her reflection sways between the ripples of the waves and wonder if she's really there or if she's simply a figment of our collective imagination. I'm prone to suggestion, after all, especially when under the spell of a storyteller who's filling in the blanks of my own life history.

The current in the pond changes course and a Tibetan thanka comes into view. Another ripple reveals a statue of Saraswati on the mantel place and brocade embroideries hanging over the doorways. Above the fireplace a mask twists and distorts with each crest of a wave. It has nine faces, each of them with bulging eyes, piercing fangs, and a crown of five skulls. "Mahakala, the Great Protector," says Tobias, staring at the reflection of the wrathful deity.

"Why would anyone have such a mask?" I wonder.

"Maybe she needs protection," he says. The water ripples again, then flattens to a glasslike surface. As the currents calm, the thanka disappears, the mask disappears, and the imaginarium across the street recedes into memory.

We walk a little farther along the shore and hear the tiniest echo of chimes in the air. Six metal tubes of varying lengths hang from the lower limbs of a Ficus tree and with each brush of wind they reverberate with the sounds of the Far East. It's a welcome sound, transporting us to a world of mist-enshrouded mountains, spiraling rock gardens, and sweeping orchards of mandarins and cherry blossoms.

Tobias picks up a flat stone, rolls it around in his hand, then skips it across the pond. The sound of splashing water is all it takes to cause a disturbance high above in the branches of the trees. *"Tswee-tswee-tswoo,"* comes the call from a golden-crowned kinglet who descends from a conifer with a flurry of feathers and a quick circling of the garden. The bird sees something in the water—his own reflection?—and swoops down for a closer look. The tips of his wings brush against the surface, creating a tiny ripple that slowly builds as it traverses the pond. The kinglet is joined by another bird, this one with a yellow tuft of hair, and then another and another, each of them dipping into the pond and sending the waves every which way. With each swell and undulation, a new story emerges. In every crest and crown, a climax builds. With each breaking of a wave, a new tale unfolds—

Chapter 6
The Momser

Six months of the cold, dark, Scandinavian winter moved with the urgency of molasses dripping off petrified conifer. I felt like I was trapped in an Ingmar Bergman black and white meditation on existential angst and human despair. Long nights morphed into short days which descended into longer nights still. I feared becoming fossilized like a fly in Baltic amber. And then, against all odds, the sun rose fully into the sky. In the giddiness of spring, my heart melted and I fled Stockholm with Annika, my new Swedish girlfriend, for the beaches of Greece. An entire new world was out there and we were going to grab it and shake it and turn it on its axis. And shake it we did, for an all-too-brief six weeks. Then came Crete, an island where an entire civilization had vanished centuries ago in a giant swell of the sea, and suddenly we felt small and insignificant again. This was history we were facing, a history that was unkind, and suddenly, out of nowhere, a black cloud appeared over the horizon and a tidal wave of emotion erupted. When it receded, Annika was gone and I was left staring into an empty sea.

With my sanity hanging in the balance, I decided to flee to East Africa in search of the elusive white-tufted rapto-rhinocerous, last seen chasing rainbows in the Olduvai Gorge. Or, if that didn't work out, I figured I could always hit the beaches of Mombasa. But first came a quick layover in my ancestral homeland. Two thousand years had elapsed since my distant relatives fled the Holy Land in search of more hospitable environs. They wandered the whole of Europe before settling in Bogoslav, Russia, a rather dubious choice since both Paris and London were available. But Bogoslav it was, a village that offered nothing but ergot-infested rye and rancid vodka. That, alas, turned out to be a temporary refuge as well when the Cossacks pillaged the village. It was time to hit the road again. And now, many generations removed, here I am, a wanderer of a different stripe, come not to settle in the land of my forefathers but rather to escape on the first boat to Ethiopia. I was, after all, seeking out not just my own ancestors but rather the roots of all humanity itself.

Upon arriving at Ben Gurion Airport I jumped into a taxi and headed for Ramat Gan, a suburb outside Tel Aviv, where I'd arranged to stay with Avram, an Israeli film director whom Michael knew from Amsterdam. From there I planned on going to Eilat, a port on the Red Sea, where I hoped to book passage on a fishing boat to Asmara. The taxi driver, a guy named Stein, was like taxi drivers everywhere, alternately talkative and morose. "It's your first time in Israel?" he said as we pulled out of the airport.

"First time," I said, gazing out at a mostly barren land-scape that stretched to the horizon.

"It's a wonderful country... so much to see... we have everything here... dead seas... ancient tombs... archeological wonders. What more could anyone want?"

"And I'm sure you've got some living things, too, right?" I said, with a weak attempt at Jewish humor. "You know, along with the tombs and all?"

"What do you think?" the driver retorted, not taking the bait. "Look at those trees. Whoever heard of trees in land like this? That's why they call it the miracle in the desert."

I glanced at a scraggly palm tree whose forlorn fronds blew disconsolately in the bitter breeze. "My parents sent money to plant a tree in Israel years ago," I said. "Maybe that's it."

"Not possible. The Americans bought cedars, not palms."

"Well, I'm looking for that tree. Maybe I'll take it back home with me."

The driver raised an eyebrow, then fell silent for the next twenty minutes. I wasn't sure if I'd offended him or if he'd simply tired of our conversation. As we continued down the highway, the surroundings seemed less like a miracle and more like any other semi-arid patch of land that had been carved out of an unappealing landscape. There were patches of vegetation, a sprinkling of olive and fig trees, and a string of nondescript buildings that stretched along the roadside. I stared straight ahead, hypnotized by the waves of heat that radiated off the highway, my mind wandering to places far from here and to a girlfriend now long gone.

Where were you now, Annika, were you kneeling at the Blue Mosque in Istanbul, were you crossing the Anatolia Plateau in a caravan, were you bathing naked in the Euphrates, were you heading south through the desert for Isfahan, were you trying on fine silk brocades along the ancient trade routes, were you riding the horse of a black-haired Afghani into the Hindu Kush, were you gazing into the sheer walls of the Khyber Pass, were you wandering through the marketplace of Lahore, were you tasting the rose water of Kashmir, were you holding the hand of some lover in the foothills of the Himalayas, were you thinking of me one time even, wondering if I was all right, remembering the night we met in Stockholm—

"Ramat Gan," said Stein as we pulled up to a plain-looking house on a quiet street. He got out of the taxi, opened the trunk, and handed me my bag. "Enjoy your stay," he said, with a faint twinkle in his eyes. "I hope you find your tree."

I walked up a neatly tended front lawn and knocked on the door. There was a shuffling of feet, a quick peek through the draperies, more shuffling of feet, and finally a slight opening of the door. "What is it?" mumbled a suspicious-looking guy.

"Avram?" I said, hoping against hope.

"What if I am?"

"Yes, well, I'm Terry. I'm here."

"Terry you say?" he said, looking at me up and down. "I don't know of any Terrys."

"I'm sure Michael wrote to you from Amsterdam—"

"Judy!" he called out to the back of the house. "Did we hear from Michael about somebody coming?"

"Michael from London?" came a woman's lilting voice.

"Michael from Amsterdam."

There was a brief pause. "Maybe," she finally said. "A friend or something."

Avram took a long look at me, then relaxed a little. "Okay, I guess it's all right. How long do you need?"

"Um, listen, maybe I should find a hotel—"

"No, no, it's too late. I don't want to drive you. You'll stay here."

"You're sure? It's not a problem—"

"You're in Israel. Everything's a problem."

Judy appeared at the door. "Don't listen to him," she said with a pronounced English accent. "It's just a little situation. We have a spare room. Please come in."

"Well, if you're sure—"

"Come," said Avram. "Don't make it a big deal. Tomorrow's a big deal. This is barely a deal at all."

I warily entered their house, where I was led to a room that had a bed, a desk, and an assortment of movie equipment. "Don't mind Avram," said Judy as she handed me some fresh sheets and a towel. "He's nervous about tomorrow. We're due in court."

"Court?" I said with a halting voice. "You mean, like, legal court?"

"Don't worry," said Judy, "we didn't kill anyone. Not yet, at least. Although that might be easier to defend." She stared off into space, as if repeating for the hundredth time a very trying tale. "You see, we're trying to get our marriage license, but since Israeli Jews can only legally marry other Jews we have to prove to the court that I'm Jewish."

"Uh-huh," I said, surprised that the famously humanistic state of Israel would have such a blatantly prejudicial law. "That's a bit—"

"Bizarre. I know. But the rabbis run the judiciary and the rabbis follow orthodox law from the Middle Ages. It's either that or we have to get married abroad. Which, of course, is exactly what I want to do, but Avram won't hear of it. He says it's a matter of principle. And what is that principle, I ask you?"

Before I could answer, Avram cried out from the kitchen, "Principle is what separates us from the dogs! You give in to these rabbis and the next thing you know we're walking around with leashes!"

"You see? This is what I'm dealing with. He's as stubborn as the rabbis."

"Sleep well, Michael's friend," Avram called out, putting to rest any further discussion. "Tomorrow we face the gallows."

⚜

I awoke early the next morning and decided to explore the neighborhood. Ramat Gan was a middle-class suburb that seemed a bit crummy, kind of like the Fairfax district in Los

Angeles. A Jewish kid rode down the street on his bicycle tossing newspapers onto the lawns. A Jewish milkman loaded a box of empties into his van. A Jewish bus driver pulled up to a stop where a dozen Jewish office workers pushed and shoved their way to the door. I bought a Jewish roll at a Jewish bakery and washed it down with some Jewish orange juice. Outside a Jewish cop was ticketing a Jewish car for being too close to a Jewish fire hydrant. A Jewish mailman delivered some Jewish mail while a Jewish road crew filled a Jewish pothole. "Jesus Christ!" I whistled, "what a lot of Jews!"

When I returned to the apartment, Avram grabbed me in a panic. "Where have you *been?*" he said. "We've been looking everywhere for you!"

"Hey, sorry, I didn't realize I couldn't leave—"

"No, no, it's not that. We've got an emergency. One of our witnesses for the court is sick and we need a replacement. Could you do it?"

"*Me?*"

"Nobody else is around. Just you and Harel," he said, pointing to a heavy set guy whom I noticed for the first time sitting in the corner of the room. "It's nothing, really. We'll tell you everything you need to know in the car. Okay?"

"No, no, really—"

"It's very simple," said Harel, who seemed bemused by the whole thing. "You just tell a couple of lies to the High Court of Israel and hope for the best. What could possibly go wrong?"

"Uh—"

"Believe me, it's just a bunch of legal mumbo-jumbo," said Avram, losing patience. "Now, do you want to help us or not?"

"Yeah, I guess so..." I said with a sinking feeling. We piled into the car and I got a primer on the life and lore of Avram and Judy, so many details that by the time we arrived at the courthouse, my head was swimming with information. Okay, let's see, Judy's from Manchester and met Avram three years ago at a two-month spiritual retreat, no, wait, it was two years ago at a three-month retreat, and it wasn't spiritual, the retreat that is, it was educational, which is not to say their relationship isn't spiritual, it's *very* spiritual, but it's educational, too, Judy, after all, is a school teacher, no, wait, Judy *wants* to be a school teacher—*what?*—oh, Judy *was* a school teacher and hated it, not that she hates kids, she loves kids, she and Avram plan on having a big family, if Avram can overcome his little problem, yes, his fondness for guys—*huh?*—no, no, I meant *goys*, he likes *goys*, but not too much, for example, he'd never dream of marrying one, that's why we're here, right, no, Avram wouldn't marry a goy if you put a gun to his head, not that Judy is violent or anything, hell, she hates violence—*hmm?*—oh, right, except when it comes to defending the homeland against the you-know-whos, no, in that case, Judy becomes a regular warrior, except, of course, on the Sabbath, she's very observant, you know, no bazookas on Saturday, but Saturday night, she's packin' heat, if you know what I mean, she'll blow your head right off—*come again?*—oh, she *gives* head on Saturday night, no wait, wait, of *course* she's Jewish, it's total bullshit that Jewish chicks don't give head, hell, I had a Jewish girlfriend who nearly blew *my* head off—

When we pulled up outside the courthouse, I was surprised to see that the building also served as a synagogue. Apparently Israel hadn't quite bought into the idea of separation of synagogue and state. Outside, a motley crowd of people pushed and shoved as they tried to get past a big, bruising guard who blocked the door. Avram deftly slipped between two old men, snuck some money into the guard's hand, and magically got us through the first barrier. Inside there was more pandemonium, with unruly lines outside the hearing rooms, prosecutors offices and judges chambers. Each step of the way required more greasing of palms. Fortunately, Avram had come prepared with a stack of bills that kept us moving forward through the lines. Finally, after bribes to the security chief, the court clerk, and the sergeant-at-arms, we made it to the door of the courtroom itself.

Avram, dressed in a black suit and tie, looked like he was attending his own funeral. Judy, wearing a doughty floral dress in the style of Golda Meir, looked like the treasurer of a Jewish fundraiser. "Wish us luck," she said as they entered the courtroom. Harel and I waited outside for a few tense moments until the door opened and a stone-faced court functionary called in Harel, the first witness. Harel winked at me, gave me an exaggerated thumbs-up, and disappeared behind the big oak doors.

The hallway kept filling with crowds of people wandering in circles. I kept seeing the same faces again and again, blank faces attached to dejected bodies walking aimlessly in a kind of Kafkaesque procession. Why were they here? What had they done? What were they charged with? It seemed odd that the orthodox rabbinate would exert such control over a country in which only a small minority was religious.

Finally, after an interminable wait, the door swung open and Harel stumbled out, looking as if he'd just faced an executioner. He glanced my way, shook his head, then quickly turned away. I was overcome by an instinct to flee and in that instant I really didn't care if Avram and Judy got married, got divorced, or got drafted into the army. I was out of my seat and halfway to the door when I heard my name called. "Terry Tarnoff!" it rang out, a name I refused to acknowledge, no, no, I'll just be going, best of luck to the lovely couple but I've got important business on the other side of town, nice to see ya, wouldn't wanna be ya, but then I felt a hand on my shoulder and I was pulled to a dead stop.

The court officer looked at me with such disdain that I shrunk to the size of a microscopic bug on the marble floor. He bore down on me with piercing eyes and the anger of Job: "Where's your *yarmulke?*" he demanded. "My yarmulke?" I said feebly. "I, uh, I must've left it at home."

He pulled me back to the door outside the courtroom, dug around inside a musty box, and pulled out a little black skull cap that would've fit some kid attending his big brother's bar mitzvah. He propped it atop my great mound of hair that grew every which way but down, then opened the door and shoved me inside. I felt it kind of floating up there unsteadily as I entered the courtroom, a room much bigger than I had imagined, a room large enough to conduct the religious trial of the century. I felt immediately intimidated, especially when I saw Avram nervously pacing behind a defendant's table while Judy sat slumped in a chair, quietly weeping. At the front of the room was an enormously high bench where three rabbis presided. They appeared to be well into their seventies, with black gowns, tallises and long flowing beards. The main rabbi looked exactly like God, the pissed-off God I remembered from Hebrew school. Sitting at a lower desk was the court scribe, an even older man with thick glasses and long gnarly fingers. He was busy catching up with the earlier proceedings, which he entered onto parchment paper with a plume pen. The whole scene was straight out of Dickens.

The chief rabbi began: "*Bevakacha tomar lebeyt hamishpat et shimcha hamale—*"

"I'm sorry, your honor," I interrupted, "could you speak English?"

He looked at me with annoyance. "You don't speak Hebrew?"

"No, I'm afraid not."

"How long have you been in Israel?"

"One day."

"And you don't speak Hebrew?" he repeated, as though I should have already picked it up. "Are you Jewish?" he said, eyeing me skeptically.

"Yes," I said in a wavering voice.

"How do I know that you're Jewish?"

This, I thought, was a rather odd question. Did I need to present some kind of evidence? A document perhaps? A certificate of circumcision? "Well," I said, after a long moment of consideration, "I guess I'm Jewish because my father is Jewish and my mother is Jewish."

"Your last name, it's Russian?"

"My parents were both born in Russia. They were infants when they emigrated."

The rabbi nodded. To be a Russian Jew was pretty good, not as good on the hierarchy as being a German Jew, but definitely better than a Lithuanian or, God forbid, a Moroccan or Egyptian Jew. "But your first name, it sounds"—he paused for dramatic effect—"*Irish.*"

"Some people do that in America, your Honor. Things get a little mixed up." As a matter of fact, I was named after a comic book hero. My mother was a big fan of *Terry and the Pirates,* but I decided not to tell the rabbi that. He might not understand. After all, even in America, not many Jews got their names from the funny pages.

"Do you know the defendant, Judy Mendelbaum?"

"Yes, I do."

"Is she Jewish?"

"Yes, your Honor, she's Jewish."

"How do you *know* she's Jewish."

My previous response to the same question had gone over so well, I decided to play the same hand. "Uhhh... because her father is Jewish and her mother is Jewish."

"How do you know her father is Jewish?" he said, throwing me a curve ball.

I was caught a bit off-guard and blurted out the first thing that came to mind: "Because he's president of his synagogue back home!" I lied.

"And where is that?"

I tried to remember what Avram told me in the car. "Manchester, England."

The room was getting hot. One of the other rabbis turned on a rotating table fan. "And how do you know that her mother is Jewish?"

"Because she keeps a kosher home?"

"Are you asking me or telling me?"

"No-no, she definitely keeps a kosher home. No milk and meat together, different plates for Passover, the whole thing."

"And how do you know this?"

"Why... because I visited them."

"In Manchester?"

"Uh-huh. Twice," I said, doubling down.

"At their home?"

"Yes."

"In—"

"Manchester."

The fan rotated my way and I could feel the yarmulke teetering on top of my head. I held it down with my hand as the rabbi narrowed his eyes. "Is Judy Mendelbaum already married?"

"*What?*"

"Answer the question."

"Of course not."

"How do you *know* she's not married."

"Because she would have told me. Judy and I are very close."

"Oh? When were you last in England?"

The fan rotated my way again. "It's been a few months, but we correspond all the time."

"Is that right?"

"Sure, between Manchester and Amsterdam, Manchester and Oslo, Manchester and Stockholm—"

My yarmulke suddenly went flying off my head. I grabbed for it, but it was too late. God was obviously punishing me, but for what? For lying to a rabbi? For missing every single religious service since I was thirteen? For taking a gentile to the prom? The yarmulke hit the floor and blew down the aisle. I ran after it and almost had it in my hand when another rotation of the fan blew it even further away. I noticed Avram watching in horror as I dove under some seats and finally retrieved it. The rabbi leaned over and glared at me when I returned to my spot far beneath him. He had me completely figured out. "Do you realize this is a *court of law?* If you are lying, you can be held for perjury!"

Perfect, I thought. I'm in Israel for one day and already they're threatening to send me up the river? Do they even have rivers in Israel? I'm going to do five to ten for telling them that a girl named Judy Mendelbaum is Jewish? Something rose up inside me, something noble, something righteous, something... Jewish. "Your Honor!" I exclaimed in a strong, clear voice. "Look at these two people. Look how they love each other. All they want to do is to get married, have a family, and lead a good life. You know that Judy is Jewish, you know she doesn't already have another husband. Why must you take what should be a wonderful and beautiful time of their life and turn it into something painful and loathsome?"

The rabbi flinched a little, looked at his associates, waited for the scribe to catch up, then leaned over closer to me. "Get out of my courtroom, you *momser!*" he bellowed. "Now!"

I jumped back, saw the fan rotating my way, and held the yarmulke to my head as I edged toward the door. *Momser* was a Hebrew word suggesting that I was the product of unwed parents, which I thought was a rather harsh epithet coming from the lips of the chief rabbi of the High Court of Israel. Harsh and blatantly untrue, I might add, although I did recall my grandmother squeezing my cheeks and calling me her little *momser*, so maybe the rabbi knew something I didn't, after all. I nodded to Avram and gave Judy a look of encouragement.

Israel, I was beginning to realize, was one tough town.

⊂℘

The misadventures continued. In Jerusalem a rabbi wrapped a tefillin around my arm so tightly that my circulation nearly stopped, then wrestled me to the ground trying to get me to pray at the Wailing Wall. I escaped into the Al Aqsa Mosque, where an imam cursed my heathen soul to an eternity in hell, then fled to the Old City, where a one-eyed dwarf tried to sell me a bloodstone ring he'd stolen from a tomb. I followed the Stations of the Cross in the Christian Quarter, had an aram sandwich in the Armenian Quarter, and bought some Lebanese hashish in the Arab Quarter. A few days later I took a bus through the Negev Desert, had an iced tea in Beersheba, and bought a ticket on a fishing boat to Ethiopia in Eilat. I slept on Coral Beach, snorkeled in the coral reefs of the Red Sea, and came eye to eye with angel fish, butterfly fish, damsel fish and trigger fish. I fell asleep, slept like a log, got robbed of all my possessions, walked naked through the wadi searching for my rucksack, cursed God, saw the sky turn red with anger, found my stuff, smoked the rest of my hashish, wandered the desert, lost my way, searched for the tree planted by my parents, considered my place in the universe, found the tree, lost the tree, missed my boat, and got trapped for a few more weeks.

The last thing I remember was wandering through the Negev Desert, where waves of heat rose off the desert floor and Annika danced between undulating columns of pure light. I followed her over a dune in the wadi where she swayed to the celestial sounds of an invisible orchestra, then shimmered, faded, and finally vanished into a mountain of sand.

I stared into a blank wall of disillusionment and realized I'd lost my bearings. In the desert there are no guideposts, landmarks, or roads to follow. There are no directions at all. Just inclinations, impressions, and wild stabs in the dark. Surely I'd find my way just over the next ridge or the next mountain range or the next bank of clouds...

Chapter 7

Fiona

As any storyteller will tell you, there are times to linger and there are times to fast forward. For example, when you look into a mirror and see the back of your own head, it's definitely time to move things along. Which is how we get to Fiona glancing into the rear view mirror of a Lexus sedan and noticing that Tsuneo, our dumpy beer keg of a driver, only had seven and a half fingers. "What have you gotten us into!" she whispered as she dug her fingernails into my arm. "The guy's a Yakuza!"

"All right, now look, you don't know that," I said, realizing full well that, *of course* the guy was a Yakuza, and a bungling one at that. What else could he be, a sword swallower? The Japanese mafia was famous for chopping off one section of a finger for each major screw-up, and this guy was already eight calamities into a very messy career. With only three phalanges per finger, he was in danger of soon driving with his feet.

"I can't believe I agreed to this," said Fiona, shaking her head.

"It's only ten days," I said, trying to put a positive face on things. "We'll be back home before you know it."

"That's easy for you to say. You're not the one going on-stage."

I tried to take her hand but Fiona pulled away and stared out at the nondescript countryside. One town morphed into another with little to distinguish them. Utsunomiya became Nasushiobara which became Shirakawa as we headed ever north. I sank against the back seat, feeling worse than I could ever remember. Was it really only two months since the protective spirits of Bali had saved me from being pulled into the sea? And was it really only a few months before that when I had prayed with the monks of Nepal for the soul of a departed lover?

Now, look at me. I was accompanying my girlfriend to a strip club in the north of Honshu where she'd be the star attraction. Oh, God, what have I done? How could I have sunk so low?

The smell of sulfur hung in the air. Like maybe the devil was afoot.

⁓

Haruki Nakamura had a million scams going on, a few of which were legal. He was a young guy with a reassuring smile and a kindly disposition that made his questionable propositions hard to resist. Nakamura was always hanging around Midori Apartments looking for a little wrinkle in the immigration laws or an oversight in prefecture regulations that he might translate into monetary gain. It was nickel and dime stuff, nothing that could really send him up the river but enough to keep him perpetually negotiating the rapids.

Midori Apartments was rented exclusively to foreigners, most of whom were stopping off in Japan for a few months to pick up some extra cash on their way from somewhere to somewhere else. Nakamura was an intermediary between the travelers and Japanese companies seeking Western hostesses, models and movie extras. None of this was actually legal since it violated the stipulation that foreigners not engage in any form of work while visiting Japan. It was a gray zone, and not easy to police, since the jobs tended to be for a week or two and the offending workers were usually long gone before the authorities got wind of it.

Fiona had been Nakamura's client ever since arriving in Tokyo. He immediately hooked her up with a club in Roppongi that paid surprisingly well just for chatting with the customers, lighting a few cigarettes, and dancing cheek to cheek. For the corporate drudges, it was a chance to experience something exotic and try out a few words of English. For the foreign hostesses, it was fast money and the occasional innocent kiss. For Fiona, an educated, sensitive woman, it was all a bit of a joke. Each night she dressed up, had a few drinks, and assumed a new identity. It was both liberating and demeaning, a balancing act made easier by being in a foreign country in which nothing completely made sense anyway.

Fiona was a beautiful woman with a gentle soul and a slightly twisted British sense of humor. It was born, per-haps, of being the product of a declining empire. What else could one do but laugh when everything around you was crumbling? The British had learned not to take anything too seriously and Fiona saw herself as a character in her own fairy tale. She had the ability to step just slightly out of her own body and watch everyone, including herself, fulfill their assigned roles. Where I fit into her ongoing story was still being determined. We'd met shortly after my arrival and were immediately drawn to each other. For her, I think the attraction was largely based upon my tales of East Africa and South Asia, where I'd spent the last two years. She was especially fascinated by the stories about Nepal, a magical place she'd long dreamt of visiting and a country to which I hoped to return. For me, I was attracted to pretty much everything about Fiona. She was smart, she was funny, and she had a refreshingly skewed view of the world.

Nakamura had also signed Fiona to a contract with Famous Models, a reputable agency whose representatives loved her red hair and impossibly pale skin. It was a peculiarly British look that was elegant, other-worldly, and just a bit shabby all at the same time. She modeled everything from spring bonnets to fashion accessories to nursing apparel, each new role only adding to the unreality of her world.

For me it was more difficult. Nakamura had gotten me a couple of auditions playing guitar in Tokyo nightclubs but there was little interest in a musician who insisted on playing only his own songs. "Very sorry, Terry-san," Nakamura would say. "Club owner say they want to hear Top Ten. You not play even Top Thousand."

"Yeah, okay," I said, realizing how misguided I'd been to think I could ever break into the Tokyo club scene with my indecipherable lyrics.

"I keep trying," he said with a hopeful look. "We make something work."

One day, Nakamura showed up with a "once in a lifetime" offer. "Miss Fiona," he said in his overly polite English, "how about you take little excursion to Sendai? Very nice seaside town. Five star hotel. A-one restaurant. Ten day, all expenses paid."

Fiona looked at him warily. "And what exactly must I do on this *excursion?*"

"Very simple. Only fifteen minutes each."

"What do you mean, *each?*"

"Fifteen minutes on, two hours off, six times each day."

Fiona didn't like where the conversation was going. "And what do I do for those fifteen minutes?"

Nakamura's eyes brightened. "You like to dance, no? Just

dance fifteen minutes, maybe take off a few clothes, rest two hours, dance again! You can even pick your own songs!"

"Are you actually serious?" said Fiona, more flabbergasted than angry.

"Two thousand dollars."

"Forget it!"

"Private chauffeur pick you up and drop you off."

"You're wasting your breath!"

"Okay, tell you what, how about you bring boyfriend? Terry could use holiday."

"Uh, wait a minute, Nakamura," I said, "You're getting a little ahead of yourself. I don't think Fiona's too interested in this."

"And you are?" said Fiona, eyeing me warily.

"No, no, of course not," I said, surprised she'd even think such a thing. "Not unless you really, really wanted to."

"If I wanted to? How could I possibly want to?"

"You couldn't. It's a ridiculous idea. It's just that it's a lot of money—"

"So?"

"No, no, I was just thinking about how we'd been talking about Nepal and how this could, well—"

"Help get us there?" said Fiona, narrowing her eyes. I couldn't tell if she was angry or tempted. "I can't believe I'm even saying this," she said, turning to Nakamura. "What kind of striptease is this?"

"It's nothing!" he said. "No touching. Audience completely in dark. You can't even see their faces! It's almost like being at home. Breasts mostly."

"Forget it Fiona," I said.

"No," she said, "I'll do it. On one condition. You'll be my personal valet. You have to promise not to leave my side for one single second. Except during those fifteen minutes. And then, you will never, ever, look at me onstage. Not even once, understand? You can just leave it to your imagination what I'm doing out there."

"Fiona, you can't be serious."

"I'm plenty serious."

Nakamura clapped his hands together. "We go now to record store?" he said, his eyes dancing with delight.

"Sure, Nakamura," she said, grabbing his arm, "let's go buy some music."

⁂

It was night by the time we checked into the Hotel Sendai Kokubuncho. Nakamura's promise of a five-star hotel was predictably exaggerated but the room was adequate for our needs. We settled in for a good night's sleep, figuring we'd face whatever was ahead of us in the morning. Thirty minutes later there was a loud knock on the door. "You on! You on!" Tsuneo shouted from the hallway.

"What? What?" said Fiona, slowly coming out of a deep sleep. "What's going on?"

"I don't know," I said, jerking awake. "I think it's the driver."

"Come on, come on!" Tsuneo shouted. "You late for work!"

"Is it morning already?" said Fiona, confused by the dark sky and a rising moon.

"No," I said, glancing at the clock. "It's like 10 PM."

She pushed herself up on her elbows and shook her head. "Does he think I'm dancing tonight? Is he crazy? We just got here!"

"Of course not," I said, pulling on my pants. I opened the door, but before I got a word out Tsuneo pushed his way inside and tossed Fiona her clothes.

"Let's go!" he said.

"Now just one minute!" she said, grabbing her coat and bag despite her indignation. "This is unacceptable!"

Ten minutes later we were outside the door of Ichiban

Gentlemen's Club, a crummy-looking joint with blinking lights and a burned-out neon sign that sputtered to life every few minutes, sent a few pink sparks into the night sky, then fizzled out. We were led directly upstairs to a communal dressing room where a couple of dancers pretended not to notice our arrival, then to a common area where three guys checked out Fiona from head to toe before returning to their card game around a kotatsu table. We heard some sharp footsteps in the hallway, a couple of creaks in the floorboards, and a tubercular cough as a side door swung open. A skinny old man in warm-up pants and wooden sandals looked at Fiona cursorily and grunted out a couple of indecipherable commands. Next thing I knew, she was being led away to the stage downstairs. "I'll... I'll be here," I called after her.

Once she was out of sight, the three guys motioned for me to join them at the table. There was a blanket tucked into the sides of the kotatsu, which barely stood a foot off the floor. As I slid my legs inside, I felt warm radiant heat envelop the lower half of my body. "You play poker?" said a heavy-set guy.

"I'll just watch," I said.

He shrugged and dealt the cards. "How many girl?" he said.

I was surprised by the directness of the question. What did they think, that I had a stable of girls I was running up and down the coast? "Just Fiona," I mumbled.

"Just one?" he said, pouring me a shot of whiskey. "She must be very good!"

"Yeah," I muttered, as we clinked glasses, "I'm sure she is."

"Me, five girl. These guys, four each. You just rookie!"

I downed the whiskey in one gulp, thinking how my descent was now complete. Oh, God, get me out of here—

❦

"Oh, God, get me out of here!" screamed Fiona when she came rushing into the dressing room exactly fifteen minutes later. "Come on! Let's go!"

"Was it that bad?" I said, sinking deeper under the kotatsu.

"Worse!" she said with a look of abject horror. "Those men! They were staring at me!"

"Staring?"

"Who looks at a woman that way? They just kept staring at me, like I was some kind of medical exhibit in an operating theater."

"This is bullshit!" I said. "Nakamura said it would be pitch black out there."

"Nakamura says lots of things."

"Well, fuck this. I'll go talk to somebody—"

"Who are you going to talk to? Nobody speaks English. And what would you say to them, anyway?"

"I'd tell them to stop staring."

"Oh, God," mumbled Fiona as she grabbed a bottle of saké off the table, turned on a dime, and went off in search of total solitude. "Fifty-nine more shows," she muttered as she left, "fifty-nine more shows."

⤎⤏

Time moved slowly. Fifteen minutes on and two hours off left us just enough time to walk around the neighborhood, have a cup of tea, or nibble on some fried tempura. Mostly we tried to escape the smell. There were sulfur mines in the hills around Sendai, and the stench of rotten eggs was unrelenting. It was the first thing we smelled in the morning, the last thing we smelled at night, and pretty much the only thing we smelled in between.

Each day we got picked up by Tsuneo, hurried to the club, and sank beneath the kotatsu. I was eventually accepted into the backstage brotherhood and gained respect as the clever American who was building an international stable of strippers. Fiona took comfort in saké, first to warm her throat, then to ward off the boredom, and eventually to fly off to some other world altogether. It was a world that I'm pretty sure didn't include me.

On the eighth day, right around noon, Tsuneo's familiar knock rattled the door. It was like clockwork now: roll out of bed, take a quick shower, jump into the back seat of the Lexus, take a deep whiff of sulfur, hurry up the backstairs of the Ichiban Gentlemen's Club, and settle in for a day of exhilarating conversation. Still, Tsuneo's knock seemed louder than usual, urgent almost, so heavy the wood panels shook with a frenzy.

"Yeah, okay, okay," I yelled out to him, "*choto matte.*"

The pounding continued unabated. I could see that Fiona was ready to come undone. "What the hell is wrong with him?" she said, rubbing her forehead.

I glanced at the clock and saw that it was the same time as every other morning. What was the big rush? Yakuza or not, this guy was getting on my nerves. "What is it?" I said, finally swinging open the door.

Tsuneo hurried into the room, went straight to the closet, and began pulling our clothes off the hangers. "You go! You go!" he shouted.

"Okay, man, take it easy. It's not even noon—"

"Police come! Immigration man!"

"Oh, Jesus," said Fiona, falling to the bed. "I knew it! I knew it! We're going to get deported for this!"

"Not boyfriend," said Tsuneo. "Pimp okay. Police after foreign dancer!"

I pulled Fiona from the bed before she completely unraveled and shoved our stuff into a suitcase. "Come on, let's get out of here!"

"Tokyo! Now!" said Tsuneo, frantically waving his seven-and-a-half fingers like pudgy little exclamation points on our morning gone bad. It was definitely time to leave.

"Now are you happy?" said Fiona as we hurried into the hallway.

We slipped out down the backstairs, tossed our bags in the trunk, and hid low in the backseat as Tsuneo headed for the highway. "I'll tell you one thing," I said from the floorboards, "Nakamura better get me a damn good gig after this!"

"Oh, God—" said Fiona, staring at me incredulously as the car hit a bump in the road and sped toward Koriyama. It was, I was quite certain, going to be a long ride to Tokyo.

Chapter 8

The Wrong Beatle

There was a painting Fiona had been working on for months that was pinned to the bamboo slats of the closet. It was a study of women out of place, of Westerners in kimonos, Japanese in miniskirts, Berbers in saris, and Aborigines in jeans. In the lower corner there was a figure I hadn't noticed until recently, a woman almost hidden in the thick brushwork. It was a disturbing face, hollow and lifeless. When I asked Fiona about it, she didn't answer for a while, then finally acknowledged it was her mother. She'd died a few years earlier in a car accident just outside Southampton. It had been a rainy night... the lights were reflecting on the M3... there was a blowout...

I knew that road. I'd been on it on the way to Lord Montague's estate.

The two thousand dollars from Sendai turned out to be considerably less after fees, tips, and deductions for services promised but never rendered. Tsuneo suggested I take it up with his bosses but I figured I'd better hang on to my fingers just in case I ever wanted to play guitar again.

Nepal felt farther away than ever. Now it was just dreams

and memories. I stared at a Zen rock garden outside our window in Shibuya and thought about a Japanese monk I'd met in Kathmandu—

Hideo was frail and walked with a pronounced limp, but that wasn't enough to stop him from undertaking the severe journey to the Himalayas. He'd become disenchanted with his native Shinto religion and had given Zen and Thai Buddhism a try, but those "Middle Paths" were only transit stops. Hideo was looking for the outer path, the bumpy path, the path of most resistance.

When he got to Nepal, he found the real thing. The Tibetan monks started him out on one-hundred-thousand full prostrations, beginning with a ramrod straight back, then down on his knees, stretched out face down in the dirt, back to his knees, up again, and down once more. Again and again, he would repeat the ritual until his bad leg burned with so much pain that he would pound it with his fist, trying to deaden the feeling as he bent down one more time.

There were chants and mantras and fasts and days of walking and weeks of silence until every molecule of Hideo's body submitted to a kind of transcendental state in which his body became his mind and his mind became a mirror. He felt himself in tune with his ancestors. He was becoming the Warrior, the Protector, the Upholder.

My reverie shifted to a few days later when I crossed the swing bridge over Kathmandu's Bishnumati River. I was right at the spot where they cremate the bodies and a slightly sweet, sickening smell hung in the air. I moved along quickly, trying to get away from the smoke and the stench, but I was momentarily blocked by a water buffalo that moved aimlessly along a mud path. As I looked for a way around him, I noticed a couple of pigs fighting over a scrap of food. Their squeals set off a chain reaction of barking dogs, bleating goats and shrieking crows that stirred a human form from out of the muck.

It was a woman, as best as I could tell. She wore a turquoise chiffon dress—the kind that little girls wear on their birthdays—and had a whole jumble of bizarre objects tied into her hair. There were bottle caps, rubber pacifiers, toy soldiers, a baby Jesus, and plastic Hindu gods wrapped in brocade. It was like she had a second-hand thrift shop on her head and when she turned to face me the whole mess clanged together. "Ciao," she said, calling to me over the commotion.

"Ciao," I said. "You okay?"

"Buona, buona," she replied in a heavy Italian accent. I was happy to see that she was lucid but that didn't stop me from thinking she was one of strangest-looking people I'd ever seen. I couldn't tell if she was laughing or crying.

"You live here?" I said, glancing into the pool of mud.

"No, no," she said, pointing to the cremation pyres along the river. "There." She stretched her arms, rearranged her hair into something slightly more presentable, and stood up to leave. Her hair clanged and her dress swooshed from side to side as she headed for the water. "Carlotta go now."

"Oh, okay," I said, relieved to end our conversation. "Ciao bella."

Several days later I crossed the Bishnumati again and found Carlotta fanning the cremation flames. But now someone had joined her. It was Hideo. He watched her intently, unable to avert his eyes. It was as if she was a vision come out of the smoke, an apparition of the ether, an angel of the fire. She embodied everything for him—suffering, desire, ignorance, understanding, thought, speech, action, livelihood, effort, mindfulness, concentration—and he fell to her feet. He did his usual round of prostrations, up, down, up, down, but these prostrations were for Carlotta and once she finally noticed him at the side of the river, she stopped fanning the flames, sauntered over to his prone body, and tied a toy airplane into his hair—

There was a knock at the door.

I thought about not answering—who could it be this early in the day?—but the persistent rapping finally forced me to respond. *"Choto matte,"* I said in my extremely primitive Japanese. I was good for about ten phrases, but *choto matte* was my favorite expression simply because of the way it sounded. *Cho-to mah-tay.* I liked the way it rolled off the tongue and kind of reverberated in the air.

The tapping on the door persisted.

The room was dark even though it was nearly noon. I'd never met a painter before who hated light, but Fiona was convinced she worked best in the shadows and never opened the wooden shades. Her stuff was everywhere. There were books, scarves, crusty dishes, a moth-eaten teddy bear she'd brought from England, dirty towels, boots, umbrellas and paper fans. These were not the possessions of a responsible adult. They were the props to a fairy tale.

The tapping became more insistent.

"Yeah, yeah, I'm coming," I called out as I cleared a couple of old kimonos off the floor. Fiona and I lived in a four-and-a-half-tatami room, that being the number of tatami mats that could be arranged within our four walls. It was a small space but there were ways of arranging tatamis that were considered auspicious and would create harmonious living conditions. There were other ways of arranging tatamis that were considered inauspicious and would bring misfortune. Then there were our tatamis, which were arranged so haphazardly as to guarantee extreme disorientation and eternal chaos.

The tapping grew louder still.

"What is it already?" I said as I swung open the door.

"Buongiorno," said Carlotta. "I new neighbor."

I stared at her familiar face and thought for a moment that the world had just slipped off its axis. No. No, no, no, no, no. This was completely impossible. The gods were messing with me. Or the sulfur from the Sendai hills was finally melting my brain. Or the rock garden suddenly had it in for me. I swallowed hard. Something seemed to get stuck in my throat. I think it was a goat. "*Ciao, bella,*" I finally responded.

Carlotta hadn't changed much from Nepal. She still sucked on a plastic pacifier strung from her hair, she still wore a frilly turquoise dress, and I still couldn't tell if she was laughing or crying. There was, however, one noticeable difference. She was at least six months pregnant. "You have maybe some *sucra?*" she said.

"Yeah, sure," I said, leading her inside. I headed for the kitchen in a daze, wondering where Fiona could possibly have left the sugar and wondering how Carlotta could possibly, at this very moment, be in my apartment.

Carlotta sat on the tatami nearest the closet and immediately began pulling on a piece of igusa straw that was unwinding from the underside of the mat. "*Bambino* love the sweet," she said, rubbing her stomach. "*I* love the sweet. *Husband* love the sweet."

"Husband?" I said, feeling that goat in my throat again.

"Hideo very *mal.* He next door. *Stomaco. Polmone. Rene. Gamba.*"

"I'm sorry to hear that. Maybe he caught something in the mountains."

"He caught me," she said with a half-sad look. "Hideo have bad case of Carlotta."

I looked for the sugar in the refrigerator and under the sink with a greater sense of urgency. Then I heard a little swooshing sound and a childlike laugh.

"*Ooooh...*" said Carlotta.

I looked over and saw she had one of Fiona's brushes in her hand. She seemed entranced with the fine hairs.

"Nice, no?"

"Very nice."

"No, no," she said gleefully. "You look painting. I make

better."

I turned with a sinking feeling to the canvas on the closet door, which was still wet from this morning's session. It didn't take long for my worst fears to come true: there, in the corner of the painting, was a deep gouge running down the length of a kimono and perfectly bisecting the face of Fiona's mother. "Oh, God..."

Carlotta saw my distressed look. "You *problema?*"

"Yeah, big problem, " I said as I hustled her to the door.

"No *sucra?*"

"No *sucra.*"

She looked at me and shrugged. "No *problema.*"

At that very instant I heard footsteps approaching from down the hall and I knew from the little hop, hop and skip that it was Fiona. Of course it would be Fiona. The door swung open. "My, a lot's happened around here since I left," she said in her lilting British accent upon seeing Carlotta's bulging stomach.

"Some unexpected company," I said, trying to defuse the coming explosion. I thought fast. Maybe a healthy display of indignation would help divert the inevitable disaster. "Fiona, where in God's name have you put the sugar?"

"How should I know?" she said, transfixed by the mass of objects tied into Carlotta's hair. "Have you looked under the kimonos?"

I quickly moved between Fiona and the painting when Carlotta came a little closer. "You make?" she said, pointing at the canvas over my shoulder. Fiona nodded. Carlotta ran her hand along some strands of hair that fell to her shoulders, untied a toy bazooka, and handed it to her. "This for you."

Fiona held the bazooka in her hand, not quite sure what to do with it. She nodded unsurely and went to put it down.

"No, no," said Carlotta, "like this." She took a thin column of Fiona's hair and braided it through the bazooka's barrel. She then let it drop and stood back. The bazooka dangled perfectly atop Fiona's left ear. *"Bella! Bella!"*

Fiona looked into the mirror, then turned to Carlotta and smiled. "I'm Fiona."

Carlotta glanced around the room with dancing eyes. "I fix for you *everything*," she said. Then, before I could stop her, she pulled Fiona to the painting. "You like?"

I stood there, waiting for the inevitable. It was too late now.

Fiona looked at five months of work, of intricate layers of texture and shadow, of theme and subtext, of the innermost expression of everything roiling around her subconscious. Carlotta's work was irreparable, a mad slash that became the sole focus of the canvas. Fiona stepped back and glanced at me. Then she looked back at the painting. And then she took Carlotta's hand and said: "I like very much."

With that, everything melted. The painting, the tatamis, and the rock garden all blended into a pool of light. I felt bathed in a transcendent glow. I don't think I've ever loved anyone as much as I loved Fiona at that moment.

⚬⚮⚬

Nakamura, feeling bad about our misadventure in Sendai, managed to get me a gig at the Omaru Club, one of Japan's most exclusive nightspots. My audition hadn't gone particularly well but the manager of the club thought I looked like John Lennon and that was good enough for him. This Lennon thing had caused me no little embarrassment throughout Asia. If anything, I had perhaps the tiniest resemblance to Lennon, and that was mostly because we both wore round wire-framed glasses with rose-colored lenses. Add a guitar case to the ensemble and that was enough to convince an entire continent that one of the world's richest and most famous musicians was sleeping in their crummy hotel or dining in their dump of a restaurant.

The night of my big gig was typical. I was decked out in a
full length leather coat, bell bottom pants and platform
shoes that made me tower over my surroundings. Once I
entered the Yoyogi Uehara subway station, it was only a
matter of time before a couple of Beatles fans appeared at
the top of the escalator. "Lennon-*san!* Lennon-*san!*" they
yelled at me, then ran off down the stairs giggling uncon-
trollably.

The subway ride was like any other—people pretending
not to stare, me pretending not to notice—and then I was in
the Ginza, the heart of the entertainment district. Ginza had
all the trappings of a bustling metropolis but few of its
problems. It was totally safe at any time of day or night,
which was nice, but in truth I missed that particular edge of
the big city. There are, after all, times when one *wants* to be
accosted, that's what big cities are for, to rub elbows with
deviants, to feel a bit of drool on your neck, to cringe at
someone's touch, to glare into someone's shifty eyes, to
wallow in the unsavory condition of mankind, it's therapeu-
tic actually, it's good to mix it up from time to time with
those who might make you question your blissful existence.
In Ginza, alas, the greatest danger was in being blinded by
the neon advertisements and left to wander in a state of
materialistic delirium. Walk through Times Square with a
guitar at night and you might never see it again. Leave a
guitar on a corner in Ginza and you might return the next
morning to find it waxed, polished, and perfectly tuned.

The Omaru Club was strangely quiet when I arrived, but
considering the prices posted at the bar, it was hard to
believe that anybody would be crazy enough to venture in.
A shot of whiskey cost a hundred and fifty dollars, a couple
of prawns two hundred. You could drop a thousand dollars
in this place without blinking. I figured that's why no one
was there except for two bartenders, a half-dozen hostesses,
and Shinsei, the manager.

Shinsei had once been President of NHK television but had fallen from grace after too many drinking scandals. Now he was seen as a cautionary tale for what happens if you don't keep your nose clean and your pants pressed. Shinsei was already wobbly from a hard night of drinking when I entered the low-lit club. He looked right past me with no sign of recognition whatsoever as I passed him on my way to a tiny backstage area where I waited for my twenty minutes of fame. That's all they wanted, a brief musical diversion that wouldn't interfere with the business of business. As the minutes ticked by I peeked out at a sea of empty tables. All the clubs in Tokyo had to close at 11:45 and it was fine with me if nobody showed up, since Shinsei would have to pay me whether I played or not. At eleven o'clock, with still no customers in sight, I packed up my guitar and kicked back. Just a few more minutes and I'd be back on the subway with two hundred bucks in my pocket. Suddenly I heard a commotion out front. There was the shuffling of feet, the banging of doors, and the creaking of chairs. Then the backstage door swung open and one of the bartenders rushed inside in a panic. "You're on, you're on!"

I grabbed my guitar and followed the bartender into the club. The place was packed with several dozen middle-aged executives who filled every table and barstool. They'd probably been to five clubs already and were at the Omaru to finish up the night on a high note. No one even noticed me as I took my place at the center of the stage and tuned up. I mumbled a few words, then started playing an original song about life in a quaint Nepalese village. The club immediately became a frozen, silent catacomb in which not one person moved a muscle. At first I was pleased to have captured their attention, but then I saw that my audience was staring at me so lifelessly that I wondered if they were dead. Was it possible? Had I actually wiped out an entire room of Japanese businessmen with my lyrics? Thankfully, the silence was broken when the Chairman of National Semiconductors belched loudly and threw a giant prawn across the room. This apparently was the signal everyone had been waiting for to descend into absolute bedlam. Shinsei fell under his table and began nibbling the ankle of a hostess. The Secretary of the Japanese Treasury howled like a wolf and emptied his glass in one gulp. The head of product development for Toshiba Electronics balanced a champagne bottle on the breasts of a waitress.

When I finished the song, there was absolutely no response. Not even a boo. Nobody even knew I'd stopped playing. The absurdity of performing in the Ginza hit me full force. Was this why I had come to Japan? Was this why I bought those shoes and pants? Was this really all there was? I grabbed a harmonica out of the guitar case, cupped my hands around the microphone, and let loose with a crazy, bluesy wail. The note careened around the room, bouncing from martini glasses to snifter glasses to shot glasses, and by the time it echoed off the mirrors and chandeliers, I had the full attention of everyone in the place. You could hear a pin drop. I played a furious solo that reached into the pits of their stomachs and when I was done, the lights came up, the place erupted in applause, and everyone streamed for the exits. I quickly gathered my things so as to not miss the last train. At the door, the bartender handed me an envelope with my pay and said, "Shinsei said to tell you. Music very hot. Everyone listen. No one drink. You're fired."

❧

The phone rang early one morning and I tried to grab it before Fiona awoke. The telephone, as usual, was buried beneath a pile of clothes, or under a pillow, or inside the bed itself, and I tried to locate its muffled ring. How many times had I told her—*"It's Japan. People don't live like this. There's no room to live like this"*—and how many times had she promised to clean up the mess before completely forgetting about it? To live with an artist is to be buried in paint, rags, brushes and bristles. It's to be a victim of the slings and arrows of artistic temperament. It's to be father confessor, mother superior and sister of mercy all rolled into one. I finally found the phone inside some ripped tights which were wadded up inside a boot. I fumbled with the receiver and tried to make sense of some indecipherable English. "It's Famous Models," I said, handing it over to Fiona. "Sounds important."

Fiona anxiously took the phone, mumbled a few words, and handed it back to me. "It's for you," she said. She looked almost as surprised as I did.

"*Moshi-moshi,*" I said into the receiver, utilizing two more of the dozen or so words of my Japanese vocabulary, and even that was an exaggeration since it was really only one word squared.

"Terry-*san!*" came a warm, mellifluous voice, "we have very important job for you!"

"For *me?*" I said, remembering how only weeks ago they'd looked at my long hair and mustache and dismissively told me they'd contact me just as soon as they had a call for a degenerate hippie. "You know who this is, right?"

"Yes! Yes! Can you come right now to Roppongi office?"

"Yeah, I suppose—"

"Very good! Everyone wait! *Moshi-moshi!*"

"*Moshi-moshi.*"

⬥

When I arrived in the offices of Famous Models, five people were waiting for me. There was a momentary hush as they examined me like a king crab in a restaurant fish tank. A photographer held up his hands to frame my face, a production designer took some quick measurements, a hair stylist fumbled with my hair, and a makeup man examined my pallor. "George Harrison!" they all agreed.

"No, actually, I'm John Lennon."

"Yes! Yes! Very funny!"

An executive from Sony Electronics came over and en-thusiastically shook my hand. "You've heard of *Rolling Stone Magazine?*" he said.

"Of course."

"They are soon publishing brand new Japan edition. We need you for Issue #1!"

Wow! Was it possible that my bravura performance at the Omaru Club had landed me in the pages of *Rolling Stone?*

Well, no, of course not. The executive explained that they were about to publish a translation of *Rolling Stone Magazine*. It would have a glossy cover, full color, nice paper—an *improved Rolling Stone*—and their first edition would be the George Harrison issue. The designer showed me the latest American cover. It was a close-up of Harrison onstage, wearing denim overalls and an old work shirt. Under the open collar was an African beaded necklace and in his hands was his vintage Fender Stratocaster. Harrison was backlit with red and yellow gels and was looking off into the distance with a serious, yet ethereal gaze. The guy from Sony giggled as he explained the concept. They were going to dress me up in the same clothes and reproduce the lighting and shadows. It was going to be some sort of parody as best as I could understand. "Harrison and Fender on front cover, you and Sony on back cover," said the exec. "Very funny!"

"Uh... you're kidding, right?"

"Yes! Kidding! Very funny!"

I felt a kind of existential anger slowly working its way up my spine. Didn't they know that I was an actual musician? Didn't they understand how insulting this was? Not to mention the utter absurdity of them confusing me with

George Harrison? "Don't you get it?" I said. "You've got the wrong Beatle!"

"Yes! Very good! Very funny!" they said as they hustled me off to a dressing room to be fitted with a pair of denim overalls, a work shirt and an African necklace. I was then led to a small stage that was backlit with the same red and yellow gels and was instructed to stand there with a "faraway look" in my eyes. I wasn't quite sure how to affect a faraway look, so I just stared off into the distance thinking about Fiona.

"Good... good..." said the photographer. "Maybe look a little more serious."

Okay, I thought about Fiona in the back seat of the Yakuza's car as we fled Sendai—

"Yes, yes, very nice, now hold guitar—"

The production designer handed me a vintage Stratocaster that I cradled in my arms with due respect.

"—a little higher... hold... hold... and—"

I suddenly felt the guitar being yanked out of my hands and a metal box being slipped in.

"—smile—"

I glanced down to see that instead of the Stratocaster I was now holding a shiny Sony CF-5700 Cassette-Corder. It looked like I was about to play an A-minor chord on the volume meter.

"—faraway look—"

"But... but..."

Click.

A cheer rang out among the half-dozen assistants. Before I knew what happened, the make-up man dabbed my nose, the photographer took a few more shots, and I was led away. "Thank you, Harrison-*san*," said the hair stylist as she escorted me out the door. "Tell Miss Fiona we call soon."

❦

Spring arrived and everything changed. The Japanese economy faltered, the advertising budgets dried up, the clubs began laying off hostesses, and the phone stopped ringing. Spring also brought the birth of Carlotta's baby to Midori Apartments. The baby cried all night, Hideo groaned all day, and Carlotta screamed at the basic confinements of her new life. But there were benefits from motherhood, too. Little *bambina* was developing tufts of hair and soon the strands would be long enough for braiding. Carlotta scoured the neighborhood for little plastic figurines, fabric remnants, and whatever flotsam and jetsam she might find that could adorn the newborn's crown.

As the days got longer, I began taking buses rather than being trapped in the darkness of the subway. One afternoon traffic moved so slowly that everything ground to a halt. As we sat at an intersection I heard a chant building in the distance and then the pounding of drums. In a city where honking a car horn was considered highly discourteous, this was highly unusual.

I leaned out the window of the bus to see a mass of people charging toward the intersection from across the street. There were thousands of them, some carrying red communist flags, others waving the black banner of anarchy. They wore bandanas across their foreheads and carried metal shields and staves which they beat together into a terrifying crescendo. At the front of the mob were student firebrands screaming into megaphones, whipping up the crowd to a near hysterical pitch. Riot police lined the streets and a battalion of cops on motorcycles followed behind with a massive show of force. The protestors began whistling and pounding the shields, and the entire street shook with the trampling of feet on the pavement. They swarmed toward the intersection, their youthful anger ready to explode, screaming at the top of their lungs, their eyes on fire. And then the traffic light turned red.

And everything stopped.

Not a single demonstrator ventured over the lines of the crosswalks. The beating of drums stopped. The megaphones fell silent. The chanting died down. The crowd stood there for exactly ninety seconds, at which moment the light turned green and the street shook again with anger. The mob charged across the road, screaming, whistling and pounding their staves against the shields. Somebody in a red headband with yellow lettering ran up alongside the bus, handed me a black flag and melded back into the mob. I waved it from the window, my own anarchic spirit revived, happy to add my voice to the maddening crowd, even if I had no idea what we were protesting.

With the bus barely inching along the road, I got off and entered the maze of tunnels and corridors known as Shinjuku Station. Shinjuku was a city unto itself where one could eat, sleep, work, marry, retire, and be buried for the price of one subway token. As my train to Shibuya was still ten minutes away from departure, I stepped inside a newsstand alongside the platform to see what the Japanese tabloids had to offer. As I paged through a few papers, a woman suddenly scurried out from behind some newspaper racks and began bowing to me. She had a positively giddy glint in her eyes as she bent lower and lower with each bow. I moved deeper into the store to get away from her, but a few seconds later two teenage girls came running in and then *they* started bowing, cooing and hyperventilating. One of them almost fainted.

I began backing out of the store, careful not to overturn anything, when I saw the display that would alter music history forevermore. On the side of the wall, covering three entire shelves, were dozens of *Rolling Stone Magazines*, all lined up side by side, their glossy covers vibrantly aglow in the fluorescent lighting. There was a guy on the front cover wearing denim overalls and a work shirt, open at the collar.

Underneath was an African beaded necklace. His head was backlit with red and yellow gels and he was holding a Sony CF-5700 Cassette-Corder as if it were a guitar.

Oh, God, no...

The Japanese read from right to left, so their front covers corresponded to our back covers, but since this was an American-style magazine, the publishers decided to be cute and do it the other way around. That might've worked except that the parody of the cover was so extensive that Sony even put the *Rolling Stone* logo behind my head, as well as the date and price of the magazine. If that wasn't enough, the publishers wound up cropping George Harrison's picture so that his guitar wasn't even visible anymore, thereby losing the entire point of the parody! By the time the magazine hit the stands, everybody assumed the back was the front, and there I was, plastered all over Japan.

"It's time to leave," I said to Fiona when I got back home later that night and showed her the magazine.

"I'll start packing," she said as she began gathering her teddy bear, her paper fans and her kimonos.

It was time to move the fairy tale to new environs.

Chapter 9

Interlude at the Bamboo Pond

Tobias and I walk along the edge of the bamboo pond, each of us lost in our own thoughts. There's something primordial about staring into a pond, as if an ancient world was submerged beneath the surface just waiting to be discovered. All sense of time disappears and the mind feels washed clean as the water laps against the shore.

The water carries mankind's history, all churned up and flowing in a thousand directions at once. We try to isolate a single moment and watch as it flickers to life, reflects for a brief moment in a wave, then dissipates back into the eternal wash from which it arose. The past is a jumble of people and places, of characters moving in and out of each other's stories, of synchronicity, of fate, and sometimes, of just pure dumb luck. Paths collide for unknown reasons, they continue on in parallel space for a period of time, then break apart like chemical reactions gone haywire. Orbits flatten and elongate, we spin like electrons willy-nilly through the universe, attracting, repelling, making contact, losing touch.

I glance at a patch of fog, feeling insecure and anxious. Tobias stares out at the horizon, relaxed and at peace. The fog wraps us in the problems of the moment. The clear blue sky invites us into the future. It's a future that Tobias fully embraces with all the optimism of the past century, while I tread more cautiously through the minefield of current events. I envy Tobias. He still believes in magic. The truth is, I'm loathe to burst his bubble of endless possibilities and grand outcomes. What's the harm of living in a dream world of open borders and universal love? What does it matter at this point? Let Tobias spin his tales and examine his life and ponder what it means. There's a certain charm to his naiveté, so long as he stays within the confines of the park, that is, because out there, brother, it's a whole other world.

We come upon a stone ancestral figure and are reminded of the eternal spirit that surrounds us all. It's a calming vision, a retreat to the earth, to stone and chisel, to soft edges and polished faces. A lotus flower trembles slightly in the wind, sending the murmur of a wave across the pool. The reflection of the stone statue dips and bobs, as if bowing to us in a greeting. "Tell me something," says Tobias after a long moment. "Why am I here?"

"You know why. I'm trying to reconnect with my memories before they fade away altogether. Your stories fill in a lot of the blanks."

"And why is that so important?"

"Because without the past, the present exists in a kind of void. It has less meaning unless you can put things in a broader context."

"Uh-huh, that makes sense," says Tobias. "But I think there's something else."

"Oh?"

"I think you feel guilty."

I turn to him with a start and laugh a bit too loudly. "Guilty? Why should I feel guilty? I'm just trying to piece together the whole puzzle."

"I think you're afraid you lost your way. You came back to the West after all those years and watched the whole thing slowly slip away. Whatever you learned in Africa and Asia got slowly eaten up and now you're not sure you even remember why you went there in the first place."

I feel the muscles in my neck tightening and a sense of impatience. "That's ridiculous," I say.

"Is it? You say you brought me back to jog your memory. I think you brought me back because you wanted to see what you once looked like. I think you like who you were back then better than who you are right now."

I have no answer for Tobias and no desire to continue in this vein of conversation. The world that Tobias knew doesn't exist anymore. One can no longer travel overland through some distant desert or across a lonely mountain pass in search of unspoiled lands and untouched people. The old routes are closed now, too dangerous to traverse or too developed to hold interest, the far corners have shed their distance and been swallowed into a kind of universal sameness, the pristine beaches have been usurped by lounge chairs and umbrellas, the naked forests have been stripped and re-clothed, the underground haunts have become well-lit and pacified. How do I tell him that the carefree days of yesteryear are now just a dim memory?

We gaze out at the reflection of the ancestral figure as it rises and falls in the crest of a wave. The stone edifice seems to come alive right before our eyes, its inert skeleton taking on skin and bone and gliding across the water like a ballerina unleashed from the waves. In an instant the entire garden comes alive with the hoots and hollers of a hundred birds. *"Pik-tuk'tuk,"* rattles a summer tanager. *"Kew-kew-kewo,"* trills a northern flicker. *"Pee-oo-ee,"* whistles a black-bellied plover. Then comes the most peculiar call of all, a bellowing shriek that resounds throughout the garden. The branches of a bush shudder, then open to reveal a blue-green iridescence that radiates through the foliage. A tail appears, then an elongated neck and a crest of blue feathers on a luminous head. The rest of the park falls silent as if astonished by the display below. A spectacular bird gazes out upon its audience of commoners, then dramatically fans out an enormous tail. A thousand eyes emanate from its shimmering feathers like an army of detectives come to spy on this quiet corner of the forest. A peacock? In Golden Gate Park?

At that instant the woman appears again in the window across the street and she's staring right at us, finally taking notice of the two intruders who've been watching her every move. Her face looks smooth and refined, aristocratic almost. Her eyebrows arch slightly with a kind of natural curiosity. Her hair sweeps back into a free-flowing stream of tresses that reaches just to her shoulders. Despite her noble countenance, there's a kind of mystery that surrounds her, an incompatible mix of self-assurance and vulnerability that keeps her slightly off-balance.

A shifting current in the pond projects another angle of her apartment and the geometric shapes of a mandala pulsate through the window as if someone were turning the lens of a kaleidoscope. The woman maintains a kind of numinous composure, her eyes dreamy pools of light, a glow emanating from her face. She slowly opens her arms as if to welcome us in. In the reflecting waters, a ray of light vibrates from her palms and I reach out to grab onto it as if trying to capture a thunderbolt in my hand.

Who is this woman? What does she want? As the water crests and topples to the shore, I see a kind of recognition in Tobias's eyes of some memory, some story, some thread that might help tie it all together—

Chapter 10
Where's Zed?

Bad ideas inevitably lead to worse ideas. It's one of the Lost Commandments and a corollary to my theory that everyone is wrong about everything. But then there are *really* bad ideas, which only the most disturbed of minds can conjure up in moments of extreme distress. These ideas are so bad they're almost good, given that they lie so far outside the norms they somehow succeed despite themselves. Which is to say, with the Japanese economy teetering, with the strippers union strapped for cash, and with my modeling career limited to Beatles impersonations, I decided to abandon Tokyo and smuggle drugs to Bali instead. It was so obvious, I'm amazed I hadn't thought of it before!

Fiona was highly skeptical of my latest brainstorm but I assured her that I had a foolproof method of transporting marijuana from Thailand to Indonesia. From there it would be a simple matter of unloading a bunch of Thai sticks to the tourists. As far as I was concerned, we'd be performing a public service. I promised her I'd take care of all the arrangements, which involved the purchasing, packaging, and concealing of the product. All Fiona had to do was to transport the stuff in her suitcase. Nobody would ever suspect her. She had the ability to transform herself into a nurse, a school teacher, or a legal secretary, whereas I looked like a walking wanted poster.

There was another issue facing us. Fiona's sister was about to get married in England and this would not only pay for Fiona's ticket to London but would leave us enough to reunite in Nepal a month or two later. Once Fiona realized we didn't have any better options, my idea didn't seem quite so outlandish anymore. And so, we packed up our stuff, said our goodbyes to Carlotta, Hideo and little bambina, and headed for Thailand.

⚬⚬

There's a certain comfort in returning to old haunts. Having been on the road now for over four years, I understood the way things worked and was able to move around more freely. I knew that in this place you smile a lot, in that place you bargain for everything, and in that place over there you don't even stop for a second. I knew the night clerk in Hong Kong who let me sleep in the closet when all the rooms were full. I knew the cashier in Singapore who let me pay later when I forgot my wallet. I knew the chef in Jakarta who put extra tofu in my nasi goreng. I also knew the desk clerk at the Hotel Malaysia in Bangkok, and when we checked in I asked him about Zed, a Turkish junkie I knew from a previous visit.

"Zed? That crazy guy?" said the clerk as he glanced up from my passport with a look of annoyance. "He just disappear! Leave all his stuff in room! What we supposed to do with all that junk? Crazy guy doesn't pay for room, what we supposed to do?"

That was Zed all right. He'd nearly burned down our hotel in Chiang Mai when his cigarette smoldered all night long in the folds of his mattress and now he'd parked his bags in a room and probably forgotten which hotel he was in. Hotels and Zed didn't mix, that was becoming evident. "I'm sure he'll show up one of these days," I said to the clerk as I signed into the registry. "If he does... don't tell him I'm here, okay?"

"Yeah, okay," said the clerk as he handed back our passports. "Fucking guy."

The truth is, I was hoping Zed had checked out long ago, back to Ankara perhaps, or to some opium den in Calcutta, or to some other hotel in Bangkok where the air conditioning was cooler and the room service quicker. I just wanted to make sure we wouldn't run into him in the hall, have to invite him into our room, and then wake up three months later in a pool of sweat and a pile of powder surrounding us.

We headed up the creaky elevator to our room. I watched the floor numbers flicker on and off as we were slowly pulled up by an uncertain mechanism that huffed and puffed and scraped and groaned. When the doors finally opened, I was relieved to have beaten the odds of being trapped inside and welcomed the escape from the piped-in elevator music. Bangkok had its own version of elevator music, but rather than the bland fluff of the West, this was something that sounded like the soundtrack to a Thai film noir. It was an ominous kind of music that always made me question what was lurking down the hallway.

The Hotel Malaysia was a shabby place that had catered originally to soldiers, then to backpackers, and now to anyone with five bucks and a high threshold for smog and car horns. We checked into my old room on the fifth floor— somehow that room was always available to me, even if the rest of the hotel was full—and looked around. The dresser was still there, still teetering on three-and-a-half legs, and next to it was the crummy leatherette chair and the sagging bed and the dented waste basket and the mirror with its warning sign pasted across the top of its cracked frame:

No Opium Smoking in Bed

"Classy place," said Fiona.

"Yeah, I know, it's lacking in a few basic amenities," I said, "but it's all part of the plan. A place like this, we just blend right in and go about our business. If you stay at the Oriental, everybody wants to know your life story. Here nobody cares about anything but their next hit. Mick Jagger could check into this dump and nobody would notice."

"*I'd* notice. I'd say, 'Mick, why don't you and I blow this joint and fly to St. Tropez.'"

"Yeah, good luck with that. Send me a postcard."

Fiona glanced at the torn sheets and discolored blankets and felt her skin crawl. She decided to escape into a deep sleep that would hopefully last until morning. I put away our stuff, turned the air-conditioning to full blast, and headed down the musty hallway.

The moment I stepped outside onto the street, I was slapped across the face by a wall of stultifying air that robbed me of all will to live. That's all it really took to return to the reality of Bangkok, a blast of heat that told me to fall in line with the natural order of things which, when all was said and done, wasn't natural at all, not when my shoes were sinking into the asphalt and threatening to entomb me like a mummy. I was a microscopic bug swimming across a sea of burning oil, a crazy-legged octopus jitterbugging on a blistering beach, a hot-blooded microbe exploding on a vulcanized Petrie dish. I was back in Bangkok, all right, and I couldn't wait to get out.

❦

When I awoke the next morning, I realized that something had changed. Fiona and I were on the road now, and that added a whole new dynamic to our relationship. Living in

Tokyo was one thing, a place where we each had our own lives and were often separated for long periods of time. Now we were truly together. That meant breakfast, lunch and dinner. I think we both liked the security of having a companion but this couples business is no easy task, especially considering that we human beings are members of an extremely flawed species. We're easily provoked, often irrational, and are built more for conflict than compromise. We're cavemen, basically, in designer clothes. That's why so few couples survive being on the road. The couple that can survive the road is destined for a long and happy life together.

Once Fiona and I got acclimated to the heat and humidity, it was time to put our plan into action. I made some discrete inquiries at the front desk and was eventually slipped the name of a top-notch "import-export specialist." Unfortunately, the guy lived in Pattaya, a beach town several hours south of Bangkok, and required a long bus trip through unknown territory. I wasn't thrilled to have to set out to find an unknown man in an unknown place, but I left a few mornings later with a bundle of cash and a large suitcase. Fiona stayed behind to shop for her disguise for getting through customs.

The bus twisted along a bumpy road to the coast. Three hours later I got off at the bus station in Pattaya and carefully followed a map the clerk had jotted down on the back of a napkin. I walked three blocks to the west, passed a little factory that squeezed oil from coconut husks, crossed a barren soccer field, turned left at a big banyan tree that had an image of Kwan Yin carved into the bark, and entered a little shop with a red awning and piles of junk lined up along the walls. "Is Prasong here?" I asked an old lady who sat on a wobbly teak chair that was missing a few slats.

"Who want to know?" she said to me through blackened teeth.

"Somboon from Bangkok sent me."

"Don't know any Somboon!" she shouted.

"Somboon... Somboon..." I whispered discretely. "You know, the friend of Chanchai."

"Chanchai?" she said, still shouting. She stared at me suspiciously, then called out to someone in the back. "Kulap!"

A young boy wearing shorts that were at least two sizes too big wandered in from the back room. The old lady yelled out some instructions to him and he motioned for me to follow. We headed back onto the street, down through some alleyways, and up to a fragile-looking structure that was built on stilts. "Prasong! Prasong!" the boy called out.

What was *wrong* with these people? Was everyone in Pattaya half-deaf?

After some movement behind a shuttered window and the shuffling of feet, a middle-aged man with slicked-back hair appeared on the porch. He was wearing a polyester shirt, tight pants with a sharp crease down the middle, shiny black shoes, and the kind of wraparound sunglasses that Thai traffic cops wore day and night. I had an over-whelming urge to flee. The guy looked like a cross between Dick Tracy and Sergeant Friday. I half-expected to see handcuffs hanging from his belt. "What you need?" he said.

"Yeah, well, I, uh, I was told you could help me. You know what I mean? Somboon sent me."

"Thai sticks? How many you need?"

Well, that was easy. Prasong was obviously a man of few words. I decided I liked that about him. At least I think I did. Actually, who knew if it was good or bad? It might've been the worst possible thing in the world. I hesitated. "Um... that depends on the price."

"One brick, one hundred-fifty baht. Hundred brick, price one-thirty."

I did some quick mental arithmetic. At these prices, and with twenty sticks in a brick, it was like buying chewing gum. "Yeah, okay. Sounds good."

Prasong nodded. All that was left was to try the product. Prasong rolled up a big joint and handed it to me. I lit up and felt a strong tingling in my throat as I inhaled. By the time I handed it back to Prasong I was already feeling stoned. Prasong took a long drag and let the smoke escape through his nostrils, like something he'd seen in a Humphrey Bogart movie. He then handed the joint to little Kulap, which I thought was a bit odd, but not really, since the kid seemed like an old pro. Kulap smoked the joint halfway down, then nodded knowingly as he passed it back my way. I wasn't completely sure what we were agreeing on, me and little Kulap, but I shared in the conspiratorial nod and then Prasong started nodding and some guy on a bicycle started nodding, and an old grandmother on the street started nodding, and even the Kwan Yin carving on the tree started nodding. That's all it took for a wave of paranoia to descend over me, not uncommon when I smoked Thai sticks, the strongest pot I'd ever tried. I looked more closely at Prasong, how his sunglasses reflected into his shiny shoes which then reflected back to his sunglasses which then reflected back to the shoes. Who but a cop wears wraparound sunglasses and shiny shoes? And pants with creases, for that matter! I wondered how soon it would before he arrested me, or the old lady informed the police, or little Kulap blew his junior detective whistle.

Next thing I knew I was agreeing to Prasong's offer, Kulap was disappearing into a darkened room, some guy was whistling an off-key Thai film noir melody, birds were dropping out of the sky, fish were floating belly up in the sewers, and Kulap was returning with a big bag of dope. Money was exchanged, my suitcase was filled, and I suddenly found myself walking alone through the back alleys of Pattaya. The whole street was staring at me, and I do mean the street: the rocks, the pebbles, and the trash cans joined in with the shopkeepers and the old ladies and the babies and the dogs and they all looked at me with one giant unblinking stare, and suddenly I felt a weird pressure in the air, like my eyeballs might explode, and now time is shifting into some kind of present tense and I'm standing at the bus station with six hundred Thai sticks in my bag and it's only a matter of time before the army, the navy, and the national guard descend upon me to execute the most spectacular bust in the long and glorious history of the Kingdom of Thailand. This is the end, my friend, oh, yes, this is really, truly, the end of the end of the end...

❧

"How'd it go?" said Fiona, when I returned to the Hotel Malaysia that night.

"Nothing to it," I said, as I stashed the suitcase under the bed.

"Good. I was getting worried."

I glanced at Fiona sitting at the edge of the bed. Something seemed a bit off, and it wasn't her anxiety I was sensing. In fact, Fiona didn't look worried at all. She looked just about as relaxed as I'd ever seen her. Her shoulders were loose, her forehead was unfurrowed, and her eyes were languid. Which didn't seem right. I looked at her more closely. "Oh, God," I said. "You're stoned."

"Yes, well, so what if I am?"

"You're stoned on powder!"

Fiona knew it was useless to try and deceive me. I'd had too many of my own unsavory encounters with China White not to be able to recognize the telltale signs. "Well, I was worried and when I came back to the hotel some guy was hanging out at the parking lot fountain and he said he had something I might like."

"Please, tell me you didn't score from some street deal-er—"

"Don't worry. I just wanted to try the stuff. I only got a gram."

"A gram is a lot! Might I remind you that we're getting on an airplane in a few days and you need to have your wits about you?"

"If I had my wits about me I wouldn't be doing this in the first place."

"Fiona, this is important. You can't be nodding out at customs."

"Well, like I said, I was getting worried."

I could see we were entering dangerous territory. "Listen, you have to believe me. There's nothing to worry about. Nothing's going to happen at customs. And if it does, I'm taking full responsibility. I'll tell them the suitcase is mine and that you didn't know anything about it."

"And then what? They take you off to jail and I just continue on to Bali for a little holiday?"

"Fiona, nothing's going to happen."

"How do you know that?"

"I just do."

Fiona leaned back on the bed and felt a new wave of relaxation roll over her. Her shoulders loosened, her eyelids fluttered, and she drifted off into an opiated dream world. This was a new fairy tale for her, a very stoned one, and I could only hope she didn't like it too much. "Know what?" she whispered, with a slightly twisted smile.

"What?"

"I miss Sendai."

"Yeah," I said, happy to see she still had her sense of humor. "Me, too."

❧

The next day I went to an electronics shop in Siam Center and purchased a Sony cassette recorder. I was a Sony man now and nothing else would do, but in fact it wasn't the recorder I cared about, it was the extension speakers. I took some measurements and decided they'd be perfect.

Back at the hotel I set to work. Prasong had thoughtfully pressed each of the bricks with an automobile jack so that they took up less than half their original space. I wrapped each one in multiple layers of plastic until there was no hint of a smell. Then, after disassembling and tossing out the speakers, I individually taped each brick inside the now-empty speaker boxes. I resealed the back covers and cautiously spaced them out in the suitcase so that nothing would shake and would fit securely amongst the clothing and travel items. I tossed in a couple of cassette tapes and some extra wires to add to the deception.

The next few days passed in a blur. All I really remember was checking out of the hotel and taking a taxi to the airport. Once we got to the terminal Fiona went into the restroom to apply the finishing touches to her ensemble, and when she came out I almost didn't see her. It wasn't just that she was unrecognizable; she was very nearly invisible. Her red hair was wrapped in a scarf and her skin, already a whiter shade of pale, had somehow been transformed into the color of air. She wore a powder-blue sweater over a cream-colored blouse and when she walked by she blended in so perfectly with the walls, the floor and the ceiling she might as well have been part of the woodwork. She could've been carrying a Bengal tiger under her arm and nobody would've noticed.

As Fiona stood in line at customs, it was as if she'd entered a black hole in which the light had been sucked out of the air and there was nothing left but a vague shadow. Had she looked into a mirror, I'm pretty sure there'd have been no reflection whatsoever. When she reached the counter, the customs agent yawned with such disregard I thought he might fall asleep right on the spot. He glanced at her passport, stamped her visa, and drew a little chalk mark on her suitcase all in one motion. The prime minister of Thailand couldn't have gotten through any more quickly.

I followed behind Fiona in the line, checked through without a problem, and caught up with her in the corridor. "You know, I'm going to write about this someday," I said as we headed for the departure gate.

"Um-hmm..." she said as she raised an eyebrow and nodded skeptically. "I'm sure you will."

I shrugged sheepishly and laughed at my own self-delusion. She was right, of course. It was the kind of promise no one ever keeps.

Chapter 11
The Shaman's Last Laugh

The sweet smell of frangipani hung in the air as Fiona and I stared out from the porch of the Bali Sky losman. Across the path stood a giant banyan tree whose limbs twisted into the evening sky. It was a schizophrenic tree growing in every direction at once, as if refusing to stay within the boundaries that nature demanded. The dissonant tones of a gamelan orchestra drifted in from the nearby forest, adding a dramatic soundtrack to the unfolding scene. *"Nam-nam-ling-ling, nam-nam-ling-ling,"* came a rumble of gongs and flutes that were both atonal and melodious at the same time. The tree, the gamelan, and the shifting light was much like Bali itself, perfectly harmonious and utterly discordant all at once.

The moment we arrived in Bali, Fiona transformed from her persona as the librarian of a British boarding school—or whatever disguise it was that she was affecting—to a free flowing beach nomad. Off came the scarf, the powder-blue blouse and the sensible shoes, and on came the sarong, the lace kebaya and the flip-flops. "I like it here," she said.

"I thought you would."

We'd gotten through customs without a glitch and could finally take a deep breath, even if we had a suitcase full of pot propping up the tea and cracker tray. From our fresh perspective in the tropics, what had seemed like such a good idea in Tokyo already felt more than a little questionable. We'd taken unnecessary risks and now had to unload six hundred Thai sticks without drawing the attention of the authorities. The locals didn't much care one way or the other, but the officials from Java were always on the lookout for drugs, alcohol, nudity or anything else that might help free the human spirit, and I knew to keep my distance.

I was happy to see that not too much had changed in the nine months I'd been gone from Legian Beach, even if I had an uneasy feeling that a page had been turned when no one was looking and that a new story was being written. I sensed that some step into the future had been taken that couldn't be walked back, that some social pact with the locals had been breached without their knowledge. Foreign investors were purchasing land at bargain prices, travel consortiums were scooping up cheap lodgings, and government agencies were pushing the development of new tourist attractions. The villages along the beach were expanding into the rice paddies, there were more cars on the road, and the merchants were ramping up production for a growing export business. Paradise, I feared, was fraying at the edges.

Fiona, meanwhile, was plunged into an artistic fairyland the likes of which she'd never imagined. Wherever she went she was surrounded by paintings, fabrics, sculpture and jewelry. For the Balinese it was only natural to carve the handle of a tool or adorn the crown of a cow or embroider the top of a basket, and art was an integral part of everyone's life. Dreary England offered nothing remotely like this, and even Japan didn't compare. Within several days her sketch pad was bursting with the visual impressions of an irresistible new world.

Bali was bathed in a perpetual glow but Fiona's pale skin and red hair were no match for the beating sun. She preferred the forests behind the sand dunes and the palm groves far from the beach. The light there was subdued, like our room in Tokyo, and she could wrap the shadows around her like a comfortable old blanket. But Tokyo wasn't in her mind anymore, not since the moment we stepped foot in the tropics. The nightclubs and subways already seemed a million miles away.

∘◦✐◦∘

"Pssst... psst..." I called out, as a couple of Westerners strolled down the path that bordered the losman. I waved a joint in the air, giving my best impersonation of a streetwise drug dealer, but my heart wasn't in it.

A handsome guy wearing linen pants and a floppy cotton shirt looked at me curiously but ambled over despite my half-hearted presentation. "Anything we might be interested in?" he said.

I could tell immediately that he was more sophisticated than the usual riff-raff I tended to associate with. Most of the people I knew had just a touch of the criminal in them, but he seemed to be more refined than most. He carried a woven bag from Dayak over his shoulder, wore a silver belt encrusted with turquoise, and exhibited a certain panache born of good breeding. "Well, I actually have a few Thai sticks," I said, already feeling embarrassed by the whole encounter.

"More than a few," Fiona interjected under her breath.

"Yes, well, probably as many as you could possibly want."

"Is it the Buddha weed?" said the guy's companion, a striking-looking woman whose accent I couldn't quite place. She was remarkably beautiful, like an Egyptian princess or a French actress or a German countess. She looked like she'd be equally comfortable on the French Riviera or the Costa del Sol. "Is it the good stuff?"

"I'm told it's from Buddha's personal stash."

"Well, in that case—" said the guy.

"You see?" said the woman. "I knew it was our lucky day! Didn't I tell you we should walk this way?"

"Um-hmm," the guy said, nodding to her while whispering to us in an aside: "She wanted to walk along the beach." He seemed amused by the whole thing. "I'm Jonathan," he said, putting out his hand to shake. "That's Anouchka."

"Terry and Fiona—"

"Your hair!" said Anouchka, gazing upon Fiona's red locks. "It's the color of a persimmon! Is it natural?"

"Yes, it's from my mother's side—"

"Wait! Jonathan! The bag!" said Anouchka before Fiona could get out another word. Jonathan handed over his satchel and Anouchka dug through it until she came up with a tiny uncut garnet that was strung on a strand of copper wire. "You must have this," she said as she handed it to Fiona. "It's the perfect match! Never lose this stone, it's very special. It comes from the mines of Burma, near the stupa of the highest saints. Only the most important people have such a stone."

"I'll cherish it forever," said Fiona, holding onto the garnet as if it were a buried treasure. I was pretty sure that it could be purchased for about a dime at any gem shop, but Anouchka made the stone seem special, and she made Fiona seem special, and she made the moment itself seem special.

"You see?" said Anouchka. "I knew we should've walked this way. I told Jonathan it was time to tingle-tangle."

"Tingle-tangle?" I said, not at all sure what she was talking about.

"Don't mind my wife," said the guy. "She kind of speaks her own language."

"How do you say it then?" said Anouchka, looking a bit flummoxed.

"Mingle? Is that what you meant? I'm going to guess mingle."

"Mingle... tingle-tangle... what's the difference?"

"None whatsoever."

"I'm dying to know something," said Fiona, already falling under Anouchka's spell. "Where are you from?"

"I come from everywhere," said Anouchka, sweeping her arm into the air.

"Well, yes, but—"

"Why does it matter? I'm tired of borders and boundaries. What good are they? They're only there to separate people. We need to bring people together. Isn't that right, Jonathan?"

"That's right, dear."

"Good! Then that's settled!"

In fact, nothing at all was settled, but she was right. Who cared where she was from, or how old she was, or what her real name was? These were all things that would forever remain a mystery. I could tell from the way Fiona was looking at her from several different angles that she already wanted to paint her. "Anouchka, can I show you a couple of drawings?" she said.

"An artist?" said Anouchka as she anxiously followed Fiona into our modest room. "I knew it! Didn't I tell you, Jonathan? I knew it!"

"Yes, you were just telling me—" he said, as they disappeared behind a beaded doorway.

"Beautiful woman," I said to him.

"Fiona, too."

"We're a couple of lucky guys."

"That's for sure."

I lit up a joint and handed it to him. "You been here a while?"

"About a month. Amazing place. You?"

"I'm back for the second time. Truth is, I'm not sure why I ever left in the first place. I spent the winter in Japan and couldn't wait to get back." Jonathan took a hit on the joint and passed it back. I watched as the smoke swirled around into a tiny cloud, hung in the air, then disappeared into the folds of my sarong. "I mean, in Tokyo I had to wear pants. Pants with *belts*. And shirts with *buttons*. And shoes with *laces*."

"What?" he said in mock horror. "What were they thinking?"

"This is where the magic is. Here... India... Nepal—"

—As if on cue, the gamelan music from the forest came drifting in, beautiful yet jarring—

"That's what we're beginning to realize. The longer we spend out here, the more we want to just keep on going. These places aren't going to be a secret forever."

Bali was hardly a secret but compared to most exotic locales it was still largely untouched. Who knew how long that would last? I took another hit off the joint and glanced up at an impossible palette of colors at the horizon. It was as if Matisse had painted the sky and still had some extra pastels he simply tossed all over the canvas.

"What were you doing before this?" I said to Jonathan, as I passed him the joint.

"I was working in Hollywood, living the good life. The truth is, I had a pretty good gig. Lots of doors were opening, a chance to move up."

"What, directing?"

"Producing. Not always the best stuff but I was getting my feet wet. Who knows, maybe I'll go back some day, try some other things, take it a bit further. I feel like there's a lot of stories to tell."

"It seems to me the best stories are right here. I mean, Fiona and Anouchka? You couldn't make up characters like that."

"That's true. Well, who knows what happens? It's all a big crapshoot, isn't it? I could stay here. I could wind up growing coconuts in Cambodia. I could run into you in Hollywood one day and wind up writing screenplays together."

"Sure, why not?" I said, taking another hit off the joint. The weed was talking now and it was leading me into another crazy fantasy.

—*Yeah, I'll move to California and become a Hollywood screenwriter. Just as soon as I write that book I promised Fiona*—

Anouchka breathlessly burst out of the room. "My God! She's a magnificent artist!" she said. "I knew there was a reason we came here!"

"You're much too kind," said Fiona, blushing from the compliment, "but I'd love to paint you."

"Of course! Of course! I will make for you a wonderful pose!" Anouchka looked completely stoned, and that was before she even took the tiniest toke off the joint. That's all she needed since she was already living on the highest of the high plains.

"Good luck getting her to sit still for five minutes," said Jonathan.

"Have you seen the sky?" said Anouchka, dreamily gazing off to the horizon. "And this crazy gong-gong music! Jonathan! It's like one of your movies!"

"Just like," he said, with an amused smile. He clearly adored his companion and waited with the rest of us to see what she'd say next.

"Who needs Hollywood?" she said. "We've got everything right here, in full color black-and-white!"

"That we do, sweetheart," he said, glancing my way with a knowing smile. "That we do."

❦

Fiona and I eased into our life in the tropics. We were awakened each morning by a chorus of finches and cipohs, and dozed off each night to the distant gamelan. By day women passed by the losman selling batiks and the occasional rare ikat blanket from Sumba or Sawu. The ikats were woven on the neighboring islands and had only recently been brought to Bali by a Westerner who traded them for horses on Flores, an island where barter was still more common than money.

The women always loved coming by our losman where they could gaze upon Fiona's red hair and porcelain skin. If they were really lucky, they might even be allowed to run their fingers through her tresses. It's hard to say who was more fascinated by whom, the women with their baskets full of antique jewelry and fabrics, or Fiona with her collection of teddy bears, fans and umbrellas.

We visited the painters of Ubud, the silversmiths of Celuk, and the woodcarvers of Mas. We walked through the rice paddies of Mount Agung, the temples of Tampaksiring, and the monkey forest of Sangeh. We watched puppet shows, ketjak dances, and cremation ceremonies. But mostly, we sat on the porch of the Bali Sky losman, waiting for customers. The days were passing, the wedding in England was fast approaching, and we were still well short of the funds needed for Fiona's ticket to London.

An uneasy tension grew between us, subtle at first, then more blatant. Fiona accused me of not upholding my end of the bargain, which was technically true, but what was I supposed to do? Go door to door with the sticks like a Fuller Brush salesman? There were other things as well. We were snapping at each other and letting minor irritations get the better of us. Things that in Japan might've passed unnoticed were exacerbated here. It's one of the pitfalls of living in paradise. Anything that's less than perfect gets magnified a thousand times when set against an idyllic backdrop.

One afternoon, as I sat on the porch strumming my guitar, a guy passed by with a cylindrical leather bag slung over his shoulder. When he heard me playing, he came right over. "Salamat, um, whichever—" he said, searching for the right word.

I understood the problem. *Salamat pagi* was good morning, *salamat malam* was good night, and *salamat jalan* was goodbye, but at this time of day it was hard to say what it was. "Uh, salamat salamat..."

We shook our heads in agreement. The guy had blond wavy hair, bright blue eyes, and an open, friendly face. I could tell from his accent that he was Italian but I figured from his looks he must be from the far north of Italy, like somewhere around Copenhagen. "Mind if I join you?" he said, pulling the case off his shoulder.

"Sure," I said, "so long as that's not a bow and arrow."

"Most people think it's a pool cue," he said, as he pulled out a shiny silver flute. "You see? Nothing lethal. But I must warn you. I don't play Verdi or Puccini."

"That's okay. I don't play anything at all. I mean, nothing anyone has ever heard."

"Perfect," he said, as he attached a mouthpiece to the flute. I tuned up, strapped my harmonica brace around my neck, and strummed a few chords. "Ah," he said, "so we are a whole band. What are you playing? It sounds kind've jazzy."

"I'm not really sure what to call these chords. They're mostly accidents."

The fact is I wasn't a very good guitar player, but what I lacked in technique I made up for in odd chord choices. It allowed me to explore new territory on the harmonica, which was my real instrument.

"Well, let me try," he said. He played a few scales until he came upon something that blended nicely.

"Yeah, yeah, that's it," I said.

We jammed a bit, then tried some other combinations. Fiona eventually came out from inside our room and introduced herself to Gino, our visitor. I could see she was distracted. She listened for a moment, poured some tea, and began pacing. I could see what she was thinking: *While he's screwing around on guitar, the sun is setting and another day is passing us by.* Fiona finally exploded. "Damn it, Terry, do something!" she said as she grabbed my shoulders. "Do you see what day it is?"

I immediately stopped playing and shrank in my chair. "Yeah, okay..."

"Yes, well, I was just leaving," said Gino as he quickly packed up his flute and disappeared down the pathway.

"Some other time," I called after him. "You sounded good."

Fiona stared at me, fed up and out of patience. I could see that it was going to be a very long night. All we needed was some off-kilter gamelan music to help set the mood. It began ten minutes later: *"Nam-nam-ling-ling, nam-nam-ling-ling..."*

⸎

And then, everything changed. First, Jonathan and Anouchka left for Thailand to continue their tour of Asia. I had the feeling their explorations were just beginning and that we'd meet again, but we agreed to meet on the corner of Hollywood and Vine at noon on New Years Day, just in case. The year was still to be determined.

Then, just like that, a guy appeared at our doorstep and offered to buy our entire supply of Thai sticks, at a discounted price of course. A quick glance at Fiona convinced me not to risk bargaining over the price, and the deal was consummated within half an hour. Suddenly, the suitcase was empty, our wallet was full, and we were on our way to purchase a plane ticket. We grabbed the first bimo to

Denpasar and tried to digest what was happening.

Bimos were local jitneys built for four or five people, but they usually carried whatever number of people, baskets, boxes and mattresses that could be shoe-horned inside. The contraptions were slapped together with discarded car parts and felt particularly unsafe on the road to Denpasar, notorious for its blind spots and out-of-control drivers. "I'm curious about something," said Fiona, sitting across from me at the rear of the vehicle as we bounced along the road. "If things hadn't gone well at customs, what would you have done?"

"You know what I would've done," I said, surprised she'd ask.

"Tell me again."

"Are you serious?"

"Tell me."

"I would've told them the pot was mine."

"Are you sure?"

I looked at Fiona for a long moment and felt something crashing down around us. "Yeah, I'm sure," I said. "I'm amazed you'd ask."

"I was just wondering," she said, brushing it off as if it were nothing.

We sat the rest of the way in silence. I stared at a giant banyan tree as the bimo took a sharp turn on the road to town and thought back to my previous summer in Bali when I ate psilocybin mushrooms and orbited high above the banyan trees with the spirits. Then, as if in a vision, I saw the man from the black magic forest lurking behind the branches, the man who'd fed me seventy-five mushrooms and launched me through the portal to a glorious, insane adventure that would forever change my life. He had that same crazy look in his eyes as he stared at me and Fiona, a crazy, demented look that told me nothing would ever be the same, that whatever had brought us together in Japan had abandoned us in Bali. As the bimo sped away I turned back to see the mad shaman laughing at me, laughing and laughing as if he'd just perpetrated his biggest joke ever.

Fiona left for London a few days later.

I never saw her again.

Chapter 12
Full Circle

I was on my own again. An empty bed. An empty porch. An empty feeling in my stomach. The entire losman felt empty, but a day or so later a gecko appeared on the ceiling, then another, and then another still, as if to fill the void. The Balinese didn't much like being alone and before I knew it, a couple of kids from Legian were playing in my courtyard and then the ladies with the batiks dropped by to chat, and then came the inevitable legions of voyeurs who came by just to come by. The Balinese were a curious people and it was nothing for them to walk down the path, make a sudden detour, swing by somebody's window, and stare at whatever or whoever was inside. It was disconcerting at first, then almost charming in its sweet innocence, and eventually more disconcerting still.

The previous summer I'd pretty much blended into an anonymous group of foreigners, even though there were often people playing music in my room until late into the night. Now, on my second visit to Bali, the locals took more interest in me and the spying became more pronounced. I was no longer just a foreigner passing through but somebody who was becoming part of the community. They wanted to know more about me, and I felt their eyes upon me wherever I went. I thought this was understandable, since the legacy of foreigners on the island was mixed going back all the way to the days of Dutch colonization and Japanese invasion.

One day I rented a bicycle from a shopkeeper in Legian and set off for town. After riding a short distance I discovered that the brakes were faulty and brought it back for one that worked. The proprietor, a short muscular guy with a quick temper, informed me that there were no other bikes available, that a deal was a deal, and that there'd be no refund. The amount of money was insignificant but the principal wasn't, not for either of us, and we got into a heated argument. Finally, when he got tired of the whole thing, he said: "You live at the Bali Sky losman, in the far room near the garden. You smoke marijuana every night."

The message—and the threat—couldn't have been clearer. "I see," I said after a moment's consideration. "Okay. You win. Keep your bike and keep your money, but I'll never shop here again."

He shrugged with self-satisfaction and motioned to the street. "*Salamat jalan,*" he said with a twisted grin.

"Asshole," I said as I headed off down the road.

⁂

Legian was a recently developed area that catered to the growing number of budget travelers who'd originally stayed on Kuta Beach. A few miles down the coast in Seminyak was an even newer development called Kayu Aya, which was being built as a getaway for the super-rich. Kayu Aya was a joint partnership between the government and an international consortium of corporations in which no expense was spared. It consisted of a dozen elegant bungalows, each with their own private swimming pools, patios and gardens. A crew of servants, gardeners and private chauffeurs was trained to provide services on a par with the finest resorts of Europe, and with prices to match.

Kayu Aya, unfortunately, never opened. Legend had it that the bungalows were built on an ancient Chinese graveyard and that the place was forevermore cursed. Whatever it was, a battle between the greedy developers and the greedy government had doomed the place to lying fallow and awaiting the encroaching jungle. There were no good guys in this argument, neither the government, which was hopelessly corrupt, nor the international consortium, which was, after all, an international consortium. As the case wound endlessly through the courts, the only sure losers were the local inhabitants of the area, who shared little in the profits and had their lives upended.

As Kayu Aya stood vacant month after month, the staff was laid off, and the jungle began to take back its natural habitat. The pipes in the swimming pools cracked, the bathroom tiles broke, and the gardens became overgrown as nature evened the score. There was nothing left but a skeleton staff that was overwhelmed by problems and watched helplessly as nature moved in.

One day an American trumpet player, who'd been staying in Legian with his wife and child, took a long walk along the beach to Seminyak. He followed an overgrown path into the forest, wandered through some old ruins, and came upon the Kayu Aya sitting there like a mythical Xanadu. One of the caretakers was snoozing in a garden outside a luxurious bungalow and when he awoke to find a bearded, long-haired Westerner sitting across from him he probably thought the spirits were playing a trick on him. But there was something engaging about this visitor and they struck up a conversation. An hour later the caretaker, who hadn't been paid in a month, agreed to rent out the whole place under the table at seven dollars per night per bungalow. The caretaker was embarrassed to ask for so much—it was, after all, an exorbitant amount by local standards—but the trumpeter readily agreed. A day later he, his wife, his young son, and a dozen friends from Legian moved in—

"There's a big party tonight," said Gino, who came by late one afternoon. "We're invited to play."

"Uh... really?" I said, uneasy about playing on such short notice.

"C'mon! Let's go!" said Gino, grabbing my guitar case and harmonicas. "I've got a bimo waiting!"

Half an hour later we stood outside a beautiful bungalow that glowed with colored lights. The walls were covered in bougainvillea, a sparkling waterfall spilled into a lotus pond, and trays of local delicacies were spread throughout the bungalow. Thirty or forty people were there, luxuriating in the swimming pool, on the patio, or sprawled out on the giant batik pillows that ringed the inside rooms.

With everyone dressed in their finest silk pajamas, flowing scarves and lace kebayas, it was the closest I'd ever come to entering a harem room. The guests were an international cast of characters, many of whom had been in Asia for years and knew each other from Thailand, Kashmir, or Goa. These were serious partiers, more flamboyant than the meditative people I knew in the mountains of Nepal or the holy cities of India. But beneath the glitzier outer layers, I recognized the same group of wanderers and seekers I'd encountered ever since Europe, albeit with better tans.

A strikingly handsome guy came over to greet me and Gino. "The band! We've been waiting for you guys! It's been much too quiet around here."

"With the stuff we play," I said drolly, "we might lull everyone to sleep."

"That's cool, too. More cream puffs for us."

"Did someone say cream puffs?" said Gino, instantly warming to our host.

"I'm Steve," said the guy, "ringmaster of this event. The woman near the door with the worried look is Laura, my wife. The little kid getting ready to poop in his pants is Anjuna, our son."

"Ah, I've heard of you," I said. Steve and Laura were well-known as two of the early travelers who had alighted on Goa, the counterculture paradise of India. "Your reputation precedes you. You play trumpet, right?"

"Yeah, Trumpet Steve, that's what they call me. Not to be confused with English Steve, Dutch Steve, or Swami Steve. I'm the real deal, straight from New York, Bombay, and Madison."

"Madison, Wisconsin?"

"The one and only."

"Don't tell me you went to school there?"

"What? You too? I graduated in sixty-four."

"I arrived in sixty-five."

"You know, the two of you look a bit like brothers," said Gino. "Do you think—"

"Can't be," said Steve, "I'm much better looking."

"That you are," I said. "And *considerably* older."

Steve laughed good-naturedly and put his arm around me. "Don't worry," he said, "you'll get there." I felt an immediate connection. We eventually discovered that we'd both majored in psychology, we'd both turned on backs on it, and we'd both hit the road around the same time.

Gino and I were introduced around and eventually pulled out our instruments. After a few moments, Steve joined us on trumpet. It was an instant blend, this most unlikely horn section of trumpet, flute and harmonica, blasting out like a Motown review while I tried to keep up on guitar. Once I felt a bit more confident I sang an original song I'd recorded on a Singapore radio broadcast the summer before and it came even more alive with Gino's tasteful accents and Steve's soaring melody.

"Nice, nice," said Steve. "You guys should come to Goa. That's where the music scene's about to explode."

"Uh-huh," I said. Sure, why not? It was just one more crazy fantasy to add to my growing list of improbable adventures.

⤳

The path that led to the beach in Legian was its own improbable adventure. At different times I'd come upon people gathering magic mushrooms, priests searching for trance-inducing herbs, and mysterious forest dwellers appearing in the shadows. One day I approached an opening in a grove of palm trees and came upon an impromptu dance rehearsal. A half-dozen Balinese girls, no more than five or six years old, were practicing the traditional legong dance. Rumor had it that the intricate moves of the dance came about spontaneously for the girls, as if by divine intervention. I always took these tales to be apocryphal, but after watching the little girls I wasn't so sure. The teacher wasn't really instructing them but appeared to be merely creating an environment for them to blossom into proficient dancers. Their eyes darted back and forth in unison as they each raised a leg parallel to the ground, then stretched out their hands and fingers in a series of symbolic gestures. All the while an old lady chanted an atonal hymn while a couple of boys kept time with drums. Thirty minutes later it all ended with a burst of laughter and the children running off in a half-dozen different directions.

I continued down the path to the beach for my afternoon swim, crossed over a mound of sand dunes, and came upon a flat expanse of white sand that stretched to the ocean. The beach was populated as usual by village women selling fruit and kids hawking cold drinks, but it seemed quieter than normal. When I arrived at my customary spot on the sand, I was surprised to find none of the usual sunbathers who normally gathered there. As I looked up and down the beach, one of the kids came running over, gushing excitedly. "Polisi! Polisi!" he said. "Take away ten people!"

"What? What do you mean?"

"Polisi arrest ten people! Take to Denpasar jail!"

"For what?" I said, looking at him warily. Like most kids that age he was a bit of a joker and I half expected him to burst out laughing.

"No swimsuit! No sarong! You lucky! Good thing you come late!"

"Yeah, good thing—" I said, tightening my sarong around my waist.

Legian was a mostly nude beach, which was fine with the Balinese but not with the authorities from Java, who occasionally issued warnings to cover up. But arrests? This was something new. Six men and four women, most of whom I knew, were arrested for indecency and forced to spend the night in jail. Their passports were confiscated and they were forced to report to the authorities in Denpasar every day until their case could be heard before a judge. A week passed, then another. A German guy missed his plane back to Frankfurt. An Australian girl missed her brother's graduation in Melbourne. An English woman got fired for not reporting to work in London. Bribes were offered and rejected, lawyers were hired and fired, and eventually everyone overstayed their visas. When the case finally came to trial the judge dismissed the charges, but the prosecutor, a strictly observant Muslim brought in from Jakarta, appealed the verdict and it took another month to be resolved. Eventually all ten were deported and never allowed back, not that any of them were particularly anxious to return to Indonesia anytime soon.

❧

I headed over to a tiny warong that was perched precariously just off the road between Legian and Kuta. The little road-side shop hadn't changed one bit since the previous summer and Kortis, a lovely Balinese girl with sparkling eyes and a good sense of humor, was still standing behind the counter tending to business. There were three stools, a little table woven from palm fronds, and a tiny kitchen just big enough for her to boil rice and cut up fruits and vegetables. "What's good today, Kortis?" I called to her from across the road.

"Frrrrruit salad good today," she responded, rolling her *r*'s with a little extra gusto to give the proper dramatic effect.

"Well, then, I'd better have a fruit salad," I said, just as I did every single day since I arrived. It was a playful routine we'd established the previous summer and neither of us could even imagine altering it. Always the same question, always the same answer.

A Western woman stepped out from behind a rack of batiks that hung along the back wall. She was wearing a skin-tight lace kebaya and had a brightly colored sarong knotted around her waist. I couldn't help staring at her. She had huge black eyes, a thin nose, and thick lips that angled upwards slightly into the hint of a smile. "Is the fruit salad really so good?" she said with a pronounced Spanish accent.

"It's the best fruit salad in Bali," I said.

"In that case I'd better have one, too," she said, smiling broadly. "You look like a man who knows his fruit salads."

"Better make that two specials," I called out to Kortis.

"Two fruit salad for Terry and the pretty lady," she called back.

"This must be my lucky day," said the Spanish woman. "A legendary fruit salad and a nice compliment all in one visit."

Kortis chopped up the fruit, sprinkled on some peanuts and coconut, glazed the whole thing with a few drops of condensed milk, and brought out two overflowing teak bowls. "When you take me to America, Terry?" she said, batting her eyelashes like a hummingbird and continuing our routine.

"As soon as Papa gives me four goats and two cows."

"Papa no *have* cows!" she moaned, still following the script, feigning disappointment.

"Well, you know the deal, Kortis, no goats, no marriage; no cows—"

"—no New York!" She looked at me with terribly sad eyes, then burst out laughing.

"You drive a very hard bargain," the woman said as she joined in the laughter. "I'm Carmen."

"Let me guess," I said. "Spain?"

"Oh, my," she said. "Is it so obvious?"

"Just a wild guess," I said. There weren't many people from Spain on the road, not with Franco still in power and keeping everyone in line. The few Spaniards I'd met were exceptional people, truly unique individuals who'd had the strength to escape.

Carmen had her own story. She came from a traditional Catholic family and lived a typically sequestered life before getting hired as a flight attendant by Air Iberia. After rigorous training, she was suddenly exposed to a whole new world, especially when the airline put her on the route from Madrid to New Delhi. There were many strange people on those flights, mostly young people from all parts of Europe. She was a bit frightened at first by their strange way of talking and dressing, but she slowly felt herself being pulled into their orbit.

"I didn't understand them at first," she said as she recounted her story over fruit salad. "They kept saying how they were searching for something. Then one day, after a very turbulent flight, I got off the plane in Delhi, got my little bag at customs, and walked straight out of the airport. I realized that I was searching for something, too. I just kept going. I just kept going on and on and that was over a year ago and still I am going, I never went back."

We were silent for a long moment as Carmen stared off into space. I could see that she was still struggling with her decision. "I think you did the right thing," I finally said.

"Yes, I hope so," she said, taking a deep breath.

As the sun moved lower in the sky, a few palm trees began rustling in the wind. Kortis leaned over from behind her chopping board. "Fruit salad is good?"

"Fruit salad is very good," said Carmen. "I'm glad I took your advice."

"It's almost time for sunset," I said. "Do you feel like going down to the beach?"

Carmen's face reddened suddenly. "The beach? Oh, no, no, I really couldn't. Maybe some other time. Yes, another time."

"Okay," I said, a bit surprised by her reaction. "Some other time."

She paid for the salad and quickly gathered her things. "Yes, it soon is dark. So very nice to meet you," she said putting out her hand.

"Yeah, me too," I said, watching as she headed off on the road for Kuta. It all felt a bit strange, too abrupt and offhanded. It reminded me of my short time in Barcelona, where nothing ever completely made sense.

❧

I saw Carmen a few more times over the next several weeks, but she always had some prior engagement or was on her way to dinner with friends or had an important errand to run. It was clear she was avoiding me, but I didn't quite know why. Then, one day, she came by in a taxi to tell me she was on her way to the airport to go back to India. "I'm off for the mountains," she said. "Or the plains. Or perhaps the deserts."

"That pretty much covers all the bases," I said.

"Yes, I suppose it does," she said. "We're all crazy, you know."

"Yeah, I know."

"I just need some time," she said, as she reached out and took my hand. I could feel her lingering a moment before she motioned for the driver to continue on to airport. "We will meet again," she said as her fingers slipped out of my palm. "I am sure of it."

Eventually we all moved on, some back to Europe, some to Australia, some to the beaches of Thailand. As I packed up to leave a few weeks later, I was thankful that I'd survived another three months in paradise without spending a single day in jail. I felt a hint of remorse settling in. Bali was just as beautiful as when I first arrived, the people were still welcoming, the art still infused every aspect of life, and the culture was still thriving. Still, I couldn't help feeling that the seeds of destruction had been planted and it seemed inevitable that things would never again be quite the same.

I stopped off at the local warong on my way to the airport. "What's good today, Kortis?" I called from the road.

"Frrrrruit salad good today," Kortis replied, batting her eyelashes and smiling broadly.

"Okay, then, I'll have a fruit salad," I said as I sat on the rickety stool across from the bamboo counter. The sun was high in the sky and a pleasant breeze blew in from the ocean. It was a moment to savor. I wasn't sure if I'd ever be back again.

Chapter 13
Interlude in a Whirlwind

Tobias and I walk along the edge of the pond, feeling uneasy in each other's presence. There's a turbulence around us, and it's not just in the water or the air but in the circumstances themselves. The fog rolls in more quickly now as great plumes of white mist descend over the park, covering first the tops of the redwood trees, then moving down to the eucalyptus and spruces. The uppermost branch of a Monterey pine briefly pokes through the haze, glistens with the refracted light of the sun, then vanishes again, as if tucking in for an afternoon nap. The birds fall quiet, the insects stop chirping, and even the distant hum of automobiles is muted by the heavy air. An uneasy peace pervades the park, a kind of truce called between the elements, a moment to recharge and reload. Nature takes a breather, maybe to rethink the whole thing, perhaps to reexamine its purpose and meaning.

As always the fog comes and goes, the clouds build and dissipate, and the wind kicks up and dies down without warning. When a thick blanket of fog settles over the pond, however, it seems unusual even for Golden Gate Park. The fog begins to swirl frantically, then funnels down toward the surface of the water as if being sucked into a void. Tobias and I fight to maintain our balance as the churning whirl-wind widens and darkens and begins to ingest everything in sight––the branch of a redwood, the stem of a daffodil, the nest of a goldfinch. The whole of the botanical garden is being swept up and spun around—pine cones, turtle shells, me, Tobias—we're all being buffeted by the winds and thrown in every direction.

And then—yes, and *then*—a woman appears out of the whirlwind riding the back of a tiger—*oh, c'mon!*—and the scene dissolves into pure madness. Her tongue is bright red, her eyes are ablaze, and she's swinging a giant sword. Everything around her shrinks—the trees, the animals, the park itself—and we feel paralyzed in her presence, incapable of movement or resistance. We're mere subjects in her realm, to be used or discarded upon her whim, the victims of an insane hallucination inflicted by forces unknown. She's toying with us, that much is evident, like puppets from a petrified forest. Then, just like that, she tires of the whole thing— what, after all, could challenge her?—and with a snap of her fingers the branches return to the trees, the water to the pond, and the birds to the sky. Tobias and I are back again at the edge of the pond and everything is exactly as it was except that now a woman is standing across from us. She looks like a mythological figure from some Hindu fable.

Surely I've seen her before. Was it at the lake in Pokhara when we stood beneath the clouds of Annapurna? Was it on the train through Rajasthan when we vanished into a dust storm? Was it on Nathan Road in Hong Kong when we got lost in a dance of the dragons? I know I've seen her some-where—*of course, I have*—she's the woman on the bus I wanted to talk to but was afraid to approach, she's the woman in the restaurant buried inside a book, she's the woman in the marketplace who disappears into an alley, she's the woman at the bar stirring her drink with a plastic straw, she's the woman on the next mountaintop and in the opposite subway and in the car in the other lane—

She's the woman from the apartment across the street. I can barely take my eyes off her as she stands before us with an accusing stare. Neither can Tobias, who seems so utterly smitten he's lost the ability to speak, not an entirely unfortunate turn of events. The tiger has disappeared into the bushes—to join the peacock, no doubt—and I can only hope they're part of the same hallucination that had me spinning like a top in a tornado. So it's just the three of us, me, Tobias, and this woman who appeared out of a cloud and is now staring at us as if we were a couple of transients slumming in the park. "What's your plan?" she says. "Is it to crash through my window and rob me of my things? Or maybe you'll smash down my door? There's a skylight, you know. Perhaps you could rappel down like they do in those museum break-ins. Of course, in those cases there's usually something of value whereas I have nothing but a couple of keepsakes, but these are desperate times, aren't they? Maybe you thought you could unload my jewelry to somebody on the street?"

"We meant you no harm," I say, stumbling for words. The truth is, I can barely move my lips. My throat is tight as a drum.

"Oh? Then what is it? Am I really so irresistible that you simply couldn't avert your eyes? It's the exotic look, isn't it, the dark complexion and the deep brown eyes and the luscious lips. You'd like to kiss those lips, wouldn't you?"

"No, no, really," I say, embarrassed by her directness.

"Yes, certainly, you'd like to taste the little beads of perspiration at the corners of my mouth and run your tongue inside the curl of my lips. Is that how you see me, as your next victim?"

"Victim? No, no—"

"How would you like it if we turned the tables? You hadn't thought of that, had you, to be victims of the beautiful woman in the window rather than victimizers? Even now you're wondering what it would be like if we were locked in an embrace. Would I be soft and pliant or would I be difficult and aloof, that's a good question isn't it, oh, yes, now more than ever you'd like to pull me into the bushes and have your way with me. I can almost taste your desire right now. But what if I were to lure you—I could do that, you know—watch as I lower the strap of my blouse along my shoulder, it's nothing is it, just the outline of my breasts beneath the fabric, but you're intrigued, you noticed my breasts right away and now you're wondering how firm they are, you imagine your hands on my breasts and your tongue on my nipples, you'd like to wash yourself in me, isn't that so, you'd like to feel every pore of your skin wet with me, oh, my, am I embarrassing you, yes, I'm afraid I am, we haven't even been properly introduced, you're wondering who this woman is, this woman who also lived in the Himalayas where she was free to drape a sari around her naked body and walk through the marketplace unmolested."

"Please, we didn't mean—"

"Surely you know who I am," says the woman as she comes a closer and stares each of us in the eyes. "I'm the woman who wrestled the nectar of immortality from the demons and presented it to the gods. I'm the woman who tricked her pursuers and turned them into mountains of ash. I'm the woman who appeared out of a whirlwind and holds you transfixed with insatiable desire—"

"Mohini," says Tobias, utterly transfixed. "The Goddess of Seduction."

"Yes, my beautiful one," she says, "you've summoned me from the waves, from the pond, from the reflections of your own memories. Do you think you're finally strong enough to possess me? We shall see, won't we? We shall see—"

Chapter 14
Nothing is Our Excuse

The snowcapped mountains glistened in the afternoon sun as we skirted over a range of jagged peaks, then plunged rapidly for the short runway that lie below. I'd been gone for a year and a half but it seemed longer as the plane descended into the Kathmandu Valley. Such is the trick the mind plays when still trying to come to terms with a previous visit that ended with the death of one girlfriend and the abandonment by another. I knew I needed to return, if nothing else to rewrite the ending of my first foray into the Himalayas. There was unfinished business in Nepal.

Kathmandu for me was the greatest challenge. The city was lonely in the winter, oppressive in the summer, surrounded on all sides by mountains so tall they both elevated and diminished the human spirit, a place both so claustrophobic and so expansive you could feel yourself suffocating on a mountaintop. It was the perfect juxtaposition of opposites that so well defined life in central Asia. Nepal took reality and stirred it into a thick minestrone of mysterious ingredients. You could find anything in that soup—yesterday's leftovers, tomorrow's appetizer, spices, gravies, condiments, skins and peals, stems and roots, things overboiled and underdone—the whole of the universe was in a bottomless bowl, roiling around, giving birth to stars and nebulae, dissolving into black holes and dark matter, and starting all over again one more time.

The airport alone was its own contradiction. It hinted at the modern world of jet engines and supersonic speeds while somehow neglecting to add lights to its runways. The terminal wasn't much different from a Himalayan bus station, with its one-story shed that looked like it could blow away in a good wind. The officials wore a hodge-podge of uniforms, most of them ill-fitting and unconvincing in their seriousness of purpose. It was as if Tolkien had joined forces with Dali in a tailor shop of the deranged. Looking around at the bare-bones baggage room and the chaotic customs office, I was reminded exactly of why I had returned to Nepal. I was stepping back in time to a place where the lights didn't work, the clocks didn't move, and the calendar pages didn't turn.

Riding in from the airport the decades fell away with each twist in the road. Cars were replaced by rickshaws, houses with huts, wooden beams with thatched roofs. As we approached Durbar Square in the heart of the city, I could see that scaffolds still surrounded the old Royal Palace and that repairs hadn't proceeded much since I'd left. Several years earlier the Palace had been nearly destroyed by a fire that erupted only days after King Birendra proclaimed hashish to be illegal. The declaration wasn't taken very seriously and was probably just a way to assuage American concerns about the growing drug trade, but it was widely assumed that the fire was the revenge of Lord Shiva, the God of Destruction and Intoxication. There were certain traditions, after all, that you simply didn't mess with.

The moment I exited my taxi, I was greeted by the Global Emperor, a destitute, distant cousin of Birendra who was convinced he ran the whole show. He stood there with his usual welcoming smile and formal salute, although I suspect he had no idea who I was or if we had talked just yesterday or years before or maybe never at all. He was dressed as always in his faded blue wool coat and black woven hat, with a garland of marigolds around his neck and a stack of newspapers under his arm. The Global Emperor wandered the streets of Kathmandu handing out calling cards with Hindu deities on one side and a painstakingly handwritten message on the other that concluded with his wondrously flamboyant signature:

From!—His Majesty the Great Global Emperor
Vishosamrat Chakravarti Raja Almighty King God Vishnu
Sri Panch Boda Mahraj Douraj Bhagwan Travokyo
Birbikram Shah Dev Sarkar God Vishnu!
Global Emperor, Military Dictator, Patron of the Globe.

It felt somehow proper that the Global Emperor would be the first familiar face I'd encounter upon my return. Nepal was many things to many people but it was the unruly cast of characters that drew me back. Kathmandu was home to a collection of poets, painters, musicians, religious fanatics, women seeking salvation, men seeking forgiveness, criminals on the run, political exiles, drug addicts, impersonators, imposters, counterfeiters, scammers and swindlers. In a way, we were all Global Emperors. We'd left behind the world as we knew it and flown off into the thin air and even more rarified states of mind at the far edge of the globe. We were all emperors in ragged coats, aristocrats in threadbare pants, and kings in tattered shoes.

☙

I checked into a three rupee room in a bare-bones hotel, then walked over to "Freak Street," where I immediately spotted the familiar faces of the merchants who ran the jewelry and rug shops. The Print Shop, operated by some Western friends, was still there, as was the Eclipse, a decidedly un-Western-style bar. A guy whom I didn't quite remember waved to me from across the street, and a couple of street kids came running up after recognizing me as a relatively soft touch. "Five paisa, sahib, five paisa!"

"All right, all right," I said, digging into my pocket. Within seconds more kids appeared from the shadows and, as always, I was cleaned out before I got to the corner.

I recognized still more people and places and felt myself already settling in. The kid from the chai shop came running over with a glass of tea, his dirty fingers submerged inside, as always. The guy at the corner had his usual supply of unsealed peanut butter, adulterated shampoo, and three sizes of batteries from India, guaranteed to last no more than fifteen minutes each. Across the street was the guy with the Chinese peas, baked beans, and roasted walnuts soaked in syrup. Another guy had a barrel of kerosene, a funnel, and a couple of bottles with crumpled-up shreds of cloth for stoppers. The shop with the cans of Nescafe, sugar and condensed milk was still there, which meant I wouldn't have to leave town the next day, since I was hopelessly addicted to coffee. How anyone could be addicted to instant Nescafe, of course, was a mystery better left unsolved. Up the street was the New Bank, a place to avoid under all circumstances, and the old newsstand, which had a haphazard collection of newspapers that were anywhere from a week to a month old.

"Look who's back," came a voice from over my shoulder as I paged through a long out-of-date Times of India. I turned to find Angus MacLise standing there, his tall gaunt body leaning precariously as if it might topple under its own weight.

"Angus!" I said, truly happy to see him. Angus was a

Kathmandu old-timer and someone I'd grown close to my first time around. "I was wondering if I'd run into you."

"Where else am I going to go?" he said. "Nobody else will have me."

"Thank God for Nepal," I said. "If they ever closed these borders half of us would be stateless."

Angus was one of the most interesting people in the Valley. He was a drummer and poet from Greenwich Village who took it upon himself to study the most esoteric aspects of Buddhism while drumming out rhythms so convoluted they were nearly impossible to decipher. It didn't seem like the most likely combination but it seemed to work for Angus, who needed at least a periodic escape from the devils of his overly complicated brain. Angus was pure mind, blessed and cursed as he was by a photographic memory that barely distinguished the important from the mundane. It was unfiltered knowledge that floated through his mass of neurons and synapses, stories of third-century Hindu kings and fifth-century Chinese dynasties and tenth-century Siamese potentates, names and statistics and countless interpretations of so many facts and figures it was no wonder he needed a musical diversion just to slow down the streams of information.

Years earlier Angus had hooked up with Lou Reed, John Cale and Sterling Morrison to form the original Velvet Underground. They first met on a subway in New York where Angus pounded out wild polyrhythms as the train screeched through the tunnels. That's where Angus was most comfortable, in the subway stations, bus platforms, and train terminals where he could absorb the sounds of the city and add his own particular touch to the surrounding cacophony. Playing with an actual band, unfortunately, was another matter. Angus was famously late to practices, often showing up a day or two behind schedule, if at all. In a documentary called *Rock & Roll Heart: Lou Reed*, filmed some years later, Reed recounted their collaboration: *"One day we got a job and Angus said, 'You mean, I have to show up at a certain time and then I'm allowed to play and then I have to stop playing?' and we said 'yeah, man, it's a gig, that's what a gig is,' and he quit on the spot. What can I say? This was the sixties."* That was Angus in a nutshell. New York was too small for his anarchic spirit and the rules too strict. He left for California in search of a gig that began in the evening, ended in the morning, and never required him to play the same thing twice.

Angus dug into a ratty old bag he carried over his shoulder and came up with a bidi, an Indian cigarette that had wedged itself inside. "Nothing's changed since you left," he said. "Paul, Ira, Petra, everybody's here." He found a box of matches, struck one that wouldn't light, struck one that flew off like a rocket and almost clipped my ear, then struck one that burned just long enough for him to get his bidi lit. "Oh, yeah, there is one new development. Hetty's in a real tizzy. You remember our son, right? Well, she thinks he's god or something. The Karmapa's coming to check him out."

"The Karmapa?" I said, wondering if I heard right. The Karmapa was one of the Tibetan's highest spiritual leaders and it didn't seem very likely that he'd be interested in Angus, Hetty, or their son.

"Listen, talk to her about it. I promise you, she's gonna tell you whether you want to hear it or not. Me, I'm agnostic about the whole thing."

"Yeah, because if she's the mother of god then you're—"

"That's right. Listen, I gotta meet somebody. We'll catch up soon."

From the glassy look in Angus's eyes I was pretty sure I knew who he had to meet. I also knew there was no point in delaying him. He didn't look well. "Okay, man," I said, as he ducked down an alley next to the newsstand. "Good to see you."

❧

Early the next morning I crossed Durbar Square and marveled once again at the ancient temples that rose from the cobblestones into the crisp, clear Himalayan sky. Nothing in the center of the old city had changed, neither the temples nor the shops along Asan Tole nor the winding streets that led to the river. Pig Alley was still there, still filthy and still occupied by the same menagerie of mud-encrusted pigs, stray dogs and obstinate water buffaloes. The same naked kids were there, a couple of years older but looking much the same, as well as the same women washing the same laundry. Bishnu's Chai and Pie Palace was still there churning out its apple and banana cream pies on what was certainly the world's most unappetizing street.

The Bishnumati River looked a bit higher and wider than I remembered, now that it was swollen with the monsoon rains. That meant the water would be a bit less contaminated than usual but still far too dangerous to drink. The old swing bridge over the river was still there, still wobbling unsteadily and still missing a few dozen slats. I held on precariously, careful not to slip or stumble, and stepped off into Balaju on the other side. I followed a dirt path along the rice paddies, passed a military barracks, and came upon a full view of Swayambhu Temple, high atop the hill just ahead. The serene eyes of the Buddha were painted on the facade and looked out in all directions as if keeping guard over the Valley.

I walked alongside a one-lane road into the village and found myself on the main drag of Swayambhu, which consisted of two chai shops, a tailor, a vegetable stall, and a tiny shop selling cooking oil, rice, flour and whatever canned goods that might be available. Across the street was Lobsang's, a recently opened Tibetan restaurant with actual tables, chairs, and something approaching a kitchen. While I welcomed this new addition to the village, my excitement was somewhat tempered by the fact that it was, after all,

Tibetan cuisine, and wasn't likely to be awarded any Michelin stars.

I walked up the stone steps of Kimdol Hill, passing the Bir Singh garden and the Tibetan nunnery on my way to my old house perched near the top of the hill. I turned off onto a dirt path, passed a few thatched-roof houses, and came upon a little clearing with two adjoining units. I glanced up to see my little three-story column of tiny rooms precariously perched atop one other, looking a bit lonely against the morning sky. The windows were closed, the door was locked, and the place looked empty. A moment later, the door to the house next door swung open and Tshering, my old landlord, came out. His eyes, still glassy from a hard night of drinking, narrowed slightly as he tried to place me. When he finally recognized me as his former tenant he snapped to attention. There was the scent of money in the air.

Tshering smiled solicitously as he unlocked the door of my old apartment. When I stepped inside, it seemed smaller and darker than I remembered. The downstairs smelled musty, the walls were moldy, and the upper windows hadn't been opened in months. Still, the place was available for immediate occupancy and I was anxious to move back to Swayambhu. I was just about to negotiate the rent with him when I noticed a house in the compound just across the way, a charming little bungalow that friends of mine had lived in years before. It too looked empty and when I asked Tshering about it, his mood darkened. I remembered that mood. The guy wasn't all that pleasant in the best of times, but when he'd drink rakshi until late into the night, he'd often return home in a rage to abuse his wife and children. I didn't much like living next to him, but houses weren't easy to come by in Swayambhu. I decided to take a chance and see if I could locate the owner of the place next door. When I told my old landlord I'd think it over, he narrowed his eyes and muttered under his breath as I headed back to the village.

᷒᷒

It was time to pay my respects to the temple at the top of Swayambhu Hill. Swayambhu was considerably taller than Kimdol and I found myself breathing hard by the time I finally made it up the three hundred and fifty steps to the stupa. The temple was twenty-five hundred years old and was one of the holiest places in the world for Tibetan Buddhists. When I finally arrived at the edge of the temple grounds, I looked out over the whole of the Kathmandu Valley and thought back to my last visit. This was the spot from which I'd departed the country, the spot from which I'd said goodbye to the spirit of Martine as her soul transmigrated through the Bardo.

It was only a few moments later that I saw Hetty McGee across the way, spinning the prayer wheels as she circumambulated the stupa. It was Hetty who'd led me through the prayers for Martine and explained how the monks would help guide her spirit through the difficult moments of the forty-nine day journey.

Hetty was an Englishwoman of high bearing who'd been a layout artist for the *Oracle*, San Francisco's first underground newspaper and a gathering spot of anarchists, revolutionaries and visionaries. It was there that she met Angus and it wasn't long before they were married in Golden Gate Park by Timothy Leary, who in addition to being the high priest of psychedelics was also an ordained preacher in the Universal Life Church, a mail order ministry that welcomed membership for the price of a self-addressed stamped envelope.

Hetty was a breathless storyteller, the beginner and ender of conversations that ranged from the utterly sublime to the completely impossible, and if they didn't all exactly add up, well, it was only a part of her charm. She was a swirling hive of contradictions, a purveyor of arcane wisdom and prosaic misinformation in roughly equal measure. "You've come back at just the right time," she said as I approached her on her walk around the temple. "Something that happens maybe once in a lifetime."

Hetty, who quite possibly had a direct connection to the spiritual masters of the universe, was always given to overstatement but even for her this was pretty dramatic. Given her fascination with all things Buddhist, I assumed it had something to do with the temple next door. Her son Ossian, after all, was a monk in that temple. He was five years old.

"Did I ever tell you about the time we were in Pondicherry?" she said. "It was a couple of years ago when Angus and I were working on a documentary about Sri Aurobindo. One day we were paging through a book about Nepal and Ossian saw a photo of Swayambhu temple and he cried out, *'Gotta go, momma, gotta go!'* I'd never seen him so excited! When we eventually got here, I understood why. He insisted on joining the monastery."

I knew this story and always questioned its veracity. Did Ossian really make this choice or was it perhaps convenient for Hetty to let the monks raise her son? And even if Ossian wanted to join, how could a child not yet five possibly make such a decision? "How's Ossian doing?" I asked, wondering where this was going.

"Ossian is doing wonderfully," said Hetty, "In fact, I'm beginning to believe that he may in fact be a tulku."

"A tulku?" I said, searching my memory. "That's, what, a—"

"A reincarnated monk," she said. "A very high monk who chooses to come back the next time around in a particular body."

"And you think that's Ossian?"

"I'm sure of it. I've been having all sorts of dreams and premonitions. Why else would Ossian lead us to this very temple?"

"Yeah, I've wondered about that—"

"There's only one person who knows for sure and that's the Karmapa," said Hetty. "And wouldn't you know it, he's coming to Nepal for the first time in over twenty years to consecrate a new temple." Hetty leaned over and lowered her voice to a bare whisper. "He's in exile in Sikkim, you know. I've already sent a petition to his monastery. What do you think happened?"

"What?" I said, feeling the excitement in Hetty's voice resonating through my bones.

"The Karmapa has agreed to perform a test to determine if Ossian is who I think he is."

"Wow," I said, feeling just a bit delirious myself. "And, tell me again, who is that?"

"The first Westerner to ever be declared a reincarnated Tibetan monk."

❧

Durga Puja was upon us. It was the major festival of autumn and harkened back to a more primitive Nepali past. The ceremony was part Hindu, part animist, and part animal worship. One day, the crow was honored. On another day, kites were flown. On still another day, cows were worshipped. The ninth day of the holiday, however, was the most dramatic. That was the day of sacrifice to the Goddess Durga, and each family was expected to slaughter a chicken, a goat or a sheep. Only a hundred years earlier, virgins were sacrificed to Durga on the steps of Hanuman Dhoka but now the King sacrificed one hundred and eight water buffaloes instead. Their necks were severed by the blow of an immense sword and the grounds of the temple ran with blood.

There was blood everywhere in Kathmandu, swathed over doorways, sprayed onto taxis and rubbed over the faces of the gods. Sometimes it was difficult to even distinguish whether an image was Hindu or Buddhist. There was a great mix of cultures in Nepal and a crossover in the styles of the temples and iconography. Wherever I went, there were monks in saffron robes, sadhus in loincloths and nuns in maroon dresses, and all of them were either chanting mantras, counting beads or offering prayers to the gods. On the last day of Durga Puja the rains came one final time. The blood was washed away and the streets were cleansed. It was a good omen.

❧

After the holidays I tracked down the owner of my neighbor's house in Swayambhu. Prasad Bhandari, a gentle man with a friendly smile, had a little jewelry shop on the outskirts of Thamel and agreed to meet me on Kimdol. The next day, as he fiddled with the lock on the door, he noticed my old landlord watching from the house next door. "Better you live here," said Bhandari. "This man no good."

"Yeah," I said. "I think you're right." The moment we entered the house, I felt at home. Downstairs was a kitchen which led to a semicircular patio outside. The shape of the patio alone was reason enough to move in. It felt like being on the bridge of a ship plying uncharted waters. A crooked little stairway led to an upstairs room that was cozy and utterly charming. There was a little trap door in the ceiling that led absolutely nowhere, but I chose to think of it as the oubliette, a secret chamber in which was stored the forgotten wisdom of the ages. "I'll take it," I said.

I moved in the next day. The house felt even more comfortable once I had a few basic amenities in place. I got a mattress and quilt from one of the stalls in Asan Tole, plus the usual straw mats, wall hangings, and kitchen utensils.

Now I could really sit back and look around. The view out my window was of Kathmandu, a few miles to the east. To the west was Swayambhu temple and in between was a horizon framed by snow-capped mountains that rose majestically to the sky. The house was completely surrounded by a wall and garden and offered me total privacy. This meant no more prying eyes of the guy next door, who I knew would be none too pleased to lose a potential renter. I sensed he might seek revenge for my going elsewhere but figured there wasn't much of anything he could really do. I decided to try and maintain cordial relations and leave it at that.

᠙

A week or two after I moved in, Kathmandu began teeming with Tibetans. There was an ever-growing influx of people from the remote valleys of Nepal and from Tibet itself, over treacherous mountain passes that could only be crossed a few times a year. The pilgrims risked death, starvation and jail as they skirted around the Chinese border guards who patrolled the closed boundary with Nepal. The opportunity to be blessed by the Sixteenth Karmapa was worth it, even if it meant waiting months for his springtime arrival.

The Tibetans from the furthermost districts arrived earliest and would have to wait the longest before the weather cleared for their return. They planned to camp out the entire winter in the villages outside Kathmandu, and one group of about forty men, women and children staked out a small space near my house on Kimdol Hill. The first time we met I stared into their round, flat faces and they stared back into my narrow, angular face, equally intrigued. They'd never seen a Westerner before, never listened to a radio and never read a magazine. A little girl came up and touched my skin, wondering if it might break like alabaster, then went back to pulling raw wool onto a spool. That's what the women did virtually all day long and, if the moon was bright enough, all night as well. It was difficult work but they did it as a community, huddled together in this strange place doing the one familiar thing that tied them to their land back home.

⚬❦⚬

A job in Kathmandu was just about the furthest thing from my mind when I returned to Nepal, but the opportunity suddenly arose when the people running the Spirit Catcher Bookstore decided to leave for the winter. The shop had been around for a couple of years now, run by a group of Western poets and writers who came and went as they pleased. That the Spirit Catcher existed at all was a minor miracle. One might refer to local mythology to best explain the dusty, musty library located at 104 Dharma Path, on the corner of Jhochen Tole Alley. It's possible that when Shiva stabbed Parvati in a jealous rage, her tears fell from heaven into a pond in which a lotus blossom bloomed and a thousand books flowered. Or maybe when Shiva cut off the head of his son Ganesh, a spurt of blood fertilized a giant banyan tree from which were cut the ten thousand pages of a thousand books. Or maybe when Shiva rode a tiger through the mountains he got tired one night and decided he needed to kick back and read a good novel. Whatever it was, the Spirit Catcher Bookstore was open for business, occasionally at least, and I was now in charge.

In my yearlong reign, I became steward of an institution that brought together all the disparate elements of our far-flung community of artists, writers and musicians. People bought books, sold books, traded books, and somehow the rent got paid and the lights stayed lit. We had a Spanish translation of the *Bhagavad Gita*, an Amharic version of *Tropic of Cancer*, a mahout's guide to Sri Lankan elephant commands, a Swahili translation of Mao's *Little Red Book*, a book of mountain climbing tips written in Braille, a compendium of long-dead currency conversions, copies of *The Tibetan Book of the Dead* in Egyptian and *The Egyptian Book of the Dead* in Tibetan, Cheiro's *Language of the Hand*, Aleister Crowley's *Magical Diaries*, Madame Blavatsky's *The Secret Doctrine*, the complete works of Herman Hesse minus the missing pages, Kazantzakis in the original Greek, Dante in the original Italian, and a book of Russian fairy tales in faded Cyrillic. We even had our own calendar featuring a Hindu god in a state of debauchery and the Spirit Catcher Bookstore slogan displayed across the masthead:

Nothing is Our Excuse

And so it was. Nothing was our excuse, not for any of us. We had nothing and wanted for nothing. We were in Kathmandu and that was more than anyone could ever ask for.

Chapter 15
A Visit from Afar

The winter wore on, getting colder each night. My windows whistled in the wind and my threadbare blanket did little to ward off the chill. I spent more and more time in the cafés in the village, bundled up over hot bowls of tea, wondering what madness had kept me away from the beaches to the south. It was high season in Goa and I could almost hear the music echoing over the beaches.

The population of travelers to Nepal dwindled over the winter months but a hardcore of semi-permanent residents stayed on to brave the elements. A few stray visitors appeared from time to time, but they were mostly mountain men, adventure seekers, or truly lost souls whose inner compasses spun wildly in every direction. One such traveler presented himself on a cold winter morning.

The Brothers' Chai Shop was already under a cloud of smoke by the time I arrived for breakfast. The brothers were two middle-aged Tibetans who looked more like monks than waiters. They were constantly reciting mantras and counting the beads on their malas, even when taking orders.

What they thought of all the Westerners who smoked chillums in their restaurant from morning to night was anyone's guess, but I had the strange feeling they didn't even realize we were there.

There was somebody new at one of the tables, a guy with the weirdest color hair I'd ever seen. It was somewhere between red and orange, but that doesn't really do it justice. It was more like the color a leaf turns just before it dies, when it shrivels up and its veins collapse. Nobody had hair that color, neither man nor beast nor orangutan. It was a shade of red that incorporated ruby, crimson and plum, with a dollop of marigold, cantaloupe and apricot thrown in for good measure. It was the color of madness.

James was from Maine and had the odd demeanor of a seventeenth-century Pilgrim. All he really needed was a pair of buckle shoes, some knee-high stockings, and maybe a black conical hat to top it all off. He took a deep hit of hashish, handed me the chillum, and sputtered something as if speaking in tongues. As I filled my lungs with a sweet cloud of Nepalese charas, I wondered if maybe he was inviting me to help in a witch dunking or a burning at the stake. I took this as my cue to leave.

My escape, unfortunately, was brief. By the time I got to Kathmandu, James was already there getting out of a taxi with an elderly, pasty-faced man to whom I took an immediate distaste. They headed straight my way. "Hey! Neighbor!" James called out. "Meet Reverend Johansen! He's a friend of the family back home! The Reverend's a missionary out here!"

"A missionary?" I said, feeling my head suddenly throb with might well have been a grand mal seizure.

"That's right, my good man," said the Reverend, sticking out a big beefy hand to shake. "I've been spreading the Gospel for over twenty years to these sad souls."

"Sad souls? Surely you don't mean the Nepalis?"

"Why, who else?"

I felt the muscles in my neck, shoulders and throat tightening. "Listen, you—"

"Just doing the Lord's work," interrupted James before I could properly register my disgust. I wasn't sure if he was serious or if he was pulling the old man's leg.

"Would you like to join us for our afternoon repast?" said Johansen.

"No, no, sorry," I said, blurting out the first thing that came to mind. "I've got to go meet my, uh, spirit guide."

Johansen smiled solicitously and patted me on the shoulder with his puffy fingers. "Beware of false prophets," he said.

"Yeah, you, too," I said as I squirmed away and disappeared into the marketplace. Nepal was full of religious fanatics but the Christian variety seemed particularly out of place in these pristine mountains. Didn't the evangelists have enough souls to save in Alabama and Georgia?

I passed the shop that sold screws and nails, the outdoor dentist who pulled teeth with a pair of rusty pliers, and the guy who typed letters on his ancient Underwood. At the kerosene stall I came upon Rajaram and Devagiri, two Western Hare Krishna disciples who'd been sent to Kathmandu to open the sect's 103rd temple. They were a curious pair who'd fallen under the influence of some of Kathmandu's more radical expatriates and seemed to be having second thoughts about their commitments. They looked particularly troubled at the moment. "Everything okay?" I said.

"A minor issue at the temple," said Devagiri.

"It's not so minor," said Rajaram.

"A few devotees have arrived—"

"—six—"

"Yes, six devotees have arrived from Europe. New ones. Babes in the woods."

"They won't shit unless you tell them to."

"Well, yes, they do need to be told what to do."

"*Should I sweep the floor?*" said Rajaram, mocking the innocent devotees. "*Can I make some tea? Is it time to begin dinner services?*"

"And you think it's easy for *me?*" screamed Devagiri.

"Yeah, well, I'm sure you'll figure it out," I said, slipping away before I got sucked into yet another religious conflagration. I was already two over my limit.

⟨⟩

I crossed Durbar Square in the shadow of the old royal palace and Hanuman Dhoka. The square had its usual clusters of pilgrims, beggars and sadhus who sat on the steps of the temples meditating, chanting and smoking chillums. Subtract the odd automobile and motorcycle and it could've been any era in the past thousand years. I felt remarkably removed from western civilization. With no televisions, few radios and only sporadic reporting in the newspapers, it was surprisingly easy to divorce oneself from the supposed urgency of current events. The only events that really mattered were what was happening in that place at that time as the modern world faded into irrelevancy.

I saw my old friend Chaz approaching from across the square. Chaz was a tabla player who'd studied for several years in Calcutta under an Indian master and was now taking a short break. With him was a strikingly beautiful young woman who glided across the cobblestones with the grace of a dancer. Her eyes were like blue sapphires gleaming through the morning haze, eyes that exuded playfulness and intelligence. "This is Lisa," he said in introduction. "We met on the bus coming up from the Terrai."

"A bus better left to the chickens and goats," she said with a perceptible Canadian accent. I found her flat pronunciation oddly endearing.

"I remember that bus," I said. "My stomach is still bouncing around in one of those mountains."

"Join us for chai?" said Chaz, picking up on my immediate interest. I couldn't tell if they were together or just
friends.

"Sorry, I can't," I said. "I'm off to work."

"Work?" said Lisa, looking surprised that anyone would
have a job in such a place. "Like nine to five?"

"More like five to nine. It's a little bookshop on the next
street over."

"I'll come visit," she said. "I'm always on the lookout for a
good book."

"Yeah, stop by," I said. "It's upstairs. On Jhochen Tole." I
watched as Lisa and Chaz headed across the square. It was
hard to take my eyes off her. What a beautiful girl.

⟨♦⟩

The Chief of Immigration was in a fury. He'd bought his
position from the King, fair and square, and was merely
expecting a decent return on his investment when the
Minister of the Interior pulled a fast one. They'd been
feuding forever and in order to prevent the Chief from
collecting the monthly bribes most foreigners paid to stay in
the country, the Minister began issuing visa extensions for
free. In a country where baksheesh was part of the price of
doing business, this was like a declaration of war.

When I heard rumors of such underhanded wheeling-
dealing, I knew it wouldn't last long. I immediately visited
the office of the Interior, passport in hand, and was shown
in to see the Minister himself. He was signing anything put
before him––passports, birth certificates, dog licenses––and
didn't even look at me as he stamped my visa with an
unheard-of six month extension. The fact that he was
gaining nothing didn't matter to him. All he cared about
was how much his archenemy was losing. As I walked
outside, I took a deep breath of fresh Himalayan air. Ah,
what a glorious, magical country!

When I first arrived in Nepal I did everything I could to avoid paying baksheesh, but once I used up all of my legal remedies it was either pay up or get out. Much as I hated the idea of bribery I justified it to myself as a kind of tax for living in Shangri-la. But it wasn't long before I discovered the *joys* of baksheesh, for there were many advantages to having a government official in your pocket. The longer a foreigner stayed, the more he paid, and the more he paid, the more he was counted on for his monthly contribution. The immigration officials had became so beholden to foreigners they began turning a blind eye to certain "indiscretions" since no one wanted to diminish their share of ill-gotten gains. There would come a time when I'm pretty sure I could've gotten away with murder in Nepal, not that I ever particularly wanted to, but still, it was nice to know that I could, just in case.

⚜

Spring arrived and there was a palpable feeling of anticipation in the air. As I walked through the makeshift pilgrimage camp that was spread out along a steep path along Kimdol Hill, I could feel the excitement building. The Tibetans chanted their mantras with renewed vigor as they gathered wool into large bundles and prepared for the long trip home. One morning I heard a harrowing scream and rushed over to the camp to find a young girl bleeding profusely. She'd nearly cut off her finger with a wool shears and her family was in a panic. When I looked at the wound I could see why. Bone was showing through and blood was gushing everywhere. I grabbed the girl and hurried down the hill, where my friend Delia just happened to be arriving in a taxi. When Delia saw the wound she ushered us straight into the cab. The girl was petrified, probably more by the cab ride, the doctor and the hospital than by the injury itself. "There, there," said Delia, soothing her as the doctor sewed up the finger. The girl's eyes softened into warm pools of trust and adoration. Delia held her as tenderly as if she were her own child.

A few days later came the moment everyone had been waiting for. Rangjung Rigpe Dorje, the Sixteenth Karmapa, was finally due to arrive. The Karmapa was the spiritual head of the Kargyupa sect of Tibetan Buddhism and was second in influence only to the Dalai Lama. Having been in exile for decades, this was a once-in-a-lifetime opportunity for his followers to be in his presence. While the main ceremony was to take place across the valley in Bodanath, the monks were to first come to Swayambhu and pay respects to the oldest Tibetan Buddhist temple of them all. Thousands of people lined the road all the way up the hill, waiting for the motorcade from the airport. The Karmapa was due to arrive at noon but the plane was late, not unusual for the Kathmandu airport which ran more on whim than any semblance of schedule. And so, we waited... and waited... and waited...

One o'clock... two... three... four... five...

The tension began to mount. A few people got unruly. There was some minor pushing and shoving. A Tibetan woman slipped into a crazed, highly sexual dance full of wild hip thrusts and breathless gyrations. People moved away from her, afraid of being possessed by evil spirits, but then another woman joined in, and then a third. Finally, a long string of cars appeared around a bend in the road. A cheer went up and everyone watched as the motorcade slowly wound its way to the bottom of the hill. The vehicles moved out of sight, but a few moments later we heard the distinct sound of horns. It was a deep rumbling that seemed to rise up from the bowels of the earth.

"Mmmmmwwwaaaaaaaaa."

The sun began to set, the full moon began to rise, and for one fleeting moment both the sun and the moon were at opposite horizons, both visible and glowing. At that very instant the Karmapa appeared. He was surrounded by eight monks carrying ceremonial umbrellas and a phalanx of bigger, beefier monks who held the crowd at bay. David Lean couldn't have choreographed it any better. The sun, the moon and the Karmapa simultaneously filled the screen in one perfect shot.

The crowd and the bodyguards engaged in a kind of throbbing, organic dance. It was a blessing to touch the Karmapa, so everyone pushed forward to get close while the guards tried to keep him from getting trampled. It was a delicate encounter made no easier by the few dozen Western Buddhists who were in attendance. Once the Tibetans had touched the Karmapa they retreated to the rear, but the Westerners seemed consumed by the idea that if one touch was a blessing, imagine what *five* touches could do.

"*Mmmmmwwwaaaaaaaaa.*"

I, too, touched the Karmapa but with a rather unconvincing tap to his shoulder. I felt slightly embarrassed but I figured it couldn't hurt to deposit some good karma into my celestial bank account. "Isn't it incredible?" swooned a Canadian woman who'd come all the way to Nepal for the event. She looked transformed by the experience, her eyes clear and beaming, her spirit so light I thought she might float off into the clouds. At that moment I envied her. I wished that I too could feel transformed by the touch of a holy man, that I could share in this once-in-a-lifetime mystical experience, but I was still too earthbound—as usual—and I was still incapable of completely giving myself over to a transcendental moment of illumination. When I touched the Karmapa all I felt was the fine weave of his silk brocade coat.

The Karmapa disappeared into the temple and the crowd began to disperse. A short time later he was whisked across the valley to Bodanath, where there were more ceremonies, invocations, and a series of teachings for the most advanced Buddhist practitioners. And then, a few days later, the Karmapa met with Ossian in his private quarters and administered the tests given to potential tulkus. Hetty waited nervously outside the closed chambers as the Karmapa set out a series of cups, chairs and maybe even a few pairs of eyeglasses. Ossian had to choose which ones were his—his, that is, from his previous life. This was the moment of truth for Ossian and, maybe even more so, for Hetty. She'd been telling anyone who'd listen about the upcoming event and was almost sick with worry. Every Westerner in the valley knew the story and waited anxiously for the results. When the doors finally creaked open there was a brief silence, a moment of reflection, and then the dramatic declaration that Ossian was indeed the reincarnation of a high lama. That lama, it was said, had simultaneously reincarnated into three separate beings this time around and Ossian was the first Westerner ever to be declared a tulku. It was a moment to be etched into history.

Hetty slept well that night, even if her life was only about to become more complicated. Her son sat on a fancy throne wearing a glorious brocade hat that almost buried his little head. Shortly after the ceremony Angus was seen withdrawing into an alleyway just across from the Hanuman Dhoka temple, where the streets wound around and around and led to untold destinations. It fit with an old Tibetan prophesy: the mother of a tulku would go mad and the father would vanish into the streets. It was perfect. Hetty was a born eccentric and Angus was known to disappear for days on end into the back alleys of Kathmandu with a drum, a kerosene lamp and an opium pipe. It may not have been exactly what the Tibetan soothsayers foresaw, but that's what happens when a tulku's parents just happen to be Angus MacLise and Hetty McGee.

Chapter 16
The Angry Mistress

Spring edged toward summer and with it the conditions in the valley quickly deteriorated. It hadn't rained in months and the rivers coursing down from the mountains had been reduced to a trickle. The Bishnumati, which originated high in the Himalayas, carried more waste than water but that didn't stop everyone in Swayambhu from continuing to wash everything in the river, whether it was their children, their clothes, or their food. It was, therefore, entirely foolhardy that I visited the new Tibetan restaurant— highly questionable even in the best of times—and risked a plate of rice and cauliflower. Lobsang, the owner and chef, chanted mantras from behind the pots and pans and I figured if that couldn't ward off the germs of our temporal world, what could? In retrospect, perhaps Lobsang washing his hands once in a while would've helped.

When I awoke the next morning I had the most peculiar feeling, as if all of my internal organs had been rearranged helter-skelter with no regard for where they should be. Nothing quite fit anymore, neither my optic nerve nor my ear canal nor the heart beating in my hand. I stumbled downstairs to look into the polished pan that I used as a mirror and saw someone staring back at me with the strange pallor of an overripe zucchini. I knew straight away that either the pan was tarnished or I was.

I staggered down the hill, struggled into a taxi, and held on until we got to the clinic downtown. The Nepalese doctor, who may or may not have studied medicine, stuck me with a needle so dull it barely punctured my skin, then drew enough blood to transfuse a horse. He ran a test in a laboratory that looked like the chemistry set I had in junior high school and then confirmed the obvious, that, yes, I had hepatitis, and no, he couldn't do anything about it. "The liver," he said, "is an angry mistress."

At a loss for what to do, I visited Dr. Mana, a well-respected homeopathic doctor who determined that I was a Kapha dosha in the ancient system of ayurvedic body types. This apparently was good news and meant I might not die. The Pitta doshas, being big-boned and thickset, tended toward meat-eating, alcoholism and violence. The Vata doshas, being thin and wiry, tended toward vegetarianism and hysteria. But we Kaphas, a less common form, combined the two qualities and led a fairly balanced existence. And that, if I understood correctly, would help me defeat hepatitis. "Lie flat on your back for thirty days," Dr. Mana said, "eat nothing but rice, plain boiled vegetables and papaya, and drink plenty of water with glucose."

"Thirty days?" I said.

"The liver needs to take a break. You must only ingest foods that don't need to be filtered through the liver."

"For thirty days?" I repeated, hoping I'd heard wrong.

Dr. Mana dug through a collection of containers and poured out several dozen pellets that looked suspiciously like deer droppings. "Here, these won't hurt you," he said, handing me a bagful of homeopathic pills that we both knew wouldn't do any good, but he didn't want me to leave empty-handed and I didn't want to make him feel bad, so I gave him a couple of rupees and clasped my hands in prayerful thanks. It was the least a mild-mannered, even-tempered Kapha could be expected to do. Even a Kapha whose liver was an angry mistress.

෨෧ఎ

I lay on my straw mattress and pancake-thin pillow staring at the ceiling, the floor, and the walls. The thanka hanging right across from me, its gold highlights glistening in the shadows, radiated malevolence. The central deity had eyes that bulged right out of his head, fangs that dripped with blood, and a tongue that hung to his feet. He wore a necklace of human skulls, swung daggers from his many arms, and danced on a cemetery from which shot the flames of hell. If I understood the symbolism properly it was a good kind of malevolence since the deity was either warding off evil or was showing me something about the illusion of the corporeal world or was simply trying to scare me into enlightenment. That's the interpretation I liked best—to be scared into enlightenment—since I'd been lying flat on my back for twenty-three days and didn't have the strength for anything else. For twenty-three days Mahakala laughed at me, spit venom into my face, mocked my fragile existence, and chastised me for asking the unanswerable and questioning the unquestionable.

Maybe the universe was telling me I shouldn't have returned to Nepal. Maybe the universe was telling me I never should've left Nepal in the first place. Maybe the universe couldn't care less whether I was in Nepal or Timbuktu. Mahakala leered at me with renewed vigor. Maybe there was no such thing as the universe. Maybe I wasn't really there at all. Maybe there wasn't really a painting on my wall. Maybe that wasn't really a wall. Maybe I didn't really have hepatitis. In which case, why was my skin so yellow and why did my eyes look like flashing caution signs?

I stared at the ceiling door of the oubliette and ran through all the forms of revenge I would take out upon Lobsang. I would tie him to a prayer wheel and spin him like a centrifuge until his eyes popped out. I would hang him from the top of Swayambhu stupa until the crows pecked at his carcass. I would swing him from a prayer flag until the wind cast his spirit to the four noble directions—

"Hey, babes, keeping up your spirits?" said Paul, appearing unannounced at the head of the stairs. Paul was one of my oldest friends in Nepal and had been there longer than any other Westerner. Like Hetty, he lived just across from the temple but Paul's interest in Buddhism was mixed with equal parts rock and roll, science fiction, art history, horticulture, gemology, astrology, astronomy, astrophysics, and psychedelic research of all shapes and sizes. Paul called everyone "babes," probably because he couldn't remember anyone's name. He showed up every morning with boiled water and glucose, a surprisingly repugnant combination given its utter tastelessness.

"Yeah, yeah, happy as a clam."

"Well, you might be better off in bed," he said, staring at me with his piercing blue eyes. "There's trouble in the kingdom. They found two bodies out near the airport."

"Bodies? You mean, like *human* bodies?"

"That's right. They were all scorched and charred and riddled with bullet holes or knife wounds. The cops weren't really sure. They're not real proficient at murder investigations."

"*Murder?*" I said, raising my head slightly from my pillow. "In Kathmandu?"

"A couple of Westerners. It's all hush-hush. Nothing in the papers, nothing anywhere. The authorities are keeping it on the down low." Paul leaned in and whispered under his breath. "Captain Narayan paid me a visit. He figured I've been here the longest and maybe I know something. So I'm putting the word out, real carefully, if you know what I mean. There's certain toes I don't want to step on."

"Toes?"

"Mafia." I took a long look at Paul, wondering what the Mafia could possibly want with our cabal of destitute expatriates. "That's my theory, at least," he said, staring out the window with nervous eyes. "The big boys are moving in on the drug trade and these two hapless kids got caught up on the wrong side of a deal."

"Paul, does that make any sense to you? Why would the Mafia come halfway around the world to kill two travelers outside the Kathmandu airport unless they'd done something completely insane?"

"You have a better theory?"

"Yeah. Maybe they got hit by lightning. How about that?"

"Sure, lightning. I'll tell Captain Narayan. Case solved." Paul pulled out a canister of filtered water, stirred in some powdered glucose, and handed me the concoction. "And now the moment we've all been waiting for."

"I'll drink it later," I said, looking at it with distaste.

"You'll drink it now," he said. "Eight cups a day. I'm guessing after this one, you'll only have seven to go."

I forced the foul liquid down my throat. It was like drinking chalk. "Thanks for stopping by, Paul."

"Happy to do it, babes. I'll check in later with news from the front." He looked at me with a rare seriousness. "You know, these dead bodies aren't a good thing."

"No," I said, feeling a cold chill down my spine, "they aren't."

❧

Early afternoon brought Billy and Suzie, who arrived each and every day with a pot of rice and vegetables so bland I could barely force them down my throat. They were two of my favorite people in the Valley but now acted as food testers, tasters and tormentors. Like most everyone else who'd taken refuge in the Himalayas, they had their own stories. Billy was the son of a high-ranking New York communist at a time when membership in the party was not conducive to one's health in the American legal system. After endless harassment, Billy's mother took him to Cuba during the time of Castro's revolution and eventually on to Poland, where he spent the majority of his youth. When they finally returned to New York some ten years later, Billy turned to Eastern religions, which much better suited his temperament. He reconnected with Suzie, a relative from Chicago who had followed much the same path, and the two of them set off for the south of India in search of a spiritual teacher.

Their trail eventually led them to Nepal, where they settled in for what was to eventually become a fifty-year stay. They found their physical and spiritual home at the base of Swayambhu Hill, where the sounds of Tibetan horns reverberated through the night. It was there that Billy became a yogi and Suzie a teacher, all the while maintaining a sense of humor and irony that eluded many of their contemporaries. Ten years in Warsaw—or Chicago, for that matter—will do that to any but the most dogmatic of disciples.

"You're really in luck today," Suzie said, appearing with her dreaded pot of boiled rice.

"Oh, God, not you again," I moaned with all the drama I could muster. I truly thought that one more bite of rice would kill me.

"He's feisty today, don't you think?" Suzie said to Billy.

"Very feisty," he concurred.

"And ready for some nourishing food."

"Very ready."

I forced a spoonful of rice down my throat and tried not

to gag. "You know what this tastes like?" I said.

"Chicken Stroganoff at Delmonico's?" said Billy.

"Yeah, Delmonico's on Pig Alley."

Suzie forced a big smile. "He's looking better, isn't he?" she said to Billy.

"Oh, absolutely," he said. "We'll have him out of here in no time."

And so it went, day after day after blessed day.

⁘

My friend Jimmy showed up one afternoon with his dad, a rare visitor from the West. Jimmy's dad was the writer of *I Love Lucy* and I imagined him cooking up a scheme for Lucy to go to the Himalayas to save one of Ricky Ricardo's hapless band members from some mad Nepalese doctor. The actual reason for his visit was to make sure his son was safe and sound, but I'm not sure that bringing him to see me in this condition was particularly reassuring. He squinted at me from afar and tried not to inhale more air than absolutely necessary. I thought that was pretty wise and often attempted the same technique myself. Not breathing, however, had its limits and so did Jimmy's dad, who exited on the first plane west after realizing his son had no intention of leaving.

Jimmy was one of the youngest among us and as such we tried to look out for him, but he was a tough kid who was more than ready to take on whatever Asia might throw his way. He dressed like a tribal warrior from Afghanistan, smoked hashish like a sadhu, and absorbed every arcane piece of Eastern wisdom into his magnificent imagination. Writing coursed through his veins as well, and he was usually seen with a thick journal into which he entered his observations of the remarkable events swirling around him. Writing was a family business. His brother Tom was one of the creators of *Saturday Night Live* and he too later came to

Nepal. With Jimmy as his guide, he filmed *The Search for Akassa,* an episode that was to become a classic segment for his *Schiller's Reel* on SNL. It was only the beginning of our seeing Kathmandu on the big screen. Several years later Bernardo Bertolucci filmed part of *The Little Buddha* in Nepal, a story partially based on the life of Angus, Hetty and Ossian. Billy and Suzie worked as advisers on that film.

⁂

Angus showed up later in the evening. He operated best at night and in the shadows. He slipped his tall, skinny frame into the corner, pulled out his opium pipe, and lit up. Angus lived in his own rarified world and I'm not sure he was even aware that I had hepatitis. He just smoked the pipe, started drumming on an Indian tabla, tamped down another ball of opium and reached over to me. "Here—"

"No, I told you, I can't."

"You... can't?"

"I'm sick. Remember?"

"You are?"

"Look at me. You see how yellow I am?"

Angus squinted behind his wire-framed glasses until his eyes became little almonds cracking through the shell of his gaunt face. "Oh, yeah, you are. I thought it was just the light."

"Why do you think I've been flat on my back for the last three weeks?"

"I was wondering—"

"Look at my arms, look at my ribs. I've lost, what, twenty-five pounds?"

Angus hunched forward like Ichabod Crane. "Better go easy on the opium for a while," he said, offering me one last chance to take a hit before slipping off into the night.

⁂

Ira Cohen and Petra Vogt lived just behind me in a big house that was filled with books, paintings, poetry, photography, bat skulls, raven beaks, and a collection of human toes and fingers that Petra had purchased in India from the Bone Man of Benares. Ira was a New York beat poet and photographer possessed of true genius and a temper to match. He was an impassioned artist whose work touched everyone with whom he came into contact. Ira was born into a home of deaf mutes and the silence almost drove him crazy. Sometimes the only sound he heard was his rubber ball bouncing off the bedroom wall—*thwack, thwack, thwack*—harder and harder he'd throw it, getting no one's attention but his own. The ball would carom around the room, breaking cups, dishes, lamps, and whatever else he had piled up on his desk. In this silence words became Ira's ally, an endless, profound, profane outpouring of words that began the moment he awoke and continued unabated throughout the day. His voice echoed over loud music, car horns and screeching subways, louder, louder, turn up the radio, turn up the TV, sing, dance, laugh, scream, let there be a great chorus of glorious noise.

Years earlier Ira had been introduced to a material called mylar, a kind of aluminum foil that NASA was using in its rocketry development. He found that by photographing a reflection off its surface he could get the perfect distortion to capture his surrealistic vision. What began as a modest experiment expanded eventually into a whole series of photographs and portraits and later an entire movie, *Invasion of the Thunderbolt Pagoda*, that was shot through mylar. He photographed William Burroughs, Ornette Coleman, Alejandro Jodorosky, Allen Ginsberg and Jimi Hendrix as they passed through his East Village loft.

Petra Vogt, the daughter of a German chemist, was born in Berlin and was being groomed for the classic German theatre. She was a modern-day Dietrich whose charisma was manifested through a high, arching forehead and eyes that pierced steel. When the Living Theatre descended upon Berlin—the same international troupe of artistic provocateurs that Margo had seen off in Geneva years earlier—the local arts community was thrown into chaos. The troupe was an irrepressible force that swept away the ideas of classic theatre and replaced them with the closest thing to anarchy anyone had ever experienced onstage. They'd been exiled from America, jailed in Brazil, reviled in England, and feared pretty much everywhere else. After witnessing a single performance of *Paradise Now,* Petra threw away her training, her pedigree and her future to run off with the circus. Under the tutelage of Julian Beck and Judith Malina she became a central member of the cast and an unforgettable presence onstage.

When Ira met Petra, an artistic force was unleashed upon the world. They were two outsized personalities draped in purple, black and silver, two alchemists of the netherworld who poked holes in preconceptions and mutated reality. It was only natural that they would wind up in Nepal, the perfect stage for their surreal explorations.

The day that Ira and Petra found out I had hepatitis they hurried over with sheets of mylar and rolls of film. "You're magnificently yellow!" cooed Petra. "It's a wonderful shade, completely inhuman, you must be part of my new collage, please, just lie back, let the shadows sink into your glorious skin, is it too light in here, Ira, do we need to close some windows, oh, this is good, this is really good, you are so wonderfully gaunt, who knew you could project such luscious morbidity!"

"Congratulations," said Ira, "you're going into our gallery of rogues, misfits, and international outlaws."

"I'm honored," I said.

"You should be," said Ira, angling one final shot of my jaundiced visage against a sheet of mylar that was twisting in the breeze. "Don't ever change."

⋘⫯⫯

There came an urgent rapping from downstairs, then the sound of the door swinging open and footsteps racing up the stairs. "Thank God, you're here!" came a panicky voice. I forced myself up to my elbows to see a familiar face, albeit one drenched in tears and perspiration. I actually wondered if I was hallucinating, but then I saw the familiar black eyes, the thin nose, and the thick lips. "Carmen?" I said, squinting my eyes, "is it you?"

"Of course it's me," she said as she squeezed my hand. "God, you're hard to find! I asked around in town. Somebody said to try the bookstore, and then somebody said Swayambhu, and then somebody gave me directions and I took a taxi immediately, and here I am. The taxi's waiting at the bottom of the hill with all of my things."

"Well... I'm happy to see you. How long's it been?"

She didn't answer right away. Her eyes kept darting back and forth so anxiously I wasn't sure if she was entirely there. "Now, listen to me," she suddenly blurted out. "You really must listen. Somebody's after me. They're trying to kill me!"

"Uh... *what?*" I said, not completely sure I'd heard right. "Who's—"

"I only barely got away!" she interrupted as she frantically paced the room, her hands fluttering, her eyes peering out the window every few seconds. Several times she glanced my way with a quizzical look, as if wondering what I was still doing in bed.

"Carmen? What are you talking about?"

"In Bangkok! First the hotel, then the restaurant, then everywhere I went—*are you sick?*—they were after me, this French-Vietnamese guy and his Canadian girlfriend—*you don't look well*—they followed me everywhere, they wanted me to buy gems—*why are you in bed in the afternoon?*—and then they took my photo and wanted to see my traveler's checks and I became suspicious—*do you want some tea?*—so I changed hotels and still they found me, I couldn't go anywhere without seeing them, they wanted to kill me—"

"Carmen! Please! Slow down!"

She finally took a breath and leaned over the mattress. "You *are* sick," she said, taking a closer look. What happened to you? You don't look well. Listen, I'm going to check into a room and come back later. What can I bring you?"

"Nothing, I'm fine."

"I'll be back soon," she said, as she bounded down the stairs. "Just stay where you are. Oh, my God, everything is so crazy!"

❧

It wasn't long before Carmen returned with an oversized papaya. I think she finally realized how ill I was and decided not to burden me with too many outbursts. "I'll make tea," she said, calmer now but still disjointed. I wasn't sure what was worse, the manic outburst or the sudden composure.

"So catch me up," I said, taking advantage of a quiet moment.

"Yes... well... I've been traveling a lot," she said. "Here and there, you know. Everywhere, really."

"What brings you to Nepal?"

"There's a Buddhist meditation course I've heard about. I think I might take it."

"Yeah, good. Nothing wrong with that."

"Unless I go trekking in the mountains instead. Yes, I think that's what I'll do."

"You'll have to wait several months—"

"Well, to Pokhara then, or to the hot springs..."

"Sure, there's a lot to choose from—"

She smiled unconvincingly. "Do you know where I can score some hash? I really need some good hash."

"Yeah, sure, I can hook you up with somebody."

"I figured you'd know," she said as she pulled a joint out of her purse and lit it up. I watched as she took a long drag. She held the smoke a moment, leaned back, and then swooned almost to the floor. I caught her before she hit her head on a lamp.

"Carmen? Carmen? Are you okay?"

"Yes, yes," she said, her voice trailing off. "I just need to lie down." I gave her some space on the mattress and wrapped her in a shawl. "Thank you," she said softly, "thank you."

"Are you going to be okay?" I said, feeling her forehead for a fever.

"I'm all right. You don't have to worry," she said as she drifted off into sleep. "Too much hash... too much thinking..."

❧

Over the next several days, Carmen came and went, always with new plans and new stories. She brought so many papayas I could barely stand looking at them anymore, but she insisted I eat every bite. "You must!" she said. "It's important! Do you want to *die?*"

Between her constant ramblings, her paranoia about being chased and her endless servings of papaya, I thought I was about to lose my own mind. There was only one way to end it. I got better.

It was a radical course of treatment, but I'm convinced that Carmen aggravated the hepatitis right out of me. She drained the yellow from my eyes and the tint from my skin until there was no trace of my ever having been sick. The virus simply couldn't stand up to Carmen's madness.

And then, just like that, she decided to leave again. She couldn't escape her fear of being followed and figured if she kept moving, they—whoever *they* were—wouldn't catch up with her. She decided to return to Bali, imagining things would somehow be better there. I felt Carmen slipping away, not only from me but from the larger world as well. Life in Asia had worn her down and she was in a dangerous state of mind. Carmen had a lifetime condition known as Franco's Spain and I had no idea how to help her out of it. We hugged as she got into a taxi to the airport. "Be careful, Carmen," I said.

"Don't worry," she said with a little glint in her eyes. "Promise you'll eat your papaya everyday?"

"Promise," I said, thinking how I'd never eat another papaya for the rest of my life.

As the taxi sped off, I headed back home. It felt good to be outside again. I realized how much I'd missed the feeling of sunshine on my face and the wind in my hair. The shops in the village were bustling with customers. A boy stood along the road selling just-roasted peanuts. The whirr of a foot-driven sewing machine resonated from the tailor's shop while the clip-clip of wool shears reverberated from a tiny carpet factory in the upstairs loft. As I headed for the steps to my house, I came upon Lobsang's Tibetan Restaurant and couldn't resist going inside. "Lobsang!" I yelled into the kitchen.

Lobsang's head poked up from behind a pot of thukpa he was cooking. *"Tashi deleg,"* he said with his usual smile.

I looked at his greasy hair, his sweaty skin, his filthy clothes, and realized, oh, God, what's the use? "One rice," I said, "hold the cauliflower."

Chapter 17

The Far Gone Exosphere

Ira was mad at me again. Ira was always mad at me for one thing or another, either because I wasn't listening to what he was saying or because I was listening too carefully, or because I hadn't responded to one of his comments or because I'd responded too quickly, or because I hadn't laughed at one of his jokes or because I'd laughed too loudly. Whatever it was, we were usually at odds and often steering clear of each other. That didn't stop me from loving pretty much everything about Ira, but it was a love from afar, love from a safe distance.

It was Petra's birthday and I wandered through the market at Asan Tole looking for the proper gift. What could I possibly give Petra? A petrified crow talon? A spider's nest? A scorpion encased in amber? Good choices all, but nothing was available. One stall had a variety of animal pelts, but when I discovered they were infested with crawling things of an unknown nature, I made a quick exit. After a few more hits and misses I came upon a miniature perfume bottle carved from amethyst. It was perfect. Petra, who wore nothing but black, silver and purple would surely appreciate the bottle, if only for its color. "How much?" I asked.

"Hundred rupees," said a guy who sat cross-legged on the floor smoking a bidi.

Okay, here we go. I had already made the mistake of asking the price in English and now I was in for the whole routine. "One rupee," I countered.

The guy looked at me as if I had offended his honor. "Eighty rupees, best price."

"Two rupees."

"Fifty rupees."

"Three rupees." We went back and forth until we finally got down to ten rupees, which was still way too much but it was for Petra, after all, so I decided to splurge.

At a party that night Petra provided entertainment on her violin, an instrument she didn't really play, but that mattered little. Just the way she held the bow was mesmerizing, not to mention the way she propped the body against her chin and the way she tuned the strings. The entire performance was so raw and wonderful as to be beyond criticism. I joined her on guitar as Ira read from his latest poem:

>*For Petra running thru the streets*
>*of Essaouira with a beating heart*
>*in her hands—*
>*To what fell black winged majesty*
>*Does your Beauty's shivering glance*
>*Owe its Silver Talon & Claw*
>*What spider more fantastic*
>*Came ever down*
>*From taut stringed web*
>*To take its prey*
>*From realms of endless dreams*
>*In streams of airy currents*
>*Where prisms are set aflame*
>*Before the dawning day.*

Ira went upstairs to retrieve her present while Petra unwrapped her other gifts. She feigned delight at the usual pouches, beads, and bundles of incense, but when she gazed upon my little perfume bottle she looked truly pleased. It was just the right shade of wanton lust. A moment later Ira returned with a small box wrapped in spidery fabric that she tore open with ravenous zeal. When she opened it, there was a moment of strained silence from the assembled guests. Inside the box was a little perfume bottle, just like mine, only made of quartz, not amethyst, and of lesser quality.

"How nice, Ira," said Petra, forcing a smile.

Ira seemed a bit disheartened by her response but then, when he saw what I'd given her, he flew into a rage. "You got her the same thing?" he stormed. "In *purple?*"

"Yeah, I know," I said, shifting uncomfortably on an overstuffed pillow that lay crumpled on the floor. "Crazy, huh?"

"I think it's wonderful," said Petra. "Both of you coming up with the perfect gift!"

"Wonderful?" yelled Ira. "What did you do, follow me? Of course, you followed me and saw what I got and then you got the same damn thing. Only better!"

"Ira, that's ridiculous. Why would I do that?"

"Out!" he screamed.

"Ira, really," said Petra, trying to calm him down.

"Out before I smash the whole damn thing!"

"Okay," I said, gathering my guitar, "we'll talk about it tomorrow."

"No, my dear boy," he said with arching eyebrows that fluttered like bat wings, "we shall never speak of this again!"

⚭

Ira and Angus oversaw a shoestring publishing house called Bardo Matrix, which put out poetry journals that were printed on handmade rice paper and illustrated with woodblock prints. In addition to his own writings, Ira also issued books written by friends with whom he'd collaborated during his years living in Tangiers, most notably Paul Bowles, Gregory Corso, Diane Di Prima, Charles Henri Ford and William Burroughs. The Bardo Matrix poetry series occupied a special shelf at the Spirit Catcher Bookstore and was to become a valued collector's item.

Thursday night was the weekly Poetry Reading and the bookstore was packed. Ira read from *The Cosmic Crypt*, Angus read from *The Cloud Doctrines*, and Roberto Valenza, newly arrived in Kathmandu, read from *The Clearing Stage*. Like most everyone else in Nepal, Roberto had an interesting story. He grew up in Staten Island, the son of a New York cop and a long-suffering mother who tried to steer him away from trouble. Despite her efforts, Roberto wound up in Rikers Island Prison for hijacking a couple of cars and joyriding through the streets of Manhattan while high on hard drugs. She was at a loss for what to do. Roberto's striking blue eyes flashed with just a tinge of madness, his Italian good looks drove all the girls wild, and his four-part harmonies on the street corners downtown were enough to break any mother's heart.

Upon his release, Roberto headed for California, where he joined a band in the Santa Cruz mountains. As lead singer he found his voice, his freedom, and the vehicle for unleashing his burgeoning talents. The band grew in popularity, shared the stage with the Doobie Brothers, and almost overnight were offered a recording contract. Their world was spinning like a top. They'd been plucked from obscurity and were thrust into the heart of the music business with barely a moment to breathe. And then it all exploded. The guitarist of the band, who was responsible for putting the music to Roberto's words, folded under the pressure and went off the deep end. Within a few days of recording, he became a religious zealot, traded in his guitar for a bible, and disappeared into the mountains. The band broke up, the record contract was withdrawn, and Roberto suddenly found himself living in his car.

It was a moment tailor made for self-destruction but Roberto was saved when a beautiful girl from the northlands appeared on the scene. Tancha, who'd grown up in the wilds of Alaska, was an independent force of nature who provided a perfect counterpoint to Roberto's big city ways. She responded to the chaos of the music scene with a gentleness and spirituality that kept the two of them grounded as they moved from place to place in the Santa Cruz Mountains.

There were lessons to be learned in those mountains and even more so in the Himalayas, a mythical spot that called out to them from the other side of the world. They abandoned their California dream and replaced it with a Nepalese flight of fancy in which they meditated, fasted and studied Buddhist texts. While Tancha held their fragile existence together, Roberto wrote poetry that explored the heights of human consciousness and the depths of human depravity. He studied Indian singing, a tonality so strange it made him reconsider the meaning of music, and then, when the temptation proved too strong, he nodded off in a druggy stupor behind the desk of the Spirit Catcher Bookstore while customers took books, left books, and made up their own prices.

As Roberto alternated lines of poetry with atonal Indian chants, I filled in on guitar while Angus played a rhythm that was completely beyond comprehension. He'd gone beyond polyrhythms and improvisations into some whole other realm that eclipsed music. Whatever I was playing on guitar and whatever Angus was playing on drums had absolutely nothing in common. He was jamming with an astral quartet in some unknown plane of consciousness while I was left to play mere chords on the guitar, chords that no matter how complex they might have been were chords

nonetheless, combinations of actual notes creating a somewhat predictable tonality. Angus wasn't playing rhythms, he
was stealing shapes from a multidimensional universe, little
pieces of trapezoids and octahedrons that flickered together
for an instant, then flew off into some far gone exosphere,
never to return again.

Throwing Petra into the mix was almost too much for
one room to absorb. We needed a studio the size of a
continent or an ocean, some space where the sounds could
expand out to infinity, because should they ever reverberate
off a wall and bounce back, the laws of nature would be
forced to rearrange. The assembled audience became
unwitting volunteers in a musical magic act in which they
might have their bodies sawed in half, their wallets stolen,
or their past lives reawakened. Billy sat there with the
straight back of a yogi and the glazed eyes of a trance
dancer. Suzie relaxed into the comfortable slouch of a
chillum smoker as she took a deep hit off a pipe and passed
it on to Paul, who leaned against a wall and took in the
scene with his blazing blue eyes. With him was his beautiful
bride Pippy, who'd just arrived from Australia and now
stared wide-eyed at the strange collection of hill dwellers
and valley denizens. Leigh the painter was there, along with
Andrea the dancer, and Stefano the jeweler. There was
German Henry, English Mina, Dutch Bob, Danish Walter,
Canadian Linda, Marie-Claude from Paris, Ingrid from
Stockholm, and Jasper from London. Andy Rogers was there,
and so was Keith Dowman and Keith Redman, all taking it
in as Roberto's voice elevated the sky, Petra's violin sliced
through the clouds, and Angus's kettle drum shook the
mountains.

❧

I went home with Marie-Claude that night. The next
morning, as she left my house in Swayambhu, I heard a

commotion from somewhere outside. As I pulled on my pants, I heard voices rising and finally a woman's scream. I rushed downstairs to find Marie-Claude standing there, shaking with anger. "What is it?" I said, grabbing her arms. "This crazy man!" she said, her eyes ablaze. "He threw a stone at me!"

"What?" I said, glancing around at the empty courtyard. "Who did this?"

"Over there!" she said, pointing to the house next door. "He yelled something to me and then threw the stone!"

"Okay," I said, trying to calm her down. In a way, I wasn't totally surprised. In traditional Nepali society, unmarried women didn't visit men overnight. Westerners, who mostly lived by their own rules, were generally left alone. This, however, was something else. As much as I tried to respect local customs, bullshit was still bullshit. "Listen, just go home. I'll see you later in the village."

"Yes?" she said, glancing around to make sure it was safe. "Okay, then. See you."

The moment she left, I went straight to my neighbor's house. Tshering was sitting there in the courtyard, hunched over a bowl of tobacco. He glanced up at me with such an exaggerated look of innocence that I knew he was guilty. I grabbed him by his shoulders and pulled him to his feet. "Hey! Asshole!" I said through gritted teeth. "I know you don't understand a word I'm saying but if you ever throw another stone at one of my friends, I'll throw your ass right off the top of this mountain!"

Tshering backed away. I was twice his size and fully ready to use it. He turned without saying a word, then disappeared inside his house. He never bothered me again.

❧

Several days later I heard a soft tapping on my door and went downstairs to find Raju, Hetty's houseboy, pacing nervously outside. "Miss Hetty send me," he said as he handed me an envelope. I opened it to find a note from Hetty explaining that she'd fallen the night before on the slippery stone steps outside the monastery and had quite possibly broken her hip. Enclosed with the note was forty rupees and instructions on how to find a Nepali friend of hers who could help ease her excruciating pain.

"Okay," I said to Raju, "tell Hetty I'll take care of it."

Raju hurried off and I gathered a few things for my trip to town. When I got to the bottom of the hill I ran into Petra, who was also going to the city. When I told her about Hetty, she insisted on going along. We shared a taxi and headed for the city. The driver crossed the river, maneuvered through some back alleys and let us off in Thamel, where he pointed to an old house that stood in the shadows of a giant chilaune tree.

As we crossed the street, I heard some doors slam and noticed several neighbors staring out from the cracks of their half-closed windows. This was no cause for alarm since Petra was inevitably a source of tremendous interest, if not fear. The Nepalis were convinced she was Kali, the Goddess of Death, Doom and Destruction, and kept a safe distance. Actually, I always thought Kali was a milder version of Petra. With her heavy mascara, purple lipstick, and black and silver cape, she looked like a sorceress out of an old German expressionist vampire film.

I knocked on the door, waited a good long time, then saw a glassy-eyed guy peeking out from a darkened interior. "Yes?" he said.

"I'm looking for Sharma."

"Yes?"

"Hetty sent me."

He paused for a moment, as if debating whether it would be more trouble to shoo us away or simply let us in. Finally he opened the door and guided us to a windowless room off the hallway. He moved a bit strangely, sliding more than walking as his feet barely lifted off the floor. The room was almost entirely dark with only the bare glow of a kerosene lamp. Other than a couple of straw mats and a medicine chest, it appeared to be entirely barren. "What do you need?" he said.

"Hetty said you'd know."

"Yes, yes," said Sharma as he studied my face. "How much?"

"Forty rupees."

"The usual," he said as he opened a drawer and pulled out a ball of opium.

"The *usual?*" said Petra, leaning in to make sure she didn't miss a word.

"Every Tuesday, every Saturday," he said.

"I knew it!" Petra whispered under her breath.

"How is Hetty's shoulder?" said Sharma as he wrapped the opium into a small envelope fashioned from a scrap of paper.

"You mean hip," I said.

"Hip?" he said after thinking it over. "Yes, well, whatever ails her. Tell her I wish her a quick recovery."

"We'll tell her, all right," said Petra, relishing the news. To have anything to hold over Hetty was sure to come in useful at some time or another.

Once outside we hailed a rickshaw. As we sat beneath the canopy, Petra kept glancing at the little parcel in my hand. "What do you think?" she finally said.

I looked at her a moment, then unwrapped the opium. Petra carefully chipped off two small blocks, one for me and one for her, and rewrapped the parcel. "For later," she said with a conspiratorial wink.

By the time I made it up to the top of Swayambhu Hill an hour or so later, Hetty was nervously awaiting my arrival. She looked relieved and graciously thanked me as I handed over the opium. I saw her eyes cloud just slightly, however, as she held it in her hand and realized it was a bit light. Hetty could've determined the weight of a feather without needing a scale. "Yes, yes, well, enjoy your evening," she said as I bid her farewell. "And be sure to give Petra my best."

⧆

There were all sorts of scams going on in the kingdom, most of which were being conducted by the government itself. There was a black market in everything from shampoo to razor blades to watch parts, but money itself was the biggest source of corruption since Indian and Nepalese rupees had virtually no value on the international markets. Everybody was looking for ways to trade rupees for dollars and then, if they were really lucky, find a safe place to stash them overseas.

In recent days, a group of Indian businessmen had discovered that a growing interest in Tibetan carpets in the West could be turned to their advantage. They reasoned that if they could buy carpets in Kathmandu with rupees, they could ship them to Hong Kong, trade them for U.S. dollars, and make a nice little profit. It didn't even matter if they made any money on the carpets themselves since turning rupees into dollars was the sole objective of the transaction.

Almost overnight there was a run on Tibetan carpets in Kathmandu. Shop after shop sold out and once the supply was depleted, the shearers, dyers and weavers were put to work day and night. Carpets were flying out of the kingdom as if by magic. For the Tibetan refugees who'd barely been scraping by, it was a windfall. Kids got shoes. Parents got radios. Teachers got books. The monasteries shared in the good fortune, as well. There was so much money around that monks could be seen drinking Coca-Colas in the cafes, comparing their new wristwatches and sunglasses.

It didn't take long for the authorities to get wind of what was happening. The idea that business was being conducted behind their backs didn't sit well, and one day a government decree was issued banning the export of all carpets from the kingdom. Wool was declared an endangered resource, or some such nonsense, and that was that. The shoes disappeared. The radios were returned. The Coca-Cola lost its fizz. In short order the refugee community was worse off than ever before since one of its only sources of income had been removed. Eventually the pared-down carpet trade was allowed to resume, but the Tibetans were to learn a hard lesson in the art of commerce, the business of government, and the strange mathematics of currency exchange.

⌒✑⌒

There was a commotion at the corner stall across the street from the bookstore. Arguments often broke out over the price of sugar or kerosene but when I heard a familiar-sounding voice I decided to go over and investigate. As I approached I saw a Westerner standing with his foot propped up on a barrel, arms folded, peering at the vender who stood stubbornly on the shop floor. "Fifteen rupees," said the Westerner, holding a can of peanut butter. "That's all I'll pay."

The shopkeeper held his ground. "No, sahib, the price is twenty rupees."

"Fifteen rupees! Take it or leave it!"

"Twenty rupees. Last price."

The Westerner steeled his jaw and stared unblinking into the vender's eyes. "Fifteen rupees or I walk," he said. I wasn't sure if he was trying to scare the shopkeeper or hypnotize him, but I recognized a familiar technique involving the positioning of the feet, the tilt of the head, and the slant of the arm that was designed to give psychological advantage. It was straight out of Stephen Potter's book, *One-Upmanship*, a satirical instructional on how to dominate one's adversaries, and there was only one person who could possibly be using it. It was, of course, my old friend Robert from Amsterdam. Only Robert would pull a stunt like this halfway across the globe.

"Twenty rupees," repeated the Nepali, refusing to succumb to Robert's subtle manipulations of eyebrow, nostril and lip. I could see the shopkeeper was losing patience and decided to intervene before things got out of hand.

"The thing is," I whispered into Robert's ear, "you can't bargain over canned goods."

"What?" said Robert, turning to me with no sign of recognition. "That's ridiculous! Bargaining is bargaining. Who gives a damn if it's in a can or a paper bag?" Robert was fully into his performance now and I'd merely become one of his props.

"You can't bargain over canned goods," I said. "That's just the way it is. You can stand here all day, but the price won't change."

"Sixteen rupees!" Robert barked at the vendor.

"Twenty rupees!" said the guy.

"Eighteen!"

"Twenty!"

"All right, fuck it, you win!" said Robert as he yanked his foot off the barrel. "You wore me out! You beat me down!" He dug into his bag, handed over the money, then turned to me with the glimmer of a smile. "I heard you were here."

"When did you arrive?"

"Yesterday. On a bus. Oh, this is Hilary," he said as a fetching young lady stepped out from the shadows of the stall. She'd been paying no attention at all to the contretemps, which made me like her already. She obviously knew not to take her companion too seriously.

"Nice to meet you," she said in a soft British Midlands accent as she reached out to shake my hand.

"How long's it been?" Robert said. "Three, four years?"

"Something like that."

"You look like shit. You lose some weight or something?"

"I had hepatitis."

Robert immediately backed away. "Jesus, you're not still—"

"Don't worry, I've been certified safe by the Swayambhu Board of Health."

"Um-hmm..."

A street kid who'd been scoping out the scene saw it was time to make his move. He approached Robert with big, sad eyes. "Sahib, no mama, no papa."

"And how much do *you* want?" said Robert, his eyes noticeably softening.

The kid, who'd been closely following the argument with the vender, had a ready answer. "Twenty rupees, sahib."

"Jesus Christ!" said Robert as he reached into his pocket. "Does everything in this country cost twenty rupees?" He pulled out a twenty rupee note and handed it to the kid.

"Sahib?" said the kid, not believing his eyes. He'd probably never held so much money in his hands in his entire life.

"Um, Robert," I said, "do you realize—"

"Yeah, yeah, I get it. What was I supposed to do, *bargain* with him?"

"Robert," said Hilary with admirable patience, "maybe we should move along before we're left penniless."

"Good idea," said Robert as he eyed a crowd of beggars approaching.

"Why don't the two of you catch up on things," said Hilary. "I'm going to take a little nap at the guest house."

"You sure?" said Robert. "I mean, you'll be okay? Maybe I should go back with you. Or at least walk over there so you don't get lost."

"Robert, it's a block from here."

"Okay, okay," he said, "But don't go anywhere else, all right? Lock the door. I'll be back soon."

"We'll get together later," Hilary said to me as she gave Robert a warm hug.

"Absolutely," I said. Robert and I stood there a moment watching as she disappeared into the crowd. "I like her," I said, giving Robert a nod of approval.

"I think I'm going to marry her," he said, straining to get one last look as she neared the guest house. "Do you think she'd marry me?"

"Of course she'll marry you. I can see the way she looks at you. You didn't do anything to her, did you?"

"What do you mean, *do anything?*"

"Well, you know, Stephen Potter—"

"Do you actually think I'd one-up my own girlfriend?" said Robert. "Are you serious?"

"No, no, of course not," I said, wondering exactly which chapter of Potter's book he'd used to win her over.

As we headed up the street toward New Road, Robert examined each and every chai shop, tailor, and food stall. After checking out the spice market we came upon a tiny alcove with a brightly painted statue of the Elephant God. "Ganesh," I said, "the Overcomer of Obstacles. It wouldn't hurt to pay our respects."

"Ah, here it comes," said Robert, nodding knowingly. "I was waiting for this. They finally got you, didn't they? Who was it, the Hindus or the Buddhists?"

"Neither."

"You sure? Because nobody will be able stand it if you come back from the East one of these days all high and mighty."

"Don't worry about it," I said, shuddering at the thought. "I know less now than I ever did."

Robert took a good long look at me. "Oh, God," he said, his shoulders drooping, "you're doing it already. I can't even get a good argument out of you anymore without you agreeing with everything I say."

"Yeah, I know. It's almost worse than Potter, isn't it?"

Robert became more serious and lowered his voice. "We heard about your girlfriend. The one who died in the plane crash in Morocco."

"Martine," I said after a moment. "That was a couple of years ago."

"You okay?"

"I'm all right."

"I mean, if you need anything—"

"I'm glad you're here, Robert. It's good to see you."

"Me, too."

⁂

I did my best to show Robert and Hilary around Kathmandu without appearing to know too much. Things had gone remarkably smoothly when I suggested we go to Pashupathi, one of my favorite places in the Valley. It was only a few days before their departure and I wanted them to meet Pani Baba, a much-beloved sadhu who was known for drinking water through his nose. Why he did this was anyone's guess but it distinguished him from the sadhu who held his arm aloft for six straight years, the sadhu who lifted bricks with his penis, and the sadhu who buried himself alive under six feet of dirt.

We found him at his dhuni, his sacred fireplace, and watched as he prepared a chillum and intoned several chants in praise of Shiva, the God of Intoxication. I could see that Robert was secretly thrilled to be there—this was a story he'd be able to tell for years once he got back to the West—and I even felt reasonably confident he wouldn't pull any tricks with the old man. The sadhu packed his chillum with a mixture of hashish and marijuana, wrapped a wet cloth around the bottom of the pipe, and handed Robert three matches. This was a real honor, to light the chillum for the sadhu, and I nodded to Robert in approval. "Just strike all three matches at once and hold them over the chillum," I said. "Oh, and don't throw them into the dhuni afterward."

"Why not?" said Hilary.

"The dhuni is holy. It's a sin to throw anything into the dhuni."

Robert rolled his eyes. "I knew that," he said. "It's not like I just got off the boat."

"I'm just telling you," I said, thinking about my own lack of etiquette the first time I smoked with sadhus. Not only did I toss the matches into the dhuni, I almost threw in the cloth as well. I thought they were going to throw me into the Ganges.

"Jai Shiva!" intoned the sadhu, holding the chillum to his lips. *"Bom Shankar!"*

"You couldn't resist, could you?" whispered Robert as he lit the matches. "You had to show me up in front of Hilary, didn't you?"

"What are you talking about?" I whispered back.

Robert glared at me while the sadhu took such a massive hit from the chillum that it briefly burst into flame. He then passed it around the circle.

"Robert, he's handing you the pipe," said Hilary.

"Huh? Yeah, yeah, okay," he said, still irritated. Robert cupped his hands around the stem of the pipe and took an impressive hit. His days in the hash clubs of Amsterdam were paying off and he did himself proud. "Here, Hil," he said, handing the chillum to Hilary.

Robert exhaled a big cloud of smoke into my face, looking quite pleased with himself. He finally gave me a little wink, the storm apparently having passed.

"You know, I kind've wish you weren't leaving so soon," I said. "I've been enjoying this."

"Passage is booked, my good man. The stage coach leaves in the morning."

We shared a warm glance, then leaned back against the hill that rose up from the dhuni. The hashish was strong and the temple began to shimmer in the distance. As we each floated off into our own dream worlds, the sadhu reached over for his cup, filled it with water, and drank it through his nose. Hilary and I looked at each other and nodded. Robert stared straight at the sadhu, witnessing an act that made no sense whatsoever. Later, when we talked about it over dinner, Robert claimed no such thing ever happened. This was, I think, one of his tried and true techniques from *One-Upmanship*. When in the presence of the inexplicable, simply pretend it doesn't exist. The insult about the matches, however, would never be forgotten. No matter how many years passed, Robert would never, ever, let me forget about the time I tried to show him up in front of his future wife and some sweet old sadhu.

Chapter 18
Interlude Through a
Bedroom Window

Push and pull, back and forth, that's how it is between Mohini and Tobias, between Mohini and me, come closer, back off, approach, retreat, we stand at the edge of the bamboo pond, the lotus flowers lean in to overhear our conversation, the magnolias droop down to eavesdrop, even the turtles paddle over for a closer look, it's quite a dance we're performing, a dance with no moves, no steps, no motion at all, it's all in the head, a thoughtful waltz, a brooding tango, an imagined kathikali, because Tobias misses Nepal as well, that's what he tells Mohini— *oh, you've been to Nepal?*—well, yes, Nepal, India, the mountains, the beaches, it seems like yesterday, but of course for Tobias it *is* like yesterday, let's hear him explain his strange rebirth to her, but she doesn't care about that, not when she's found someone to talk to about the good old days in Asia, and okay, they *were* good, but the world moves on, things change and ideas evolve, it's perfectly fine if you want to endlessly relive the past, but it's not for me, not anymore, Mohini looks at me with a touch of pity, like I've turned my back on my own history, while Tobias falls deeper under her spell, a quarter of a century has passed him by and Tobias doesn't understand a bit of it, that's why we're in the park, it's the only thing that hasn't changed, neither the pond nor the redwoods nor the magnolias, they're all just as they were, but outside this botanical garden is a whole other world, the modern world, and it's off-limits to Tobias until he exhibits some sense of coming to terms with the present reality, and that, sad to say, just ain't gonna happen, they talk about the old days as if they'd traveled the same roads together, good god, look at them, two peas in a pod, and now her finger brushes against his shirt sleeve, an accident perhaps, but he notices it too, and just like that they're sitting on a log next to the pond, staring into the water, reminiscing about all those walks along the Ganges they never took together, the meals they never shared, the places they never visited, it's a bit sad really, a shared nostalgia for something that never happened, ah, but everything Mohini does is calculated, every gesture, every look, every innuendo, and Tobias is the perfect patsy to fall under her spell, well, excuse me for a moment while I take a little stroll around the park, the truth is, I'm a bit jealous of all the attention they're giving each other, let them clear the air and let me clear my mind, because all this talk about the past is making me dizzy, maybe I'm threatened by all these thoughts of our shared history, maybe I feel guilty for abandoning a part of my past, maybe I feel there's something still unfinished from an eight-year journey that ended long ago and yet maybe didn't end at all, maybe I'm threatened by Tobias's passion for the old days and Mohini's refusal to adapt, yes, let me walk a bit through the Andean Cloud Forest and the Garden of Fragrance, okay, that's enough, leaving those two together for more than a few minutes is just asking for trouble, I'm getting an anxious feeling, like who exactly is this woman and how did she show up in the first place and what was

that business with the tiger and the peacock, I hurry past
the ancestral figures and the stone carvings and suddenly
I'm right back where I started, staring into the bamboo
pond, watching the reflections in the waves, wondering
where the hell Tobias and Mohini could possibly have gone.

⤳

It's been over an hour now and I have no idea where they
are, and okay, a joke's a joke, but this stopped being funny
about two minutes after I returned to the pond, right
around the time I screamed out to Tobias that if he didn't
get back here immediately there'd be hell to pay, come
back, come back, a great storm is brewing, the volcano gods
are angry, the forest spirits are on the warpath, but nothing
works, my shouts to the heavens are met with the silence of
mockingbirds and the hush of butterfly wings, it's just me, a
lonely soul calling out to the universe, oh, lord, why have
you forsaken me, have I really fallen off the path, have I
forgotten all those lessons of yesteryear, have I alienated
even my former self and the woman under whose spell he's
fallen, of course it was Tobias to whom she gravitated, he's
younger and more handsome, his back is straight and his
eyes glimmer with optimism, okay, I admit it, the world's
his oyster while for me the shell is closing fast—*Tobias,
damn it, come back!*—don't you see what trouble that
woman is, she'll lead you down the path of ruin, you're
blinded by her beauty, you can't resist her, you have no idea
what the modern world is about, times have changed,
there's no point in looking back, forget the old texts and the
ancient wisdom, forget the shamans and the sadhus, they've
had their day, it's time to look forward and see what the
future portends, the fact is, nobody has the slightest idea
what's going on, not one of us, and whether you meditate
all night or walk in the desert for forty days or chant into
the wind until your voice goes mute, the results are the

same, you're right back where you started, a kid with big eyes wondering what it's all about—*Tobias, it's dangerous out there!*—if you want to know what it's about, I'll *tell* you what it's about, there are two twelve-year-old kids out there, they're crazy with anger and anxiety, they're on the verge of puberty and their hormones are pinballing from one crisis to another, they're a couple of little shits to be honest, and their parents give them a new computer game just to get them out of their hair, it's called *Masters of the Multiverse* and the little jerks are fighting over the world, they manipulate everything, they rig elections, they create monopolies, they establish royal houses, they build religious institutions, they even invent musicians to inspire the masses and poets to move the soul, but don't ever forget that these kids are real brats, they'll fry an ant under a magnifying glass if they want, or wipe out a whole country with a tsunami, and do you know who *we* are, folks, we're the players in that game, we're little computer chips with virtual bodies and a consciousness granted us by our twelve-year-old overlords—*Tobias, where the hell are you!*—I look everywhere, in the garden, in the bushes, in the trees, a hummingbird flies over the pond and I see the reflection of two people embracing each other tenderly, it looks like a man and a woman, he brushes his fingers through her hair and she runs her hands down his neck, they're kissing now, a deep, prolonged, passionate kiss, I can see their bodies moving in the curl of the waves, they move together as if they were a single entity, joined together, unified, a singular expression, and suddenly my attention is drawn to the building across the street where I see the silhouette of two people cast against the wall—*they've left the park, they've broken the one and only rule!*—it's Tobias and Mohini, locked in a passionate embrace, making love for the whole world to see.

Chapter 19
The Chicken Chop Suey
Murders

There are rules and then there are rules. James, who seemed to be on the verge of a mental breakdown from the day he arrived, finally went over the edge and broke every rule in the books. In the course of one particularly bizarre week he went from smoking too much hash to muttering on the streets to waving a walking stick over his head to raving biblical prophecies to eating his own excrement. That, alas, was the point of no return. There's no doctor or psychiatrist in the world whose therapy allows for the eating of one's excrement. Someone (I think it was me) once said: "Eat your own excrement, prepare for a shitstorm of trouble."

I arrived in the village one afternoon to find James screaming at a group of people like a raging, red-haired John the Baptist: *"Behold!"* he intoned mightily while shaking his staff into the air, *"For the kingdom of God is upon us!"* The moment he began swinging his staff over their heads, several women grabbed their children and a few men picked up rocks in self-defense. I hurried over to find a Nepali policeman cowering in fear as he tried to grab James before he clobbered anyone.

At that very moment another Westerner arrived on the scene. He was a barrel-chested guy who looked like he could take care of himself. "Do you speak Nepali?" he yelled to me as he grabbed James around the shoulders.

"Barely," I said, trying to get hold of James's arm.

"Well, you talk to the cop. I've got this guy."

The crowd was becoming more agitated as I approached the cop with a respectful greeting. "*Namaste,*" I said.

"Jail going!" he replied.

"Yes, well, this man—"

"Jail going!"

"Okay, of course, but you see, this man hasn't really been eating or sleeping—"

"Jail going!"

I knew that in Nepal the way to deal with madmen was to throw them into jail and beat them until they died or came to their senses. James, I feared, was never going to come to his senses. I pulled out a ten rupee note and tried to hand it to the cop. "Listen, we'll just take the man—"

"*Jail going!*" screamed the cop, swatting my hand away.

"*Cast them from the holy temple for they have defiled my land!*" screamed James, finding the worst possible moment to add his two-cents worth.

"James, you dumb shit!" I yelled. "You're baksheesh-proof!" I turned back to the cop and saw a blank look in his eyes. That's when I knew it was all over. When a Nepali's eyes go blank, it's time to give up. The argument is finished. The cop mumbled something, then pointed to a taxi that was parked at the side of the road.

"Taxi?" I said. "You're taking him to the jail in a *taxi?*"

"*Taxi going!*"

"Unbelievable," I said to the guy holding James. "Listen, maybe we should go along. At least we can find out where they're taking him."

The guy nodded and looked at James sternly. "Okay, James, listen up. We're going for a little ride here—"

"And lo! From the heavens came manna—"

We pulled him over to the taxi, struggled to get him in, then bracketed him on both sides in the back seat. James was squirming and babbling and it was all we could do to keep him from fleeing. The cop, meanwhile, didn't seem to be in any rush. When I glanced back and saw that he was still talking with the villagers, I instinctively leaned forward and yelled to the driver, *"Kathmandu going! Jeldi! Jeldi!"*

The driver screeched out and tore down the road. I held on for dear life as I turned back to see the cop running after us in a cloud of dust. "Way to go!" the big guy applauded as he stuck out his hand to shake. "I'm Walking Horse," he said.

Walking Horse? Is there no one, not one single person in Nepal, named Bob? As the taxi barreled around Kimdol Hill, I saw that we'd left the cop far behind. "Stop!" I yelled to the driver.

"Stop?" he said, not sure if he heard right.

"Stop!" I repeated. As we hustled James out of the back seat, I handed the driver five rupees. "Kathmandu going."

"Kathmandu going?" he said, looking thoroughly confused.

"Jeldi, jeldi!"

He glanced at the empty back seat, nodded, and sped off for the city.

⚬⚭⚬

Rajaram and Devagiri weren't thrilled to see James when we arrived at the Hare Krishna temple a few minutes later, but when I pointed out that it would give the six new Western devotees something to do with their time, we were welcomed in. After locking James in a room with Tandu, Kumar, Tripada, Acharya, Bhima and Keshi, we considered our options. "I know a little about this," said Walking Horse.

"I have a degree in psychology and interned at Bellevue Hospital in New York—"

"James is eating his shit," I said.

"Ah," said Walking Horse, taking a step back. "I see."

"Why don't we just call the Embassy and get him repatriated?" said Rajaram.

"Do you know what that means?" said Walking Horse. "The embassy hires a doctor and a nurse to accompany him on a plane to the States to make sure he doesn't flip out along the way. First class all the way. Then, when they arrive, the State Department confiscates his passport until he can pay back all the costs. Do you have any idea how much that could be? He could be trapped in America for years."

"So, what?" said Rajaram, showing a notable lack of compassion. "At least he'd be out of our hair."

"There might be one other way," I said as I headed for the door. "I'll be right back." Once outside I followed the stone steps to the Buddhist nunnery across the way, where I convinced the abbess to use her phone. Phones were a rarity in Nepal and the numbers easy enough to remember. The nunnery's number was nine. After looking through a flimsy directory I called every Christian relief agency in Kathmandu until I finally located Reverend Johansen. Just hearing his voice made my skin crawl. When I told him about our little problem he didn't seem particularly concerned, but he finally agreed to meet at the temple that night.

By the time he arrived we were all worn out from trying to keep James from leaping out the door or digging through the floor or flying through the window. When I tried to warn him about James's condition, Johansen cavalierly brushed aside my concerns. "Yes, yes," he said dismissively. "I am well aware of James's history. That's why I'm in contact with his family, to keep a watchful eye over the boy."

"This has happened before?"

"Certainly. James can be rather excitable. A few words from me is all he needs."

"Uhhh... I think he's beyond a few simple words."

"Why don't we just let *me* make those determinations, shall we?"

"Okaaaay... he's in here."

I opened the door to James' room. The six initiates were still inside watching over their charge, who'd calmed down a bit after they'd chanted *Hare Krishna* to him for five straight hours. The moment he saw Johansen, his eyes lit up. "Reverend!"

"Hello, James, how are you?"

"I'm fine, thank you. How are you?"

"Just fine, James. Now, what seems to be the problem?"

"Problem? I don't think there's a problem."

"I see." Johansen shot me a knowing glance, looking irritated that I'd made him come all this way for nothing.

"There hasn't been a problem at all... *not since I fucked the Virgin Mary.*"

Johansen turned quickly, as though he hadn't heard right. "P-pardon..."

"Fucked her good," James roared, *"for within me is the seed of salvation, walk carefully, those who would dare look upon me, for thou shalt be struck dumb and blinded by the light—"*

"Stop, James! You blaspheme the Lord!"

"Fuck you, Reverend, fuck you and bow down to me, for it is I who hold the key, it is I who is touched by the golden hand—"

Johansen gingerly took a half-step toward James, putting out his hands. "James, my son, remember who I am, I am here to help you—"

James suddenly leapt from his cot and spit out his words like venom. *"Fuck you, Rev, I slay the enemies with my great sword, bow down and worship me, you heathen scum of the underworld!"*

With that, Johansen rushed for the door. I was barely

able to catch up with him in the hallway. "Hey! Wait!"

"This situation... it is out of hand... I will pray for him."

"*Pray* for him? What are you *talking* about? We've got to *do* something."

"Call the embassy," he yelled from the doorway, and then, like a bat out of hell, he was gone.

⚜

"Breathe deeply," said Walking Horse. "Feel the energy rising up along your chakras and out through the top of your head. Breathe and feel the pulse of life, in and out, deeply, deeply, feel the heartbeat, relax the mind, purify yourself of all negative thoughts, release yourself, feel the flow, release yourself—"

"Thanks," said Rajaram, calming down as Walking Horse massaged his shoulders, "now let's get that asshole out of here!"

It was midnight, a taxi was waiting for us, and an Australian doctor was on call at Shanti Bhawan Hospital. We carried James kicking and screaming down the hill, drove him across town, and got him admitted into the emergency ward. "This will make you feel better, James," said the doctor as he approached with a syringe.

James seemed to barely notice him. *"And Jehovah said to his followers, rise, rise ye one and all!"* he proclaimed, the words pouring out of his mouth like molten lava.

The doctor slid the needle into James's arm. "Just a few moments, James, and you'll forget all about this," he said as he slowly pushed on the plunger, then retracted the needle. James immediately passed out. We were rewarded with no more than two minutes of blissful silence, however, before he suddenly erupted again—

"For the beast is at the door and we shall do battle!"

"James? James?" said, the doctor, looking shocked that he was awake so soon.

"He's all jacked up on Jesus," said Walking Horse. "Better zap him again."

"This is amazing," said the doctor, as he prepared another injection. A few seconds after getting the booster shot, James stopped ranting right in the middle of a syllable. His body went limp, his tongue fell to the side, and his eyes rolled back in his head. "I've never seen anything like this," said the doctor. "He'll be out for a week."

It was only a moment before James awoke again and the doctor, looking like he'd encountered the Creature from the Black Lagoon, jumped back. "This is bloody impossible!" he said. "We just made medical history!"

"Do him again!" said Walking Horse, grabbing James's arm. "He's not human!"

When the doctor gave James a third shot his body shook violently several times until his apricot-marigold-cantaloupe head of hair finally sunk into the pillow. His face was twisted like a demented fox in a petrified forest, but he was out, all right, right out of this world.

⚶

A month-old issue of *Time* magazine appeared one day at the newsstand. Despite my best efforts to remove myself from the modern world, I couldn't occasionally resist catching up on the news. I brought the issue home and devoured every word, whether it was a headline about the famine in Ethiopia or the fine print regarding subscription rates in Singapore or South Korea. The news was mostly depressing, of course, with endless catastrophes and calamities, and I parceled out the reading over a full week. One night, just as I was about to go to bed, I turned the page and came upon a very strange headline:

The Chicken Chop Suey Murders

This, I thought, was simply too bizarre to pass up. I read the article about a bright, charming Indian-Vietnamese guy named Charles Sobhraj, who'd learned to speak eight languages and had developed a strange pull over people. He used his talents first as a petty criminal and then as an accomplished conman, moving from city to city and jail to jail. In Bangkok, he met an impressionable Canadian nurse and developed a scheme in which the two of them would befriend young travelers and invite them to his favorite Chinese restaurant. Once there he'd recommend the chicken chop suey, a house specialty whose sauce just happened to disguise the taste of the poison he'd slip in when they weren't looking. Once they fell ill Sobhraj would take them back to their rooms and magically come up with the perfect antidote to the poison. Having gained their trust and gratitude, he'd then use them as pawns in a gem scam he was running.

I began feeling queasy. Gem scam? Bangkok? I read on.

Once the travelers had served their purpose, Sobhraj would take them to some out of the way spot, mutilate their bodies beyond recognition, steal their passports, change their photos, forge their travelers checks, and fly off to wherever their outbound tickets went. He even had an embossing machine to make everything look official.

Carmen was right all along... she really was being followed...

Sobhraj and his girlfriend would travel under their victim's identities until the money ran out, then find their next set of victims. They went from city to city to city, from Hong Kong to Singapore to Kathmandu.

The bodies at the airport...

At the end of story there were three case histories of the victims of the rampage. The first told of an English couple found murdered in Penang. The second was about a German woman who disappeared in Calcutta. The third told of a guy found in a field between Bangkok and Pattaya. He'd been beaten and disfigured and then set on fire while he was still alive. When his girlfriend from Paris came looking for him and started asking too many questions, she became Sobhraj's next victim. Her charred body was found on a nearby beach. It took the police months before they were able to figure out who they were. The article included a picture of her murdered Turkish boyfriend. I stared at it for a long moment. It was... Zed Habib!

Zed, whom I traveled with to the opium fields of the Golden Triangle. Zed, who almost burned down our hotel in Chiang Mai. Zed, who mysteriously disappeared in Bangkok, leaving all his stuff in his room at the Hotel Malaysia...

I thought back to when we parted in Chiang Mai, how Zed returned to Bangkok and I continued on to Laos. I thought about how easily it could've been the other way around, how easily it could've been me...

⚬⚬

"Hey, babes," said Paul when I showed up at his door in Swayambhu. "What's up?"

I dropped the magazine onto a low-lying table and watched as it fluttered open to the article about Sobhraj. "You need to see this," I said.

"Uh-huh... okay..." he said, as we settled in cross-legged on the floor. Paul had been in the process of preparing a chillum when I arrived—Paul was pretty much always either smoking a chillum or preparing the next one—and it wasn't always easy to gain his attention. He could see I was dead serious, though, and he immediately began perusing the article. It didn't take long before I saw his eyes widening and his face going pale. *"Shit... Jesus... what?!?"*

"Yeah," I said. "They've found twenty-three bodies all throughout Asia. They think there could be as many as fifty."

Pippy appeared from their tiny kitchen alcove just down the hall and Paul and I immediately fell silent. "Chai?" she said, with a friendly smile. Pippy had recently discovered she was pregnant and had a glow emanating around her.

"Love some," I said. "Everything okay?"

"No worries, I reckon," she said with her usual Australian optimism as she patted her stomach.

I thought back to Amsterdam, to my friends Jerry and Kathy who'd been awaiting their own child, and how difficult life would be on their houseboat. From this vantage point, their cold running water and irregular heat seemed downright luxurious. Paul and Pippy were essentially living in the sixteenth century, with a door to keep out the rain, a window to shield the wind, and not much else. I admired both of them, Paul for his refusal to compromise with the modern world and Pippy for undertaking an adventure she'd probably never even imagined when living back home.

Paul closed the magazine so she wouldn't see the article, then got up and held her with unusual tenderness. "I'll make the chai, babe," he said to her. "You take it easy."

"Aren't I the lucky one?" she laughed.

"Yeah," he said, helping her to a pillow, "it's good to be alive."

⁓

And then there was Lisa. She was a regular at the chai shops, the temples and the bazaars, and always with a coterie of male followers. I was, alas, not the only one enchanted with the beautiful girl from Halifax, Nova Scotia. It was as if Florence Nightingale had descended upon the Himalayas to bandage the injured and comfort the weary. Lisa took in wounded souls the way some people took in stray dogs. There was no one too damaged for her to turn away.

It seemed that everyone in Nepal was in sudden need of her attention. Whether it was a physical complaint, a drug problem, or a crisis of the spirit, Lisa was the answer, as if she possessed a magic balm. I became jealous of their ailments, wishing that I too had some debilitating illness that could only be cured by her tender touch.

Lisa grew up in cities big and small from one end of Canada to the other, always leaving when things got a bit too sticky, as they were guaranteed to do. Her father was an unpredictable sort who sped up at yellow lights, passed on curves, and tried to outrun trains at railway crossings. It was all great fun for the kids, who hung on in the backseat, but not so much for his wife, who suffered through his moods and brushes with the law. More than once they were forced to pack up and leave town in the middle of the night. Nothing was stable in Lisa's childhood, neither home nor school nor relationships, but she turned despair into comedy, danger into adventure, and shame into honor. "Don't ever lose your dignity," she would say. "It's the one thing you can never regain."

When Lisa met Ira, a strange and beautiful alchemy was unleashed. It was like a father meeting his daughter in some alternate universe, a place where two unique personalities could come together through a shared spirit and intellect. For Ira, life was an opium dream and Lisa a dancing flame that curled into the ether. She soaked up his knowledge and reveled in his humor and delighted in his most outlandish tales. At the same time, Ira dared not go too far in the presence of this pure spirit, as if realizing that his rants and raves might well break the very chalice he was filling with the spark of genius. To see this nineteen-year-old girl calm Ira with a simple glance of disapproval was to witness a rarefied magic of its own kind. But calm him she did, this avatar from a mylar universe with eyes of sapphire, ruby red lips and a chalice made of crystal.

It came as no surprise that Lisa became one of Ira's favorite photographic subjects. He captured her holding a bouquet of dried roses, through a window draped in gauze, and wandering the recesses of an ancient shrine. One day the three of us visited a cluster of temple ruins on the outskirts of Kathmandu. The ancient stones were shattered in some places, crumbling in others, and indistinguishable from the encroaching forest in others still. Ira was particularly drawn to the faces of the deities that were rubbed raw from the wind and rain of five thousand monsoons. Decaying gods were the perfect metaphor for his surrealistic vision, for what could be more surreal than the image of an eternal, everlasting god in its final moments of existence?

Ira positioned us in various broken alcoves, hanging onto splintered beams, praying to faceless statues, turning away from gods of unknown origin. Lisa and I were always looking in different directions, whether by Ira's plan or our own inclinations. My east was her west, her north my south. If I was needy, I wasn't needy enough. If I was damaged, I wasn't damaged enough. To capture Lisa's heart one needed to take on the entire weight of the world.

With each click of his camera I could feel the scene dissolving, first the beams, then the statues, then the columns of the temple. A cold wind blew in over the mountains. I felt the loneliness of the Himalayas and the stillness of the rarified air. Winter was coming again. I'd been in Nepal for fourteen months straight and I felt the mountains closing in on me. I wasn't sure if I could get through another season of cold and isolation. It was time, at long last, to go to Goa.

Chapter 20

Once Upon a Time in Goa

I stood on a stage at the far end of Anjuna Beach facing the Arabian Sea on one side and a natural amphitheatre on the other. A full moon glistened in the water like a great beacon from above, a shining light that illuminated the paths of a thousand wanderers who'd made their way to this secluded grove at the edge of the world. There were people as far as the eye could see, groups of them huddled around fires, stretched out on straw mats and wandering along the water's edge, but most of them were dancing, great masses of people moving with abandon, dancing alone, dancing in couples, dancing in groups, hundreds of them performing a kind of spontaneous ballet in the sand. The music pounded through the night air and the sound of guitars, bass and drums wafted over the local village, up along the coast and, for all I knew, all the way to Africa. That's what I liked to imagine, my harmonica caught on a great sonic wave and carried right across the Indian Ocean to the coast of Africa. That's where I'd been years earlier, playing with an African band on the coast of Kenya facing this same body of water. I was on the other side now, wondering where this next musical foray would take me.

Roberto, recently arrived from Nepal, grabbed the microphone and sang a soulful plaint to Tancha, who danced with a tambourine at the edge of the stage:

> *I want to love you,*
> *Like the sea touches the sand*
> *I want to love you,*
> *Yes, do the best I can.*
> *Your starry smile, your lips like fire*
> *You don't bring in me no desire*
> *Just pure love, just pure love.*
> *You're gone, you're back, I recover*
> *You're gone again, and I wonder*
> *About sea, sand, space & time*
> *And your love, your love.*

That's when Alexandro, who may or may not have been the cousin of Francisco Franco, came running across the stage with a dagger trying to stab German Peter, who may or may not have stolen his money. Amsterdam Dave, who wasn't from Amsterdam, tried to intervene but Bombay Brian, who wasn't from Bombay, refused to get out of the way. Johnny Cairo, who was just out of jail in London, egged them on while Mexican Mike grabbed the knife before the whole stage collapsed under the weight of the ensuing chaos. Meanwhile, I was playing a harmonica solo, a jazzy interpretation of *Sketches of Spain*, and when I opened my eyes there were two bulls actually locking horns at the edge of the mountain as if we were on the plains of Andalusia. Nilda, an Italian straight out of a Lina Wertmüller romp, grabbed center stage and began lip syncing to the music— only there were no words so what was she singing to?—no matter, she was living out a fantasy in front of three thousand people, so why not? There was Krishna, the entrancing Parisian actress who'd given up the stage to follow a guru, and Shaki, the Munich model who'd stepped off the pages of Vogue, and Massimo, the millionaire hashish dealer with eight passports, and Coco, the French-Algerian drummer who was about to lose his mind, and Neil, the English guitarist who was about to lose his life, and Fantuzzi, the Puerto Rican conga player who acted as master of the circus, and Chandra, the Dutch-Indonesian backup singer who sparkled on the stage, and Scottish Joanne, the talented vocalist who joined her in perfect harmony, and Gilbert, the guitarist straight from stardom in Copenhagen, and Paco, the Spanish keyboardist who would leap to his death, and Cowboy, the Greek flim-flam man who married a Polish princess, and Belgian Brigitte, who dressed up as a fairy princess every full moon, and Goa Gil, the guitarist who'd been in Goa so long it became part of his name.

We were the last of the beatniks and the first of the hippies. The inhabitants of Goa, a former Portuguese colony in the heart of Hindu India, left us alone since they had absolutely no idea what we were up to and, for the most part, neither did we. It was an off-the-cuff sociological experiment to see what happens when people are granted absolute freedom to do whatever they wish. Let a thousand flowers bloom, let the mind wander and roam, let ideas percolate and philosophies abound, let it all flourish beneath a full moon that lights the path and offers guidance for anyone lucky enough to bask in its glow.

⁓

Goa was an experiment in living. It had all sorts of people, some good, a few bad, but almost all of them interesting. For some it was an experiment gone bad, but for most of us it was the adventure of a lifetime, an opportunity to put into practice something we could only dream about back home. What would really happen if you brought together several thousand people from all nations and all backgrounds, people from every imaginable religion, race and political system? Would they naturally gravitate to their own kind and form little Balkanized states on their own stretch of beach? Would language prove to be too much of a barrier and cultural biases too much to overcome? Or would they find common ground somewhere beyond their individual backgrounds and willingly band together?

This experiment, which arose naturally and without guidance, was greatly influenced by a shared aversion to authority, a libertine attitude toward sex and drugs, and a widespread acceptance of all kinds of behavior, morality and spirituality. It had all the ingredients of a laboratory test ready to explode into a million pieces, but somehow it didn't. Whether by good fortune or an auspicious conjunction of the stars or something altogether unknown, the better nature of humanity won out. From this jumble of disparate parts arose a group of people who cared about each other, looked after one another, and loved each other. If it was a gathering of souls who were far from perfect, it was a noble attempt to put into action what philosophers and social scientists could only argue about.

I looked out upon these people from all over the world and felt a swelling of pride in what we'd created. Perhaps it wouldn't last forever. No, certainly not. That's not the nature of the world. But for this period of time in this particular spot, people lived together as never before, and whether there were deaths or breakdowns or moments of madness, it was a community that ultimately banded together in a grand experiment of human possibilities.

❧

I'd only been on the beach for a few days when Eight Finger Eddie, the first of the Western expatriates to step foot in Goa, took me to a house where a band was practicing. Eddie was a legendary character who'd developed a cult-like following despite his insistence that he just wanted to be left

alone on the porch of his house. The more he insisted that
he had no wisdom to impart, the more indispensable his
pronouncements became. Eddie finally gave up trying to
shoo his acolytes away and just watched with amusement as
their numbers grew. What Eddie knew was music—he'd been
a bass player years earlier in a jazz band—but that was in
his past now and he had no intention of resuming his career.
It had nothing to do with those eight fingers, either—they
were a full two more than anybody really needed to play
bass—it was simply that Eddie was in his fifties and would
just as soon play paddle ball in the morning than jam all
night in somebody's smoke-filled room.

The band played with the heady enthusiasm of five guys
who knew they'd be the center of attention on the next full
moon. I was introduced as the new guy in town and was
begrudgingly invited to jam on a blues song, since all
harmonica players are expected to play nothing but the
blues. I'd actually moved away from the blues into more of a
jazzy hybrid but, okay, if it's blues you want, I can play the
blues in my sleep, when it's in tune, that is, but it wasn't in
tune, no, the guitars were all a half-tone flat and when I
suggested we modify things a bit they assured me that was
out of the question since they'd already spent half an hour
tuning up in the first place, so, okay, let's play the song out
of tune, which is not my favorite way to play since it can
only sound absolutely horrible, but that's what we did, we
played a twelve-bar blues out of tune and it sounded
absolutely horrible. Everyone kind of stared at the ceiling
and it was suggested that we play another blues, since of
course I was a harmonica player, and when I again proposed
a modest adjustment of the strings the drummer quickly
counted in the song and we played a twelve-bar blues and it
was completely out of tune and it sounded horrible. Everyone then stared at the floor until the guitarist suggested
they try the next song without the harmonica, whereupon I

was shown the door. Which I welcomed dearly.

Five days later came the full moon and I approached the beach with great curiosity. I was surprised to find a stage towering high over the proceedings and a thicket of bramble bushes separating the audience from the band in case anyone dared to get too close. It was the kind of stage one might expect at Wembley Stadium, not on some secluded beach in India. When the band launched into their first song they were met with a smattering of applause—it might've been somebody swatting away the mosquitoes—but they were so far away from the audience they mistook the silence for reverence. The second song was met by dead quiet and then several boos—boos in Goa?—and then a lot of boos, more with each song, boos, hisses, hoots and catcalls, mixed in with some noticeably pointed threats.

I stood at the back of the crowd, thinking how grateful I was not to be on that stage. This was the great music scene in Goa I'd heard about for all those years? This was the place I'd hoped to play with a band for the first time since my three-month gig in Mombasa? I swore then and there I'd never get near that stage, that my dreamed-of music career in Goa was over, and so much the better. I would swim. I would bask in the sun. I would walk the hills. But I would never, ever, play with a band in Goa again.

❧

I had a two-room cottage on the south end of Anjuna Beach. That in itself was a small miracle since it was nearly impossible to rent anything in Anjuna, especially on the south end of the beach. That's where the hardcore of the original scene lived and it was an exclusive club to which not many were invited. South Anjuna included some pretty grizzled veterans who looked upon newcomers with disdain. You needed to prove yourself, either through a long line of mutual friends or by possessing some unique quality that would add to the betterment of the community. Having been on the road for five years helped, as did being a musician, but the main reason I was able to live in South Anjuna was because Rick and Brigitte, two old-timers I'd met in Kathmandu, grabbed a spot for me right next to the restaurant they'd opened near the beach. Rick, a burly Canadian, ran the kitchen with a kind of long-suffering detachment, as if it were his fate to spend his days and nights over steaming pots and pans while everyone else lounged around on the sand. He had a family to feed and Brigitte, his Belgian wife, wasn't above reminding him of his place as breadwinner-in-chief. They were devotees of a Sikh religious offshoot that I never quite got the name of, and were the hardest working people I knew. With two young kids to feed, they were up at dawn and in the kitchen by noon. The restaurant was a bit of an oddity. It provided some variety from the standard Goan fare, but what it was that Rick was dishing out was open to interpretation. It was strictly vegetarian but I remember there always being a lot of ants in the food. There were ants in the soup, ants in the rice, and ants in the gravy. There were ants crawling on the silverware, ants on the cups, and ants on the plates. I'm pretty sure the ants were unintentional but with Rick one couldn't always be certain. He once insisted they were nothing but formic acid.

My cottage was part of a compound of a dozen houses that were set back a hundred yards or so from the beach. What made the compound a bit unusual was that it had a higher number of heroin addicts than the average Anjuna community. Of the dozen households probably five of them never opened their doors by daylight. The junkies were easy to identify since they weighed eighty pounds, had skin the color of chalk, and eyeballs that hung out of their sallow cheeks. Other than a certain propensity for skull rings and demonic possession, they actually seemed to be completely normal. Nice people, mostly, if a bit difficult to wake up in the morning.

Why anyone would do heroin in Goa was a mystery to me. Nobody does a line of heroin and then goes down to the beach for a swim. That's the last thing you'd want. The beach to a junkie is like sunlight to a vampire. Kathmandu, at least, I could understand. It's cold, it's isolated, you're driving yourself crazy trying to decipher the Buddhist texts, maybe a line of heroin isn't such a bad idea. But Goa's another story. It's hot, you're on the world's most beautiful beach, why would you want to lock yourself inside a dark room and stare at the ceiling? Better to get addicted in Kathmandu and then come down to Goa to clean up. Not the other way around.

Anjuna Beach had no plumbing whatsoever and barely any electricity. My compound had an outhouse—quite a luxury in India—but it took a bit of getting used to. Actually, more than a bit since the outhouse also served as the feeding grounds of a band of crazed Goan pigs. Goan pigs, famous throughout India for their savory sausage, had developed a particular fondness for human excrement and had the run of the village to empty the outhouses whenever the urge overtook them. They were nature's janitors. It was simple enough for the pigs since the outhouse was nothing more than a semi-secluded stall with an open backside, which allowed them easy and instant access. Whether because of some kind of genetic mutation or digestive disorder or psychological aberration, the pigs of Goa were in a constant state of readiness for their next meal. I learned to do my business quickly and get the hell out of the outhouse.

Which would've been fine were it not for my junkie neighbors. Junkies are known for their erratic toilet habits and it was only natural that the pigs would grow impatient with their irregular feeding schedule. Especially considering that their diet contained just enough unprocessed heroin in the stool to create a little society of pig heroin addicts who were not only hungry but strung out as well. As the season wore on, the pigs became more aggressive until they'd actually be waiting at the opening of the outhouse. To squat down and see a pig staring straight up at you—and pigs have very disturbing, human-like eyes—was disconcerting in the extreme. I carried a pointed stick with me and more than once did battle with a particularly cranky sow who seemed to have it in for me. That she eventually wound up on someone's dinner table gave me no particular pleasure. Nor did the idea of ever tasting Goa sausage.

❧

A few days after the full moon, I sat on my porch strumming guitar and playing harmonica when a voice called out from the path outside my house. I looked up to see Gino, the Italian flute player I'd met in Bali a couple of years earlier. What a welcome face! It was a real relief to see that big smile, the long blond hair draped over his forehead, and those glistening blue eyes. We exchanged greetings, caught up on our travels, and reminisced about the legong dancers and gamelan orchestras of Bali. "You still playing flute?" I asked.

"What do you think?" he said, pulling a silver flute from the satchel that was strung over his back. "Do you remember that jazzy thing you used to do in B-flat?"

"You mean—"

I played a couple of major seventh chords and Gino immediately added a bossa nova melody over the changes. We traded riffs on flute and harmonica until neither of us had a breath of air left. "Wow," said Gino, "just like the old days!"

"You sound good, man, better than ever."

"Yeah, really good," came another voice from somewhere beyond the porch. We looked over to see Trumpet Steve approaching.

"No way!" said Gino. "What are you doing here?"

"I've been asking myself that question for five years now. What took you guys so long?"

"Believe me, I've been trying to get here forever," said Gino. "You go to Italy, they sink their teeth into you and they don't let go."

"Not me," I said. "I was afraid if I left the mountains I might get social anxiety disorder. After a couple of hours at that party the other night, it turns out I was right."

"Ah, the music," said Steve. "It's been, um, a bit disappointing."

"*Disastro totale,*" said Gino. "I thought the audience would kill those guys. Actually, I thought *I* would kill them."

"Have patience," said Steve. "Everything in Goa is ebb and flow. It's like the tides. One day you're sinking to the bottom, the next day you're riding high. You'll see. Nothing lasts too long."

"Talk, talk, talk," said Brigitte, calling over from the kitchen next door. "You guys going to play or not? Rick needs some entertainment."

"Oh, well, in that case," I said, winking to Gino.

As we picked up our instruments, Steve chimed in: "You guys are in luck. My trumpet's just over at Joanne's house."

"Joanne? What happened to Laura?"

"Yeah, well, that's a bit of a story," said Steve, looking suddenly despondent. "She tossed me out. She and Anjuna have their own place. I'm just kind've floating around."

"Sorry to hear that."

Steve sank deeper into a depression, then peeked inside my cottage. "Got an extra room?"

"In this dump?" I scoffed. "Only in an emergency."

"I'll get my trumpet."

As Steve headed down the path, Gino whispered to me. "Uh, is he moving in?"

"Of course not," I said, "there's barely room for me in there."

"Um-hmm," said Gino, "*buona fortuna.*"

❧

A day or two later Fantuzzi, a whirling dervish of a performer, showed up with Neil, a lead guitarist from England, and Harry, a bass player from Germany. Word had somehow spread to Vagator Beach and just like that my little shack was suddenly full of musicians. Fantuzzi was another guy I'd first met in Bali but had heard about ever since Amsterdam. He was famous for his "blowouts," wild performances in which he'd put together musicians and dancers from around the world and create an instant happening. Sure enough, after we played a few songs, I heard applause drifting in from outside and glanced out to see a dozen people listening from a grove of palm trees just beyond my porch.

Just like that, everything changed. Steve moved in, more musicians came around, and the audience in the palm grove grew. It was like a spontaneous combustion that erupted out of thin air. We played day and night and my head was spinning with all the new names and faces. The music was good, if disjointed. And then, no more than one week later, Fantuzzi suggested we play on the beach. We'd outgrown the shack and the crowd outside was spilling into the woods. My memories of the full-moon disaster were still fresh, though, along with my pledge never to get anywhere near that godforsaken stage. "Not me," I said in no uncertain terms. "No way in hell."

Fantuzzi wouldn't hear of it. He argued and sweet-talked and finally unleashed his full package of Puerto Rican charm. "C'mon, man," he said, "you can't go against the flow. It's the will of the people. It's our duty."

"All right, all right," I said, giving in despite my reservations. "But not on that stage. It's got to be somewhere else."

Someone suggested a natural amphitheatre that was carved out of the side of a hill and plans were hatched for a gathering that very evening. I was utterly terrified of the whole thing. We were nowhere near ready to play and I looked for any avenue of escape. There was none. It was one of my first lessons of Goa. In Goa there are no avenues of escape. That night five hundred people appeared from out of nowhere and crowded around our modest clearing on the beach. They were there to hear this "great new group" that was going to save the music season in Goa. *Oh, god. Oh, god, oh, god, oh god. How did this happen?* When we got to the amphitheater we discovered that someone had run a gas generator from behind the hill and had hooked up an entire set of microphones and amplifiers. As if by the wave of a magic wand—*shazaam!*—we were transformed into a ready-made band with Fender guitars, Gretsch drums, and a Yamaha keyboard. I looked around in complete awe. Was this even possible? Sure enough, the generator kicked in, the amplifiers began to hum, and I counted in the first tune. We played a collection of original songs that were ripe for disaster but somehow we got through it, even my own unconvincing attempts at guitar and singing, and when it was over the audience roared its approval.

The whole thing seemed incomprehensible but the tide had risen and there was nothing to do but ride it. We had the stage torn down and rebuilt at a third its height. The bramble bush was removed and the sand smoothed out. Three weeks later, on the next full moon, the newly formed Anjuna Jam Band took the stage. The drummer pounded the skins with a polyrhythmic beat. The guitarist played the jazz chords of a samba. The bassist infused a kind of reggae inflection. We were from all over the world and had absorbed the flavors of South America, Africa, and Asia into our music. Whether by accident or design the sounds blended into an early version of "world beat" long before there was such a term.

As I stepped off the stage Johnny Cairo handed me a chillum. Johnnie was one of the "heavies" on the scene and to be accepted into his good graces was the highest of honors. It was official. The community was behind us. The sky was the limit. What could possibly go wrong?

Chapter 21

The Hiss in the Amplifier

I'd always felt a special affinity for the Indian Ocean. I'd spent a year on the sundrenched beaches of Kenya, Tanzania, the Comoro Islands, Madagascar, and Mauritius. I'd taken an eleven-day voyage across the breadth of the ocean to Karachi and Bombay. I'd been on the ocean's far eastern reaches in Singapore, Java, and Bali, where the seas get all churned up and mixed together. But this little stretch of sand—Anjuna Beach—was my favorite spot of all. The water was warm, the sky was clear, and the sand was as smooth and white as polished porcelain.

Twice a week I swam from one end of the beach to the other in an effort to get away from the music, the gossip and the intrigue. It was a long swim, maybe a mile or so, and required paddling out beyond some reefs and then swimming parallel to the shore to the other end. The only danger was about halfway across, where the ocean was dotted with a cluster of jagged rocks that made swimming to land nearly impossible. This was the point of no return, where to continue on meant swimming several hundred yards before it would be safe to ride the waves to the shore. It was a good place to take a break and float on my back and gaze into the endless blue sky. That was my favorite part, just floating there. I could float forever in this ocean, the waves holding me up with little fingers and massaging my shoulders into a kind of watery bliss.

I wondered if that's what we were all doing, just floating by—the band, the audience, the people in the village—were we simply there because of some random confluence of events? If that's all it had been, just a moment in time floating by, then it had been a pretty good float job. For me it had been seven years floating out of America, seven years of floating up and down through this sea and that, seven years floating after something or other that was always just slightly out of reach. What had I learned in those seven years? Well, floating is better than sinking, of that I was pretty sure. I'd come close enough to sinking on too many occasions and too many friends of mine had sunk in numbers far greater than I'd ever imagined.

I swam further out past the reef, then headed for the other end of the beach. The figures on the sand were indistinct now and, in a way, so was my entire life. From this perspective it was like looking at everyone as subjects in a jar, subjects to be studied—and I was one of them—even from this distance I could see the whole bunch of us as if under a microscope. None of it really seemed possible. Were we really living in this idyllic paradise? Was any of this really happening? I kept swimming, getting lost in the weeks and months, images of naked bodies, painted faces, swaying palm trees and sweeping sand dunes, and finally I began to tire, it was too much, the panorama of images was becoming a crazy kaleidoscope in my mind, and I glanced in and saw the shore, still far away, and I decided to try a shortcut for the first time, backstroking to save energy, taking a diagonal path toward the beach, and that's when my hand hit something protruding from the water and my arm tore against something jagged and my back ripped against something immovable, and I realized I was in the rocks—I was in the rocks and the tide was coming in and each wave was pushing me from one jagged edge to another—and there seemed to be no way out, there were sharp, serrated peaks in every direction and the waves were gathering force, and I felt myself being pulled under, I no longer had the strength, there was nowhere to go, and I glanced back and saw a wave and knew this was it, it was do or die, I couldn't linger another moment, my arms were scratched, my back was bleeding, my lungs were on fire, and as the wave bore down on me I started swimming, arm over arm, and I felt my body lifting on the crest of the wave as I skirted inches above the rocks and was deposited in one great surge of the ocean onto the welcoming sands of Anjuna Beach.

Was it a sign? A warning not to float too free? Had my life itself reached the point of no return? Other than a short visit to see my ailing mother, I hadn't been back to America in seven years. Was it finally time to dip my toes in Western waters, if only for a brief moment of time? Yes, maybe it was. If nothing else just to keep myself from completely floating off the planet.

❧

The Anjuna Jam Band played every full moon and on other special occasions. Each performance drew ever larger crowds that spread further down the beach. The people who lived on Vagator and Baga Beaches trekked over the jagged hills by day and stayed all night. They built bonfires that warmed them through the chill night air. A contingent of Goans from the local villages set up little chai shops that stretched along the edge of the sand. The glow from their kerosene lamps cast an otherworldly shadow over the elongated forms dancing on the beach.

Through it all I'd been thrust into a position of unlikely

influence—until I wasn't, that is—and for the moment I was the arbiter of all things musical. That meant the band, the stage, the set lists and who played when. That was the easy part. More difficult was deciding who was allowed to be onstage, backstage, or nowhere near the stage. This was a delicate matter given that egos could be bruised and, sometimes, a lot more. No one, for example, would dare suggest that Alexandro not be allowed onstage since Alexandro might well stab you in the neck just for clearing your throat.

Being new to the scene I had no idea who was who and found myself in constant jeopardy of offending the wrong person. That's when Steve stepped in. Steve had been in Goa for years and knew everyone. He became a constant voice in my ear, directing me from one potential crisis to another.

Like all bands, alliances formed and broke between the musicians, tensions mounted and dissipated, romances grew and fell apart. We started later and later each night, until finally it wasn't until midnight that we'd make our first appearance. Taped music and a second group filled in between our all-night sessions. Around four in the morning, the energy would begin to lag, both from the musicians and the dancers. Still, everyone forged on, dancing to stay warm, playing to stay awake. Then, around five in the morning, a tiny crack of light would appear over the mountain behind us. It was like a shot of adrenalin. The music picked up, the chai shops reopened, and more people appeared from their houses or the groves of trees or wherever they'd spent the night.

As founding member of the band I insisted that we play nothing but original material. If we were ever to become anything more than a beach band I knew it had to come from our own songs, but not everyone was onboard. The music was often raw and the audience was sometimes forced to listen to us essentially rehearse onstage. But there were glorious moments as well. Neil blossomed before our eyes.

Roberto held the audience captivated. Fantuzzi whipped the crowd into a frenzy. Gino added the perfect accents. Coco and Harry kept a steady beat. Steve and I held our own.

And every once in a while I'd think of the monks of Kathmandu and the sadhus of Pashupathi. Of the Tibetan horns and the Indian tablas. Of Shiva and Mahakala. How easily it's all forgotten. How easily put aside. How quickly everything changes.

⤬

I walked along the rice paddies where the Birmingham Boys were sleeping off another raucous night, past a chai shop where a momentary spurt of electricity activated Joe Banana's juicer, across an open field where a Goan girl was washing Dr. Bobby's sarong, through the coconut grove where Jimmy the Knife had stabbed Trumpet Steve in the chest, and down the rocky path toward the middle of the beach, where Norwegian Monica and Dutch Fredo were lying naked in the sun.

The jagged little pellets that once nearly shredded my bare feet barely registered now. I'd been down this path a thousand times over the past six months, every morning for a swim out past the reef, every evening for the sunset, and most afternoons in between. I was just about to turn down the steep incline that led to the outer cove when a voice called to me from the bungalow at the edge of the cliff: "Hey, harmonica man." I looked up to see Alan leaning over his porch. Alan was an older guy, an American who was living a big life in a big house overlooking a big beach. "You guys playing tonight?" he said.

"Yeah, sure," I said, "there's still a moon."

"How's the equipment?"

This was a touchy subject. The heat and humidity had played havoc with the amplifiers and it was always anyone's guess as to what might work and what wouldn't. Steve

Madras, a brave and generous soul, had managed to import all the gear a year earlier and it still felt like a miracle that it was there. If there was a saint in Goa, it was Steve Madras. Talking his way through Indian customs was reason enough for deification.

"The Fender's okay," I said. "The Ampeg has some weird hiss. The P.A. sounds like somebody left it underwater overnight."

"Well, I just might have a way around that problem," said Alan as he waved for me to meet him inside the house. By the time I got there he was sprawled out in a hammock, fanning himself with a woven palm frond. The heavy air moved an inch or two, then collapsed of its own inertia. Alan forced himself up onto his elbows, precariously balanced on the cross-hatching of the ropes. "You hear about that guy over in Vagator who got bit by a cobra?" he said.

I felt my tan losing at least three shades of color. I hated snakes and was in perpetual fear of stepping on one in the middle of the night. "What happened?" I said, with due wariness. I wasn't sure I really wanted to hear this.

"It crawled out of the thatching in his roof and got him in his sleep."

"Christ!" I shuddered, thinking about the strange sounds I'd been hearing in the thatching above *my* bed. Then I thought about how my mattress was pretty much nothing more than thatching itself and how a whole family of cobras was probably slithering around in there, just waiting to come out all at once and bite the shit out of me. "What happened to him?"

"He died of a heart attack. His neighbors found him lying on his floor the next morning with his hands wrapped around the snake's neck."

"And the snake?"

"They smoked it."

"Somebody shot it?"

"No, they *smoked* it. Jack the Chemist cut the venom out of its sac, put it in a pipe, and everybody took a hit. Said it was their best high ever." Alan and I caught each other's eye and couldn't help having a good laugh. "Anyway, you'd better check out that hiss."

"Yeah, good idea," I said as I ran through a dozen horrific scenarios, each of which ended with me being bitten, paralyzed, or squeezed to death by some hideously reticulated monster that had crawled out from inside the amplifier.

"So listen," said Alan, reaching over for a letter, "this just came from some guy who owns a club in Bangkok. He says he can guarantee you guys three nights, plus a weekend show in Pattaya. If we can get a couple of venues in Singapore and Hong Kong, it almost starts making sense—"

Alan had been talking for months about the band touring Asia and for the first time it actually seemed possible. I tried to imagine the Anjuna Jam Band boarding an airplane, all twelve of us, plus the roadie, the sound man, Alan and his two wives, Black Johnny, Mescaline Bobby, Blind George, and whoever else could force his way past customs.

"—which brings us back to the equipment," Alan said. He pushed himself out of the hammock, walked across the room, dug through a bag of laundry, and pulled out a little cloth satchel. He looked at me for a long moment, as if deciding if it was all right, then motioned for me to come over. Alan was one of those mysterious Westerners in India, a guy who always had money but no discernible source of income. I learned not to ask too many questions of guys like Alan, figuring it was probably better not to know too many details anyway. He pulled the drawstring, then tipped the satchel upside down and poured the contents into my hand. "Sri Lankan blues," he said. "Top of the line."

I stared at twenty blue star sapphires glistening in my

palm. They were oblong cabochons, big ones, maybe six to ten karats each. "Nice," I said, duly impressed.

"Nice?" said Alan, expecting maybe a little more of an enthusiastic response. "What do you see when you look at these?"

"I don't know, I guess I see a nice cut, good color—"

Alan shook his head, as if the last thing he was interested in was hearing some harmonica player's opinion of his sapphires. "Let me tell you what *I* see," he said, as he held up one of the stones. "This one I see a plane to Paris." He dropped the sapphire into the satchel and held up another. "This one I see a hotel for two weeks... this one I see miscellaneous expenses... this one I see a little nest egg for my Swiss bank account... and this one," he said, holding up one of the larger stones, "you know what I see in this one?"

"No, what?"

"This one I see a new P.A., a couple of guitars, a drum set, and two tambourines for my wives to shake on the side of the stage."

"You're kidding," I said, wondering if he could really be serious.

"You're going back to the States this summer, right?"

"Right," I said, trying to sound nonchalant about my somewhat dubious decision.

"Well, get your shopping list together. As soon as I take care of business, I'll wire you the money."

I stared at that stone in Alan's hand and for a moment I really did see a whole truckload of gear rolling out of the cargo hold of some jetliner. What I didn't tell him was that I actually knew a bit about sapphires and had even bought a few in one of my lamebrain schemes to try and raise some cash. Needless to say, the stones in Alan's satchel were a whole lot better than the ones I had bought. Still, the stars seemed slightly off center, the lines a little squiggly, and the blue a bit pale. But what did I know? I knew about guitars. I knew about harmonicas. Sapphires were Alan's bag.

⤖

Alan was one of the older guys in Goa, part of a group of "elders" who had particular influence over the running of the community. Alan had lived for years in Paris and was known for his Sunday salons, literary and cultural events that harkened back to the glory days of Paris in the 1920s. It was the continuation of a tradition that he adapted to his spacious front porch overlooking the beach. Alan had his hand in everything and was known as "the mayor of Anjuna Beach." If you had a problem you went to Alan, who had developed beneficial relations with certain authorities in Goa and often acted as a go-between in matters of particular delicacy.

Living down the path from Alan's compound was Bombay Brian, Alan's bête noir and archrival. If Alan was the mayor of Anjuna Beach, Brian was the nightmare. Brian was a tough Irish kid from New York who acted as contrarian-in-chief as he threw cold water on all of Alan's plans. With his intimidating appearance and manner, he looked the part. He had an armful of tattoos long before they became fashionable and had served as a helicopter pilot in the Vietnam War. This was not the most popular subject in Goa and was rarely spoken of, least of all by Brian himself.

Brian had lived for years in Bombay, conducting his rather nebulous business affairs from a desk in a Colaba carpet shop. What was stashed between those carpets was anyone's guess. Whenever I visited Brian in his apartment in Malabar Point I was always struck by how spotlessly clean it was. Tattoos, helicopters and compulsive neatness didn't really seem to go together but this was India, after all, where nothing ever made much sense anyway.

Brian caused Alan no end of problems, raging on and on,

usually as the sole voice of opposition to whatever Alan had planned. But there was always a twinkle in Brian's eye, like he was just having a bit of fun with everyone, and he often surprised me with his compassion and acts of kindness. Years later Brian would become one of the earliest supporters of the elephant sanctuaries in Thailand and was to donate significant time and money to the cause of animal rights. It felt only proper that when a Bruce Willis movie called *Rock the Kasbah* was released, Willis's character was named "Bombay Brian." Willis played a tough guy with a mysterious background who walked and talked just like Brian. Such was Brian's legacy that they'd heard about him all the way back in Hollywood.

Further up the path was Jerry Schultz's compound. Jerry was another elder and a legend in his own right. In the mid-1960s he opened Slugs' Saloon, a jazz club on the Lower East Side of Manhattan. Third Street between Avenue B and Avenue C was one of the toughest blocks in New York and the club had a reputation to match. It was a late night joint where New York's greatest jazz musicians gathered after their gigs at the more respectable Village Gate and Village Vanguard. At Slugs' they could really let loose and play late into the night. When I came upon the place in 1967 and heard Charles Lloyd for the first time I thought I'd found jazz heaven.

Slugs' gained a different kind of notoriety five years later when Lee Morgan, one of the great trumpeters of the jazz age, was murdered onstage. He was shot by his wife and bled to death while Jerry Schultz watched from behind the bar. Soon after, Jerry closed the club and headed straight for India. Now he was content lying on his hammock and recounting endless stories of his days in New York with Herbie Hancock, Pharoah Sanders, and Charles Mingus.

Eight Finger Eddie, of course, was the ultimate elder. Eddie had arrived in Goa in 1965 and was to spend the next forty-five years on Anjuna Beach. Eddie made such a name for himself that when he died his cremation ceremony was broadcast live over the internet. A short while later the Goa Brewing Company named a beer after him that was distributed all over India. "Eight Finger Eddie" was a top quality India Pale Ale with "the whiff of mangoes, citrus and pineapple." The label featured a fanciful drawing of Eddie intertwined with an octopus whose eight arms reached out as if to embrace all the travelers still to come.

❧

I headed past Alexandro's bungalow, through the coconut grove, and over to Joe Banana's shop, where three Goans were leaning over a cow that had collapsed on the ground. "Very bad," said Joe Banana. "Very, very bad."

"What happened?"

"*Naga*," said one of the guys with a distant voice and a hollow look in his eyes.

My Hindi wasn't very good but I knew what naga meant. "A snake did *this?*" I said, quickly stepping back.

"What to do?" said Joe, feeling a vein in the animal's neck. "Cow will die."

Joe and I headed for his shop, which served as the central gathering place for the Westerners living on Anjuna Beach. I figured I'd have a fruit salad and try to forget about what just happened. After all, if a snake could take down a six-hundred pound cow, imagine what it could do to me. Yes... a fruit salad... that would make everything better.

Life is like a mango, it occurred to me, as I took a bite of fresh fruit. It's sometimes sweet and sometimes sour, sometimes ripe and sometimes rotten, sometimes plain and sometimes pulpy, yes, life is an exotic fruit that blossoms in spring and withers in fall, grows by day and rests by night, reaches for the sky and tumbles to the ground—wait a minute, what was I *thinking?*—life is nothing at all like a mango, not even close, a mango at least makes a little sense sometimes, you can put your hand around a mango and give it a little squeeze, you can cut it up into rectangular slices, or squish it into a glass of juice, whereas life is something altogether unknowable, life is a puff of smoke inside the wisp of a cloud floating in a mist of vapor.

I finished the fruit salad and headed back to the beach for sunset. We had a gig that night and it was important to clear my head. The Ampeg, after all, was acting up again and I figured maybe it was time to find out what was making that damn hiss.

Chapter 22

The Rose Window

The Guitar Center on Sunset Boulevard reminded me of the Calcutta train station, minus the trains and people. Which is to say, it was nothing at all like the Calcutta train station but such was my frame of reference upon returning to America from India. The store was huge, though, and that was the best comparison I could come up with on my first day in Los Angeles. It took me a while to get used to the idea that there were no images of Ganesh in the windows, no cows sleeping in the intersections, no guys pulling rickshaws down the street. I already missed the cracks in the walls, the pealing paint, and the collapsing canopies. I missed the guy spitting streams of red saliva from his betel nut chews. I missed the lady sweeping the path in front of her lest she step on an innocent bug. I even missed the kid at the chai shop with his thumb in my tea.

Now, instead of being transfixed by mounds of cardamom, turmeric and coriander, I was hypnotized by an entire wall of electric guitars. There were Fenders, Gibsons, Gretsches and Rickenbackers, and then a roomful of amplifiers, a whole island of drums, and so many PAs, microphones, speakers and accessories I barely knew what they were for.

I jotted down a preliminary shopping list that topped out around $12,000, just about the price of one of Alan's blue star sapphires. It seemed like a ton of gear, which got me thinking about the challenges of shipping all this stuff to India, but that was for later. Now, all I needed to do was pick up Alan's wire transfer at Western Union and cash the check. All Alan needed to do was send it.

The Guitar Center was overwhelming in the mere scope of its offerings. There was ten of everything and more still in the warehouse. Things were piled from floor to ceiling and overflowing out the doors. But this was only the beginning of my sensory overload. Every shop I entered was stocked with an endless variety of products, many of which were entirely new to me. In the years I'd been away there'd been an explosion of consumer goods that would've been unimaginable in Asia or Africa. Just the bread counter at the supermarket was a mind-bending experience. Growing up there'd been three, maybe four varieties of bread. Now there was white, wheat, whole wheat, cracked wheat, buck wheat, crushed wheat, rolled wheat, and some kind of flourless wheat which begged the question as to what wheat even was. In the adjoining aisles I came upon a wild variety of mysterious canned goods, the smallest size of which was extra jumbo. There were pumped-up pieces of overfed chickens revolving on a rotisserie, yogurt that had been whipped and frozen, and kernels of corn that could be instantly popped in a device called a microwave. There was something called Eggos that wasn't really eggs and Mayo that wasn't really mayonnaise. And I thought the East was mysterious! In India at least an egg was an egg, even if might come from a platypus.

⁂

The guy at the Western Union office was lost in his own world. He was dancing to disco music that was pumping from his boombox and was so busy studying his moves in the mirror he barely knew I was there. He was pretty good, I thought, even if I wasn't entirely sure what all the flexing and pumping was about. When I finally got his attention he begrudgingly glanced into his ledger of incoming telegrams. He ran his finger down a couple of columns, shook his head, and shrugged his shoulders without missing a beat. At first I thought it was part of his dance but I eventually took it to mean that nothing yet had arrived for me.

Feeling like a visitor to some strange outpost of civilization, it was comforting to know I had a friend in town who could help ease my transition. I hadn't seen Michael since his houseboat days in Amsterdam, but I'd heard he'd split up with Lois and had moved to Hollywood to try his hand at screenwriting. I admired his bravery. Hollywood was famous for chewing up screenwriters for breakfast and spitting them out at lunch. It bought and sold writers like castoffs at a bazaar. It drained their last ounce of creativity and then buried them in the *Hollywood Book of the Dead*. Or, as Michael would say, "Nice work, if you can get it."

Michael was a tall, strapping guy, a handsome New Yorker with a big heart who lived in a little shoebox of an apartment right next to the Hollywood Freeway. More vehicles sped past his window in one hour than I'd seen in the last five years. There were sixteen lanes, some going north, some going south, and some going no direction at all; they just circled around and around until they simply corkscrewed themselves out of existence. Michael shared his shoebox with Lulu, a beautiful madwoman who got up each morning, turned on the stereo full blast, and threw great gobs of paint onto a canvas. Lulu was textbook bipolar, which meant she was pretty much like everyone else in Hollywood. Everything in Hollywood was urgent, whether it was your latest painting, your sure-hit song, or your latest groundbreaking screenplay. And that's exactly what Michael had just written. "This is the one," he said. "I can feel it in my bones."

"I'm so proud of him!" said Lulu. "It's sheer magic. Any day now we'll be moving to the Hollywood Hills!"

"And in style," said Michael. "I'm leasing a Mercedes 240."

"A gold one!" said Lulu.

"Well, I don't know about gold," said Michael. "Let's not overdue it."

"Michael, you promised!"

"Silver is classier."

"Gold matches my hair," said Lulu, suddenly despondent. I could see it didn't take much to dampen her mood.

"All right, all right, we'll see," said Michael, quickly defusing the situation. Lulu brightened immediately and went back to her painting.

When I read *The Rose Window*, I could see what the excitement was all about. Michael had taken his love of history and his flair for the dramatic and turned it into the story of Nazi Germany's plan to dismantle the Notre Dame Cathedral and move it from Paris to Berlin, where it would be rebuilt brick by brick for Hitler's personal pleasure. It was an outrageous idea perpetrated by the German High Command to show their absolute dominance over occupied Europe. They brought in engineers, architects and an army of workmen to attempt the most ambitious act of cultural thievery of all time. It was a story that left me utterly amazed. Why hadn't I heard of this before? How had one of World War II's darkest secrets been buried all these years? How could such a reckless plan slip between the cracks of history?

Perhaps because not a word of it was true. It was all hatched in Michael's remarkable imagination during his sleepless nights beside the freeway. It was an audacious idea

but it had the kind of internal logic that was perfect for a
Hollywood movie. Just as important, it had great starring
roles in the characters of Franz, a young German artist
forced into the army, and Martine, a Jewish woman leading
a secret life in Paris. Franz and Martine met whenever
possible in a room overlooking the famous stained glass
portico of the Notre Dame, the Rose Window. Their love
affair was a classic tragedy in the making.

Michael imagined Franz and Martine as the next Bogart
and Bergman. He'd managed to get the screenplay into the
hands of the Hollywood agent who represented David Bowie,
the perfect actor to play Franz, and was waiting breathlessly
for his response. A poster of *The Man Who Fell to Earth*,
Bowie's latest movie, hung over the sofa like a sacred
tapestry in a cathedral. Lulu kept a candle burning beneath
it night and day with all due reverence.

I didn't know much about Bowie but it seemed like his
playing a German soldier was a bit of a stretch, especially
when Michael informed me of his recent notoriety. Bowie
had arrived in Hollywood under the guise of Ziggy Stardust,
an androgynous rock god who carried urgent messages from
extraterrestrials to the masses. It wasn't long before Bowie
began to believe his own messages and completely went off
the deep end. In true rock star fashion he became so addicted to cocaine there was a trail of white powder that followed
him right down Sunset Boulevard.

If that weren't enough, he suddenly and brazenly transformed himself into "The Thin White Duke," a character who
would've fit in perfectly in 1930s Berlin. With his close-
cropped hair, icy blue eyes and stern demeanor, he looked
more like a Nazi storm trooper than an intergalactic savior.

After a series of scandals and brushes with the law, his
wife finally convinced him to go back to England before he
wound up in Forest Lawn Cemetery. Bowie reluctantly agreed
but his troubles were only beginning. When he arrived at

the London airport there was a slew of reporters waiting for him. *"Tell us, David, are you really a Nazi?"* they demanded as they pushed microphones into his face.

Whether it was jet lag or coming down from drugs or simply his twisted sense of humor, Bowie responded in the worst possible way: he gave them the Nazi salute. It was all caught on camera, of course, and the next day his face was plastered all over the newspapers. He became an instant pariah, harassed wherever he went. People searched his garbage cans. They stole his leftovers. They left death threats. Finally he couldn't take it anymore. He had to get out of London.

"Now me, I'd go to some quaint little village in Yorkshire," said Lulu, "and disappear in the peat and the bog. But not Bowie. Want to guess where he went?"

"I really have no idea," I said. "The Gobi Desert? The Sahara?"

"Berlin," Michael whispered under his breath.

"Berlin?" I chuckled. "No, really."

"No. Really," said Michael. "That's where his agent mailed the script."

I wasn't completely sure I was following. Had I been gone from the West so long I'd lost the power of reasoning? First the Guitar Center, then the supermarket, now this. I tread carefully: "Do you really think Bowie would want to play a German soldier after that scandal in London?"

"That's the whole point!" said Michael. "What better way for Bowie to make amends than to play a *good* Nazi? The implications are mind-boggling."

"Uh, Michael, does any of this actually make sense to you?" I said.

"This is Hollywood. I'll tell you what makes sense. What makes sense is whatever anybody *says* makes sense."

I needed to think that over for a moment. It almost *did* make sense. And that was a disturbing thought. Hollywood,

I was beginning to understand, was even crazier than
Bombay.

❧

The guy at Western Union was still disco dancing when I
returned a few days later and Alan's telegram still hadn't
come. No matter, I headed back to the Guitar Center and
took a second look at the gear. It was time to get serious. In
addition to the instruments I had to consider guitar strings,
extra tubes, microphone stands, and countless cables and
connectors. Once I got a rough estimate of the weight, I
found some quotes for the shipping charges to Bombay. My
God, was I really doing this? Things were suddenly becoming more real.

A few days later Donna Summers was blasting out of the
boombox but Alan's wire was still bouncing around somewhere between Paris and L.A. I could see the clerk was
getting annoyed by my interruptions and returned to the
Guitar Center, where I met with the sales manager. Like
every music store employee in every music shop in the
world, he was an insufferable ass who was convinced it was
cooler to sell guitars than play them. We haggled a bit over
the price before he disappeared for a two-hour lunch.

The Bee Gees greeted me at Western Union the next day
but Alan's wire, alas, was still stuck somewhere in the
grooves. Undeterred I returned to the Guitar Center for a
second round of negotiations. When the manager agreed to
throw a couple of harmonicas into the package I figured I'd
totally outsmarted him. Harmonicas! Marine Bands, no less!
What a dope! That's when a letter from Alan arrived. It was
scrawled in pencil, like maybe he was writing it while
running down the Rue de Rennes:

> *Sorry, man. Paris trip less than expected.*
> *Turns out that the star sapphires were slightly*
> *off center, the lines a little squiggly, and the*

blue a bit pale. I'm going with rubies next time.
Next summer for sure...

And that, as they say down at the local disco, was how the boogie lost its woogie and the music skipped a beat. The harmonicas would have to wait.

৵৵

It was becoming obvious that Los Angeles was simply too much for me, so I decided to seek a more stable environment. After much deliberation, I escaped to San Francisco and my friend Amy's hideaway cottage on Russian Hill. Amy had been back from Nepal for a couple of years now and was trying to make sense of things as well. She did her best to adapt to the West by working as a landscape artist by day and practicing Aikido by night. It was her way of keeping one foot in each world and not completely succumbing to the madness of America. San Francisco was a good place to try and maintain one's balance. It was a city where you could disappear into the cul de sacs, hidden alleys and tree-shaded stairways of the distant past.

Amy took comfort in her garden, a quiet, leafy spot that let her escape into a world of her own making. I spent so much time in that garden I was in danger of rooting, seeding and photosynthesizing. Amy's neighbor, Lorraine, came down once in a while to make sure I didn't develop Dutch elm disease. The night before my departure back to the East she dislodged me with a spade and a hedge clipper and invited me out for a drink.

We headed to the other side of Russian Hill in search of a quiet bar. I was nervous about the long flight to Hong Kong, the layover in Bangkok, and the final leg to Bombay. The thought of almost two days on airplanes left me feeling jittery and out of sorts. When we came upon a little neighborhood park and stopped to admire a Japanese cherry blossom, I noticed something stirring in the grass. I was instantly transported to the jungles of Kenya and the deserts of India. To black mambas and cobras.

"What is it?" said Lorraine, who could feel me tensing up.

"Listen to me," I said, trying to stay calm as I saw more movement in the leaves. "Don't talk. Don't move. Don't do anything."

At that instant an indistinct brown form rolled into a coil and lurched a good six inches into the air. It shot right toward us, this blur in the night, its eyes red and malevolent. In the dark shadows, it seemed at least four-feet long, its tail lashing this way and that as it bore down on us.

"Oh, how cute!" said Lorraine, as she bent down and put out her hand.

"Don't touch it!" I screamed, wondering if she'd lost her mind.

"What's the matter? Don't they have squirrels in India?"

"*Squir*-rels?" I said, slowly focusing my eyes. "Oh, right... squirrels... heh-heh. Listen, why don't we find a bar before it gets too late."

"Mm-hmm," she said, trying to keep a straight face. "Good idea."

We came upon Lord Jim's, a trendy bar that was nearly suffocating with ferns hanging from every square inch. This was the latest trend in San Francisco—ferns, Piña Coladas and fake tiffany lamps. Thankfully, it was a quiet night and we were able to sit next to a big bay window and sip our drinks. "Feeling a bit better?" said Lorraine.

"Sure, sure, it was nothing at all—"

At that moment a huge full moon rose over the Broadway Tunnel. It seemed bigger than usual and lit up the street like neon. As if on cue, there was a sudden influx of customers into the bar and a hum of activity. Lord Jim's was a pickup joint and the full moon beckoned like a Siren. Moments later I caught the reflection of a white stretch limo pulling up outside, a chauffeur coming around, the side door opening, and a handsome young couple getting out. There was a momentary hush as everyone strained to catch a glimpse as they entered the bar and headed for an empty table just across from us. The young man, a picture of cool elegance, sported a silk sharkskin suit that looked like it was sewn right onto his body. On his arm was an attractive woman who was wearing an impossibly tight leather skirt, a floppy black beret, and a red and white striped blouse that hung low off one shoulder. She looked like a Parisian streetwalker.

Lorraine watched them intently, her eyes slowly widening. "Isn't that David Bowie?" she finally whispered to me urgently. The guy did look vaguely familiar but Bowie had gone through so many incarnations it was hard to say if this was him. "And the woman he's with," Lorraine continued, "it's got to be Angie—"

I had no idea what Bowie's wife looked like, but the woman standing not ten feet from us certainly had the look of rock royalty. She had those slightly glassy eyes that welcomed gawkers in while keeping them at a distance at the same time. As they seated themselves beneath a couple of pampered ferns, the couple showed no sign of being overwhelmed by all the attention. Within moments everyone in the bar was circling around their table and I had the strange sensation of being on a ship that was listing dangerously starboard. That's when I remembered. "It's not him," I said.

"What do you mean?" said Lorraine, a hint of disappointment in her voice.

"David Bowie's in Berlin."

"How do you know?"

"My friend knows his agent. They just sent him a script."

Lorraine narrowed her eyes. She didn't look convinced. She glanced over at the couple again. "Well, I'm telling you—"

The crowd suddenly parted and a starry-eyed woman wove her way through the throng and shoved a pen and paper into the guy's face. Lorraine leaned over to take a peek as he jotted something down. "Your friend is wrong!" she said, grabbing my arm. "It's him all right! I saw his autograph!"

And with that, with all doubt removed, the place erupted. The owner of Lord Jim's appeared from a back room to introduce himself to the famous couple. A waitress arrived with a tray of hors d'oeuvre. The bartender sent over complimentary drinks. Bowie, meanwhile, graciously signed autographs, shook hands and reveled in all the attention. It went on for five, ten, maybe fifteen minutes before he ducked down, dug into his pocket, and pulled out a small bottle. He surreptitiously removed the lid, tapped a mound of white powder onto the webbed area between his thumb and forefinger, and snorted it right off his hand. I don't know if he thought no one would notice, but when he threw back his head the whole place erupted in applause. Bowie smiled sheepishly, then signed a few more autographs with renewed vigor. Angie watched the whole thing with cool detachment, probably stoned on some concoction of her own making.

The bartender, not to be outdone, snorted his own coke and seconds later *Heroes* came blasting through the sound system. Bowie looked pleased. He pulled a bottle of Scotch out of Angie's purse, knocked back a swig, and then, to everyone's amazement, he leapt up on his chair and began lip-syncing and dancing to his latest album.

"*I, I would be king...*" the record blasted out, "*And you, you would be queen...*" Bowie mouthed each word as he shimmied on the chair. "*For nothing would ride from the wave... we can beat them just for one day... we can be heroes just for one day.*" It was incredible. It was like being in David Bowie's living room, watching him perform for a hundred of his closest friends. "*And you, you can be near me... and I, I'll drink all the time...*" he lip-synced to Angie, "*'cause we're lovers, and that is a fact... yes we're lovers, and that is that.*"

The place went crazy. Bowie stood on that chair like he was eight-feet tall and we cheered his every move. I'd never realized just how good he really was, but now, sitting only ten feet away, I was in awe of his talent. It was him all right, David Bowie, potential star of Michael's movie, and when the song finally ended I knew I had to talk to him.

"David," I said, leaning over his table, "I'm really sorry to bug you but I have to ask you something. Have you ever heard of a screenplay called *The Rose Window?*"

"*The Rose Window,*" he said a bit ambiguously in that distinctive Brixton accent of his. "Yes... yes..."

"Oh? Because the writer is a good friend of mine."

Bowie looked at me more carefully, then leaned in closer. "*The Rose Window* is a damned fine piece of work."

"*Really?* I mean, you've actually read it?"

"I wouldn't say I read it. I ingested it. I feel it in every pore of my being."

I couldn't believe my ears. David Bowie *ingested* Michael's screenplay? This was the most exciting news I'd ever heard. "And the role of Franz, you liked it?"

"Liked it? Franz is the character I've been waiting to play my entire life."

"God, that's great, because there was some concern about you playing a Nazi."

Bowie turned to Angie. "Hear that, luv?"

"That's the only role you *haven't* played, my dear." Angie edged over just slightly toward me in her chair. "David's always had certain fascist tendencies, you know."

"But in a good sort of way," he interjected.

"Of course."

We all had a good laugh.

My head was spinning. Here I was, laughing it up with David and Angie while all I could think of was how excited Michael was going to be. Bowie reached into his pocket again. He pulled out the vial, tapped some powder between his thumb and forefinger, and took a long snort. Then he poured some more and reached out his hand. "Like some?"

I glanced around at a hundred pairs of eyes zeroed in on us. "Sure," I said, as I leaned down and snorted a glistening mound of cocaine off of David Bowie's hand.

"Uh-*hum*," came a voice from just behind me.

"Oh, sorry. David, this is Lorraine. She's—"

"—a *big* fan," said Lorraine, grabbing his hand before I'd completely finished the pile. I was embarrassed to see a stream of powder floating down onto his shoe, but David didn't seem to mind, and if he didn't mind, who was I to complain?

Bowie motioned to the waitress. "Two more glasses for my friends," he said, then picked up the bottle of Scotch and ran his fingers over the label. "We had this flown in from Glasgow just this morning. There's really nothing quite like it."

Angie ran her tongue around the rim of her glass. "David's so *promiscuous* with his money."

When the glasses arrived, Bowie proposed a toast: "*To The Rose Window.*"

We drank, snorted, and drank some more as the music blasted out. People came and went, autographs were signed, photos taken, kisses delivered, and then, in a flash, David and Angie pushed back from the table. "On to the next adventure!" he said. "Want to join us?"

"Oh, man, you have no idea how much I'd like to," I said, shocked that he'd ask, "but I've got a plane to catch in a couple of hours."

"I don't!" said Lorraine, pushing between us.

"Yes, well, another time," said Angie, taking Bowie's arm. And then there was a jumble of movement that happened so fast it was as if the whole thing were an apparition. The vial disappeared, the bottle disappeared, Angie disappeared, and Bowie was but a blur against the ferns.

"David, what should I tell my friend?" I called after him.

Bowie turned back, smiled, and said: "Tell him that David Bowie *is* Franz."

And with that, he was gone.

⁓

"Michael! You're not gonna believe who I was just with!"

"Huh? Huh? Who is this?"

"Wake up, will you? It's me."

"What time is it?"

"It doesn't matter what time it is. C'mon, guess."

"How should I know? Probably one of those insane friends of yours from India. Aspirin Dave or Johnny Beirut or Eight Rib Eddie."

"Yeah, close. I was with David Bowie."

"Okay, good. I gotta go to bed now."

"Listen to me, will you? I just spent the last thirty minutes with David and Angie. Michael, he wants to make your movie!"

There was a short pause before Michael responded in a slow, deliberate monotone: "David. Bowie. Is. In. Berlin."

"No, David Bowie is in San Francisco. I just snorted cocaine off his hand."

"What?"

"Michael, he read *The Rose Window*. He's crazy about it... the artist... the Nazi stuff... the whole deal. You know what he said?"

"What? What?"

"He said, and this is a direct quote: David Bowie *is* Franz."

"I *knew* it!"

"Congratulations! You did it!"

"I told you, didn't I? Didn't I tell you I could smell it? It's finally happening! I'm getting out of this rat hole. I'm moving up into the hills. Forget the Mercedes. I'm buying a Ferrari!"

"Okay, good, I just had to tell you. I'm leaving for the airport in a couple of hours and I'm with this girl and, well, you understand—"

"Gotcha. I'll call Bowie's agent in the morning and tell him the news. I mean, what kind of agent is this guy not even to know where his client is?"

"Look, who cares? That doesn't matter now."

"Yeah, you're right. Okay, have a good trip. And listen... thanks."

"My pleasure."

Chapter 23
Interlude Through a
Glass Skylight

I wonder if they have any idea how insane this is, making love in front of an open window, is their passion really so strong they can't even take the time to close the blinds, it's utter madness, that's what it is, but I see the look in Tobias's eyes, talk about being mesmerized, the guy is putty in her hands, all she has to do is snap her fingers and he'll come running, and as for Mohini, does she really think she can kidnap Tobias right under my eyes, does she think I'm just going to sit here in the park while she ravages my buddy, well, sorry, that's not going to happen, and with that I flee the bamboo pond, the rhododendron grove, the gates of the Botanical Garden, and arrive at the building across the street—"*Tobias! Tobias!*"—but it's no use, the window to Mohini's apartment is too high to reach, the door to the building is locked, and buzzing the doorbell is utterly useless—*now what?*—I head around the side of the building and discover a fire escape, okay, whatever it takes, I climb the slats one by one, past the first floor, past the second floor, then finally right to the top of the building where, sure enough, there's a skylight, just as Mohini said, a

skylight peering right down to her bedroom—*where they're
screwing!*—watching the two lovers together is enough to
make my stomach churn, given how preposterous it is, this
insane charade in which Tobias has completely fallen under
Mohini's spell and is barely a shadow of his former self, but
Tobias is so wildly enthralled he'd run through the bedroom
wall to get her a glass of water, yes, water is what he needs, I
need to dunk him in the pond and hold him under for five
or ten minutes until he finally comes to his senses, but the
pond might as well be on the other side of the world, no,
we're here, in the belly of the beast, the den of iniquity, the
bedroom of seduction, and I have no influence whatsoever
on this lovelorn interloper—*"Tobias! Get out of there!"*—
finally a bit of luck, one of the panels of the skylight is loose
and I'm able to squeeze through, directly below is a chandelier hanging from thick iron rings and, okay, I know this is
crazy, but I shimmy down the chain to a spot closer in,
maneuver my hands and adjust my feet, and then, out of
nowhere, I hear a rumbling, a creaking, and finally the
shrieking sound of metal separating from plaster, the
chandelier gives way, and now I'm flying through the air, a
bird without wings, a skydiver without parachute—*shiiiiit!* —
I miraculously land with a bounce and a thud on the very
bed upon which Mohini is having her way with the hapless
Tobias, and now we become the most unlikely coupling of
bodies, me, Tobias, and Mohini, arms and legs akimbo, flesh
everywhere, hair entangled, mouths agape, and intermin-
gled among the various body parts is the iron chain of the
chandelier, all twisted and tangled and locking us in a most
unwanted embrace—*unleash him, temptress!*—the two of
them are locked in a gaze like teenagers on their first date,
unblinking, unthinking, unaware of anything but themselves,
well, guess what, people, I'm actually here, wrapped as I am
inside the chain of the chandelier, and I may have climbed
through the skylight like a cat burglar and fallen like a

wingless bird onto this dog of a bed, but I cannot allow this madness to go on, who does she think she is anyway, she's got him wrapped around her little finger and plays him like a marionette, jump for me, Tobias, jump higher, open the window, close the door, rub my foot, bring me tea, look at him, he's like a puppy with drooping eyes and a tongue hanging to the floor, finally he heads for the shower and I can only hope he avoids the laptop and the internet, because if he were to engage with these objects of the modern world he might surely implode, so now I'm left alone with the enchantress, okay, you'd better listen and listen good, Tobias is not who you think he is, actually I have no idea *who* you think he is, but he's not him, understand, he's not available for whatever you have planned for him, to be your butler or chauffeur or gardener or whatever it is, it's simply not going to work, so why don't you let him cool off in the shower for a few minutes, then we'll get him dressed and simply be on our way, oh, but no, she says, it's not quite that simple, and then she asks if I'm aware of the sacred Hindu texts, and yeah, I say, I guess so, and here it comes, she tells me I'd better watch out because as namesake of the great Goddess of Seduction she's granted Tobias special powers of his own—*anybody whose head he touches will be turned into a pile of ashes!*—and what? is she completely mad? oh, yes, one touch from Tobias and you'll be burned to a crisp, okay, now I see how serious this is, I've managed to engage with an absolute madwoman who'll stop at nothing, good God, why him, why me, and now she lowers the boom, she says I'm just jealous, that I'd give anything to be in Tobias's place, but she doesn't want me, no, certainly not, I've lost my way, I've given up the path, I've become Westernized, whereas Tobias is still pure of heart, he holds to the old ways, he hasn't been corrupted by the modern world, well, *of course* he hasn't been corrupted by the modern world, the guy's been dead for decades, but she doesn't know that and truth be told, I'm not sure how to explain it anyway, no, I've got myself a real problem, speaking of which, here he comes, my problem, Tobias returns with a towel wrapped around his waist and bounds into the bedroom holding something in his hand, oh, wonderful, it's a smart phone and he says, get this—*what's this Twitter thing?*—and Mohini looks at him like he's a rube who just fell off the turnip truck, and he laughs and she laughs and even I laugh, and now he's down on his knees at the side of the bed, nothing can stop him, he's got something to say, and he clasps his hands together in prayer and looks upon his seductress with misty eyes—*Mohini, will you marry me?*—oh, no, I'm too late, the die's been cast, he's lost his mind, one brief tango between the sheets and she's hooked him like a breathless puffer fish, and how do I explain that this union cannot last, that this was never meant to be, that this is fraught with consequences too vast to comprehend, no matter, Mohini brushes aside the chains, the plaster, and the broken glass—*yes, Tobias, I will, and we'll marry the old-fashioned way, in the park across the street, we'll dance to the coming union of two glorious souls*—okay, that's it, it's time to drop the bomb, even if I must do it gently, no need to anger anyone unnecessarily since the idea of my being turned into a pile of ashes is rather unappealing, I'll just whisper a little something into her ear—*you see, Mohini, the thing is, Tobias isn't really real, I mean he's here and all, sort of, but when you actually get down to it, well, Tobias is nothing more than a literary device*—and she looks at me with a hatred beyond loathing and I look at her with a sadness beyond remorse and Tobias looks at the smart phone with a curiosity beyond fascination and all that's really left is for the chandelier to turn itself on and give us all the shock of our lives, which is exactly what it does.

Chapter 24

The Circle of Fifths

The opening chords of *Baksheesh Boulevard* echoed through the cool night air and wafted over the sand dunes and coves along the coast. It was a jazz progression that jumped through different keys and time signatures, inspired by the chaos of Bombay. Bombay might not have been often associated with jazz, but what better way to reflect the discordance of life on the streets of India's biggest city than by a free-form improvisation? The band was experimenting with new sounds, learning some basics of jazz theory to expand our horizons. One of them was the Circle of Fifths, an elegant connection of the jazz scales. In much the same way Bombay had its own rhythm and modulated through its own circles of chaos and connectedness.

Baksheesh Boulevard was Neil's song to shine and he attacked the guitar strings with a frenzy as he soared through the changes. Neil had grown as a musician by leaps and bounds since coming over from Vagator Beach a year earlier. Then, he was an unassuming Englishman thrilled just to have a few people to play with him. Now, he was the center of attention as lead guitarist of the Anjuna Jam Band.

His Fender Stratocaster sizzled in his hands as his fingers
ran up and down the fretboard with wild abandon, building
a melody, repeating it, taking it further, then pushing into a
realm where no one knew what next to expect. When Neil
exhausted his solo Fantuzzi jumped in with conga and
attempted to pull together our band of loose fragments, a
coat whose threads had unraveled and blew wildly in the
breeze. Trumpet Steve, lurking off to the side of the stage,
edged to the microphone and delivered a soulful improvisation that echoed down the beach. Chandra sang backup
with growing confidence. German Harry stood glued to the
stage, holding it all together with his bass. Gilbert Garcia, a
talented multi-instrumentalist, filled in on drums with
metronomic precision.

The song necessitated my alternating harmonicas from
one chorus to another, a cumbersome technique, but once I
got the hang of it I was able to trade solos with Neil as we
went through the progressions. And then, somewhere
around two in the morning, it hit me. I was back in Goa,
back on the stage, and I wondered for a moment if I'd ever
left. Had I really just spent the summer in California?
America and India were at such opposite poles that I was
having trouble digesting which was which and what was
what. India, with five thousand years of practice, had so
successfully mixed illusion with reality that you couldn't
distinguish them anymore, but in America illusion and
reality were considered two different things and I could
never tell which was which.

The band played through the night, taking breaks every
hour or two for another group to take the stage or for an
interlude of recorded music. Around four in the morning
there was the inevitable draining of energy, both onstage
and in the audience. The music became mellower and the
dancing more restrained. People huddled together around
fires to ward off a chill in the air and even the chai stalls

closed up for the evening so that the Goans could get at least a few hours of sleep. The Western residents of Anjuna often slipped away under the cover of darkness to catch a short nap, but those who'd come from Baga or Vagator were forced to wait at least until daybreak before making the trek back to the outlying beaches.

It was a struggle to stay awake for the next hour, much less to play music. The band went into a kind of mechanical mode while the dancers swayed in a somnambulant trance. Then, around five, the first rays of the morning sun peeked over the mountain just as the moon began to sink into the ocean. A tiny patch of blue sky appeared, illuminated from behind like a halo, then slowly expanded across the horizon. With it came a surge of energy so palpable as to animate the entire beach. People arose from the sand as if being lifted by a puppeteer, each new ray of light a string to pull the weary into the embrace of morning. The band, too, came alive. Moments before, it felt impossible to play another note; now, it felt impossible to stop. Musicians rotated in and out—Samesh, the Jamaican jazz guitarist who kept pushing the music in new directions; Ras, the drummer from Trinidad with dreadlocks halfway down his back; Philippe and Dominique, the French guitarist and bossa nova singer; Nipper and Kenny, the British rock'n'rollers; Goa Gil, the longtime Anjuna Beach guitarist; Kazuki, the Japanese Jimi Hendrix—we played and played until the sun was directly overhead, and then we played some more.

I felt as if we were all floating a few inches above the stage. As I gazed out upon a great mass of bodies moving to the push and pull of the music, I recognized a certain glint of the eyes, a placid smile, an ethereal glow that emanated from everyone on the beach. It was a glow that passed from the band on the stage to the dancers in the audience to the children playing in the sand. It was a glow shared by the Goan girls who sold chai and the ladies who fried samosas and the boatmen who waited along the shore. It was one all-encompassing glow that spread over the palm trees, up along the beach, and into the ocean itself.

❦

Goa felt both timeless and on the cusp of incredible change. The community was growing and word was spreading fast to the rest of the world. "Goa Full Moon" parties began appearing on the beaches of Mykonos and Ibiza during the summer monsoons, brought there by Westerners who'd fled the rains in India. It wasn't long before "Goa Full Moon" parties started popping up in London, Paris and Amsterdam, and it didn't even matter anymore if there was a full moon, a half-moon, or no moon at all. The parties began late in the night, continued into the dawn, and were a nonstop orgy of dancing and psychedelia. Eventually a whole new generation fell under the spell and they made it their own by adding an electronic beat to the music. From the seed planted on Anjuna Beach, a new phenomenon known as raves was about to be born.

Meanwhile, news filtered in from abroad about tragic losses that had befallen our community during the monsoon. Paco, a Spanish synthesizer player, leapt to his death in Madrid. Cecile, a French enchantress, died of a heroin overdose in Paris. Coco, our exuberant drummer, was shuffled off to an insane asylum in Algeria.

Inevitably word came from Kathmandu that James had been repatriated back to America, where he wound up in some nineteenth-century sanatorium in New England. I couldn't imagine what they'd do with him there. James was well beyond psychoanalysis, behavior modification or cognitive therapy. He was one of those hapless people who was simply mad and no amount of drugs or counseling was going to cure him.

Ah, but James was crafty in his craziness. He somehow

escaped the lockup and got himself back to India before the monsoon had even ended. He even talked his way through customs. Perhaps the immigration officers in Delhi were so hypnotized by his shock of red hair they didn't even notice that he'd been banned from Nepal. Whatever it was, he gave everybody the slip and headed straight for the Kulu Valley, a mountainous vicinity in the far north of India. Kulu was similar to Nepal in many ways, with its snowcapped mountains, supplies of hashish, and communities of Tibetan refugees. James settled right in, but it didn't take long before he was seen wandering the hills, brandishing a large wooden staff, and screaming threats to whomever he encountered.

Maybe there was no place in the world for someone like James. Maybe he really was a Pilgrim from an earlier time when entire societies lost their collective minds. Maybe he simply fell between the cracks of religion, the cracks of psychiatry, and the cracks of the hills themselves. A few weeks after returning to the Himalayas, his body was found in the rugged mountains north of Manali, his head smashed in by local villagers.

⁂

I moved into a spacious house just behind Joe Banana's shop and right next door to Eight Finger Eddie's porch. Joe would deliver a hot cup of coffee each morning and Eddie would wander over to pull up a bucket of water from my well. We'd built a little outdoor shower using woven palm leaves that rose just to eye level so we could look out upon the landscape while bathing. The shower consisted of a bucket of water that had been left in the sun to warm and half a coconut shell tied to a stick that was used as a ladle. To soap up and wash off under the cloudless Goan sky was one of the happiest times of my life. Nothing could compare to the freedom of standing naked in nature with a ten-cent bar of soap, a dollop of shampoo, and a bucket of sun-warmed water.

My house became a way station for friends who passed through Anjuna Beach. Jimmy came down from Nepal after filming with his brother and disappeared into one of my bedrooms for five straight days. Jonathan and Anouchka, my friends from Bali, were living on the next beach over but spent a couple of nights around each full moon to soak up the all-night parties on Anjuna Beach. Lisa arrived from Kathmandu and stayed for a while in the next bedroom, always just slightly out of reach. I didn't see much of her. Goa had even more needy people and her services always seemed to be required for one ongoing crisis or another. She finally moved into a bamboo hut on the beach to be nearer those most at risk. I worried sometimes that she might become one of them herself.

⁓

The Anjuna Beach Flea Market was born that fall. It started simply enough, when a couple of people gathered on Eddie's old porch one day and laid out several items of clothing to sell. A tabla player joined them, then a flutist, and then somebody showed up with a stack of books and tapes. They returned a week later and cleared a larger space beneath a tree to accommodate an astrologer and palmist. Word spread quickly and by the third week so many people showed up they had to move to a larger clearing down the beach. It became a place to exchange goods that people had picked up from all over Asia, but even more it was a place to socialize. It soon served as a central gathering point for residents of the adjoining beaches.

Like everything on Anjuna Beach, word spread quickly. A couple of Goans set up their own little stalls and then, no more than a week or two later, some Gujarati tribeswomen showed up with embroidered pillows, a Kashmiri vender unloaded stacks of wool shawls, and even a couple of Tibetan traders trekked down from the mountains with coral and turquoise. The clearing was suddenly bursting with a glorious array of colors and patterns from all over Asia. Sarongs blew in the breeze. Kurtas draped from the branches. Silver bracelets glistened in the sun. The Thursday Flea Market became a thriving event that brought people from all the corners of Goa. I saw people I hadn't seen since Japan and Bali. One of the first was Haya, an ex-sergeant in the Israeli army, who showed up in an eighteenth-century kimono and reminded me of our escapades at the Midori Apartments in Tokyo. Haya was a singular force unto herself, a woman who'd left the sheltered confines of Israel to experience an entirely different world. She became a committed world traveler and noted anthropologist who explored and chronicled the remotest parts of Africa and Asia.

Dominique, a beguiling French-Moroccan whom I'd met in Amsterdam, sat beneath a palm tree with three other women wearing Islamic hijabs. I wasn't sure if they'd undergone a religious conversion or if they were returning to their roots, but their wide black eyes peaked out from behind the scarves with the allure of a Baghdad harem room. There were others I knew more by sight than personal experience. Jacques and Odile, a Moroccan couple, inspected a collection of woven sari borders brought down from Rajasthan. Georgette and Vivian, two beauties from France, looked absolutely radiant as they nursed their newborn babies in the shade of a banyan tree. Migel, Bobby and Wendy, siblings from Brooklyn, howled over some inside joke while Irene, Migel's Swiss girlfriend, and Sarge, his boyhood friend, tried on embroidered vests from the Hindu Kush. They came from everywhere, gorgeous Yael from Israel, elegant Monika from Germany, charming Carla from Canada, dozens of faces from dozens of countries, an endless procession of friends from the past and friends still to meet. Whatever was happening in the rest of the world faded away. It didn't matter anymore. It was Thursday afternoon, it was the flea market in Goa, and it was an indelible moment that sat frozen in time.

⚬⚬

Through it all the music continued, coming together, falling apart, coming together again. The equipment choked and wheezed but somehow we were always able to squeeze out one more song from the speakers. Sharing an amplifier with one of the guitars was too much for the tubes to handle, so I reluctantly played through the PA system instead. Eventually even the PA had trouble managing both the vocals and the harmonica, so I relied on solos and the occasional fill-in between the verses. I felt restricted at first but it gave me a whole new view of musical minimalism and was valuable in its own right.

One night I was in the middle of a solo, feeling lightheaded and out of breath, when I glanced into the audience. My eyes locked upon a woman of extraordinary beauty who exuded an otherworldly tranquility. I knew her from the distance as a French woman called Krishna who'd been in Goa for years and possessed an air of mystery. I stared into her hazel eyes and continued playing, feeling a momentary rebirth, a surge of energy, and then, our eyes still locked together, I heard an unusual melody, something brand new, and I wasn't sure if I was playing it or she was playing it or if it had simply dropped out of the sky.

When the set ended I looked for her, but she'd disappeared into the crowd. I walked out to a bonfire in the dunes and stared into the flames when I felt someone touch my shoulder. I turned, certain it was her, but was greeted instead by a guy who looked vaguely familiar. I couldn't place him at first but then I saw the elephant hair bracelet from Kenya, the Guelmim beads from Morocco, the long, perfectly groomed hair, the warm eyes and the beatific smile: "Nice one," he said, pointing to the harmonica.

"Pete?" I said, feeling suddenly transported to another land. "Really?"

"Amazing, isn't it? The last time I saw you was in Lamu," he said in his mellifluous English accent. "That must've been four or five years ago. I remember you waving to me as my ferry left for the mainland."

"Yeah, you were heading off for a ship to India."

"So I was. Well, I've got something to tell you."

"What's that?"

"I made it."

"So I see."

"Mombasa to Bombay on the *Star of India*."

"I took the *Karanja* a year later. All I remember is eleven days on the sea, twenty-two thalis, and thirty-three cups of chai."

We caught up on the intervening years. Both of us had been in Asia the entire time but had somehow managed to miss each other. Until now, that is. Our paths finally intersected, just as they had in Lamu. "I remember you playing music at the shamba," Pete said. "Those were some of the best times. You, me, Big Ali, Little Ali, Sultan."

I thought back to the shamba that Pete and I had shared. We had a broken-down house on fifteen acres of land, a thirty minute walk from the port through sandy fields dotted with palm trees and the occasional baobab. I remembered how the land rose slightly and just inside a bamboo fence was a mango tree in full bloom, its ten thousand seedlings dividing and subdividing like zygotes.

"You know, I still think about those guys," I said. "I wrote to Sultan a few times but, well, you know how it is. I don't know if the mail ever got through."

Pete looked at me uncomfortably, then glanced away. "You didn't hear?"

"Hear what?"

"Sultan died. A few years ago."

I remembered how Sultan had taught me about the critical first weeks of the mango season, how if the rains didn't come, the flowers would wither and die and fall barren to the searing ground, and how if it rained too much, they'd be lashed by the wind and blown to the edge of the sea. And how that year, inshallah, looked like a good year.

I was struck numb by the news. "What did he die of?" I said.

"Old age, I think."

"Pete, he wasn't even sixty—"

"Like I said, old age."

I remembered how a half-dozen palm trees surrounded our house, their long thin fronds shimmering in the breeze and brushing together like an orchestra of raindrops falling from the sky. I remembered how the breeze diminished the heat of late afternoon and carried with it the scent of jasmine from the sea. How the last rays of the sun would hover for an instant and then, like the flick of a switch, it would be dark. How a kerosene lamp flickered at the end of a long hallway where a heavy carved door hung slightly ajar. How a candle cast the silhouette of a flame that danced up along the wall and across the ceiling. How Sultan would stand there, unsure whether to approach, entranced by the shadows that reached across the room like fingers inviting him in—

The guitars began tuning up onstage, followed by several thumps from the bass drum and a clang of the cymbals. I recognized the opening chords of *Baksheesh Boulevard* modulating from key to key. The Circle of Fifths was calling to me, a circle that kept expanding and encompassing all of us, a circle that stretched all the way to Kenya and connected us all together.

All these characters, floating in and out of concentric circles, overlaying, overlapping, connecting the seas and continents, expanding, ever expanding.

"Pete, I've got to get back for the next set," I said.

"Of course, of course," he said, looking overwhelmed by all of the sudden activity around the stage. "It looks like you're in the middle of a whole production here."

"Listen, we'll meet again soon, okay? There's a lot to talk about."

Pete nodded to me just the way he'd done when getting on the ferry to the Kenyan mainland. "Nice one," he said, as he slipped away into the crowd.

It was the last time I ever saw him.

Chapter 25

Christmas in Goa

It was snowing in Goa. A layer of thin white powder blew over the beach and landed right on top of the stage. There had previously been occasional flurries from time to time but this was a full-blown blizzard and it arrived on the jet stream in a big suitcase from Peru in the possession of a fast-talking Greek named Cowboy. His name alone should've been warning enough. Who ever heard of a Greek named Cowboy? What was he, a sheep wrangler at the Acropolis?

Cowboy appeared out of nowhere with an insatiable desire to be at the center of the action, not so easy for someone just arriving in Goa. Most newcomers lived on one of the outer beaches, then slowly gravitated to the south end of Anjuna, but Cowboy was an impatient sort and found his way in by offering to be roadie for the band. Since we weren't really on the road, it was hard to say what function he'd serve but he convinced us that he was absolutely indispensible, even though he hadn't the slightest idea how to string a guitar or change an amplifier tube. What he did have was a seemingly endless supply of pure Peruvian cocaine and a willingness to share it with the band. Eventually he even learned where all the wires went, how to operate the generator, and where to string the lights.

Cowboy loved those lights. His high wattage personality positively erupted when under the glare of the spotlight. He also had an undeniable charm, a common characteristic of most hustlers, connivers and schemers. Cowboy could charm a cobra right out of its venom. I knew from the instant I met him not to trust him with anything more important than my comb, and even that probably wasn't a good idea. He'd likely sell the teeth to someone as ancient boar bristles. He was a flim-flam man through and through, which was perfectly fine so long as you were aware of the flim and constantly on guard against the flam. Cowboy's sworn duty was to keep the band going day and night and he became an indispensible presence onstage. When offered free, unlimited cocaine, most musicians—not the most discerning of individuals to begin with—tend to overlook certain character flaws.

⁂

The band was playing more often now and Krishna appeared in the audience every night. I imagined her as my personal beacon of inspiration. Her eyes glistened in the moonlight and everything in her gaze told me, yes, you can do it, keep playing, keep reaching, play something you've never played before, play it for me, I'm here for you. It wasn't long before fantasy became reality and she became an inseparable part of my life.

Krishna was one of the earliest Western devotees of Rajneesh, an Indian guru who had developed a huge following. Rajneesh's teachings went beyond traditional Hinduism and incorporated Western philosophy and psychology into a much broader world view. He promoted many of the same ideals of personal transformation and liberation that had drawn so many people to India and his vision of the reborn man held great appeal. His ashram in Poona became a thriving center of spiritual development.

For those so inclined, that is. Not only did I have no desire to attach myself to any one guru or religion, I found something about Rajneesh disturbing. His devotees all wore malas around their necks with a picture of Rajneesh and every time I glanced into his eyes I was left with an uncomfortable feeling. It was an ambiguous feeling, not based on anything in particular, but uncomfortable nonetheless. Something cold and alienating and just a bit distrusting.

Krishna never proselytized her beliefs, even when she moved into my house. The fact that she wore the traditional orange robes of a sanyassi was reminder enough. Whenever we made love the picture of Rajneesh dangled over me and I wondered if she was cheating on him or I was cheating on her or if we all were cheating on each other. As the days wore on I found myself wearing more black to counteract Krishna's orange and hiding her malas under the mattress. Somehow she always found them.

❧

A letter came from Michael. I was surprised to see the return address as his old place on Cahuenga Boulevard, right off the Hollywood Freeway. Shouldn't he be living in the Hollywood Hills by now? It was a short note, indistinct in several places because of the stray droplets of paint from Lulu's brush. Michael wrote that he'd taken my advice and called David Bowie's agent the morning after our late night talk. He said the agent insisted that Bowie was still in Berlin and when Michael insisted that Bowie was in San Francisco, they got into a terrible argument. The agent finally hung up on him and refused to ever take his calls again.

Included with the letter was an article from *Rolling Stone Magazine* about a David Bowie impersonator who had fooled everyone up and down the coast of California. *Wh-wh-whaaat?*

Robert Van Cleve, some guy from Cleveland who just happened to look a lot like Bowie, came out to California and met a woman who just happened to look a lot like Angie. Van Cleve, a lifelong fan of the singer, knew every word to every song, could duplicate all of Bowie's dance moves, and had even mastered a British accent. The woman, who was unhappily married to a rich car salesman, saw an opportunity to live out a truly crazy dream. She fled her abusive relationship, absconded with a quarter of a million dollars, bought a suitcase full of cocaine, and got Van Cleve and herself all decked out as rock and roll's most famous couple.

They set off on a wild adventure that took them to California's finest hotels, finest restaurants and finest clubs. They left hundred dollar tips for the elevator operators, bonuses for the chauffeurs, presents for the maids, and became the most popular couple in town. It was a masterful masquerade that fooled everyone, made possible by the fact that the real David Bowie was holed up in Berlin, staying out of sight.

Staying just below the radar, they traveled from Los Angeles to Las Vegas to San Francisco, always leaving after a day or two, before anyone caught on. Eventually news spread and Bowie's managers finally got wind of the charade. The couple was in Hawaii, running out of money, running out of cocaine, and running out of time. One night they partied at the wrong club and the police were called. Van Cleve seemed almost relieved when he was arrested. "I'd give my right testicle just to be the real David Bowie for ten minutes," he said as they took him away.

I put the article down and stared into the fronds of a palm tree. Wow. What a spectacular mess I'd made! There was surely a lesson to be learned from all this but I wasn't quite sure if I knew what it was. Something about illusion and reality, I figured. Whatever it was I felt terrible for Michael and even more so for my role in the whole thing. I'd built up his hopes and popped his balloon all in one short evening. But, God, that Van Cleve guy was good! The accent was flawless. The dancing was impeccable. The vial of cocaine suited him perfectly. And the way he threw back my questions about *The Rose Window!* The guy *was* Franz!

I wrote to Michael with profuse apologies but offered him an idea in return. What if he were to write a screenplay about a David Bowie impostor? It would be the story of one chameleon playing another. And who would play the role of the impostor? Why, David Bowie, of course! David Bowie as a David Bowie impostor would be his ultimate role and sure to be box office dynamite. Now, if only Michael could get Bowie's agent to answer the phone...

◈

Another story appeared in the local newspapers, this one generating a giant sigh of relief. Charles Sobhraj had been caught. He'd continued his string of murders throughout Asia but when he got to India, he really outdid himself. He checked into a pensione in New Delhi and poisoned an entire group of French students at the hotel restaurant all in one go. When the students began falling ill, the hotel chef called the police in a panic. Amazingly, an Indian detective had just read an Interpol report about all the missing foreigners in Asia and became suspicious. The astute detective hurried to the pensione and arrested the one person in the hotel who wasn't vomiting from the poison. It was Sobhraj.

Still, this wasn't to be the end of Sobhraj's story. He spent twenty years in jail in India, where he lived like a king. Using his magnetic charm he bribed the guards and the warden and became a jailhouse celebrity. He even broke out of prison for a while—this was for the third or fourth time—probably just because he could. Meanwhile, he was wanted in Bangkok for his previous string of murders but he arranged for his Indian term to be extended until the statute of limitations ran out on the charges in Thailand. When his term was up he got deported to France but it wasn't long before he was right back in the game. Eventually he went back to Nepal, the site of his favorite casino, where he was recognized by a journalist from twenty-five years earlier. He was captured, sentenced to life in prison, and tossed into a Kathmandu jail cell, where he lives to this day. At least until further notice, that is.

⤜⤛

The stage on Anjuna Beach was festooned with decorations for the upcoming Christmas Eve party, but that was still a few days off. First came the December full moon, which was reason enough for several thousand people to gather along the shore. There was a sudden influx of people, some from as far as Europe and America, who came just to spend the holidays in Goa. "Christmas in Goa!" had become a rallying cry for travelers throughout Asia and I marveled at how quickly the numbers had grown. Our once-secluded, faraway beach was fast becoming an international destination. For me, a relative latecomer to the scene, the whole thing was mindboggling. I couldn't even imagine how Eight Finger Eddie, Bombay Brian and Goa Gil must've felt.

For the band it was becoming difficult to keep an even keel. With larger audiences came increased expectations and growing pressure. Our largely freeform performances often featured lengthy jams—as our name suggested—and we'd go on and on with improvised lyrics and riffs. Sometimes it was a real cacophony, and probably unlistenable, but then something would magically coalesce, the drums and bass would gel, the guitars would come in, and off we'd go.

Meanwhile, Cowboy had staked out a position at the edge of the stage where he carved out an endless stream of cocaine for the band. "Let's play right through until Christmas!" he said, urging us on as we snorted line after line. After all, Christmas was only two days away and it seemed entirely possible that we could simply keep playing for two straight days. And so, as the sun rose the next morning, the music kept going, through the morning, through the afternoon, and right through the next night as well. Other musicians alternated in and out, supplemented with periods of taped music, but a wall of sound descended upon the beach and it didn't let up, not for a minute, not so long as Cowboy maintained his post at the edge of the stage.

⤙⤚

Christmas Day arrived and Eight Finger Eddie made his traditional early morning appearance. The moment he took the stage, everyone gathered around with a kind of reverential silence. Would he tell a story? Preach some kind of absurdist sermon? Tell a dirty joke? Everyone waited breathlessly as Eddie pointed to the band, counted in an old jazz standard, and began scat singing to *All of Me*. The truth is, there wasn't much of Eddie. To call him skin and bones would be to exaggerate the skin part of the equation. He was in fact bones and more bones, and his internal organs, if he had any, were likely hidden inside the little shoulder bag he carried with him wherever he went. No, Eddie was all bones, bones protruding every which way and often at impossible angles, and when he danced around the stage we were all in danger of having our livers lacerated by one of Eddie's flailing elbows. But dance he did, a wild, uncontrollable skeleton dance in which he twirled, swirled and scatted to the song as if the spirits of Sarah Vaughan, Ella Fitzgerald and Betty Carter had been poured into his emaciated body. In truth, Eddie would've made a good toothpick for any of those ladies, but none of that mattered as he danced off the stage to a roar of applause. It was Eddie's yearly gift to the community, something that could never be fully repaid.

By the end of the day, Neil's fingers were bleeding, my lips were rubbed raw, and Trumpet Steve's mouthpiece was cracked right down the middle. None of us had slept more than an hour or two at a time and Cowboy, I'm pretty sure, not even that. He was always at the edge of the stage, day and night, cutting up lines of coke, keeping the whole operation going. Whatever else that operation might've entailed, I have no idea, but I remember seeing a lot of shady-looking people around the stage whom I'd never seen before.

We were ready to finally pack it in when Cowboy said, "Let's keep it going through Boxing Day!" I wasn't quite sure what Boxing Day even was, but I knew it was the day after Christmas, that it was celebrated throughout the Common-wealth, and in honor of our British and Jamaican band-mates, we decided to play one more day. This, it turned out, was not only not the end, it was barely the beginning. Cowboy kept coming up with excuses to prolong the festivities. It was either a Greek ceremony to the Goddess of Debauchery or a Roman salute to the God of Intemperance or the perfect conjunction of Mars and Saturn or the numerologically auspicious night for extended guitar solos. Whatever it was, Cowboy and his endless cocaine somehow won the day, the night and everything in between. The music went on, and on, and on. One day... two days... three days... and then, somehow, in what seemed like one long, sustained hallucination, it was New Year's Eve.

⚜

Steve and I stood atop the hill behind the stage and looked out over the beach. This was the biggest gathering of all, perhaps five thousand people in all, extending down the beach as far as the eye could see. It was a moment to reflect and reminisce. We talked about our similar pasts, how both of us had graduated from the same university with degrees in psychology, though four years apart. Now we stood at the top of a mountain in India, our eyes held open by unimagi-nable amounts of stimulants, and wondered if we'd truly gone insane. Given all our courses in behaviorism, experimental psychology and child development, we had all the tools for self-diagnosis. No matter how you analyzed it, it was pretty obvious that we perfectly fit the textbook definition of madmen. We'd traded in our sheepskin diplomas for a trumpet and a harmonica and wondered what our professors would think if they saw us right now standing on that hill overlooking the Arabian Sea. Thousands of naked and semi-naked bodies were writhing in the sands below, fires and kerosene lanterns lit up the horizon as far as the eye could see, and a vast multitude of castoffs, oddballs, and social misfits stretched from the sea to the stage. Would our professors prescribe a lengthy convalescence with extended group therapy and experimental drug treatment? Hey, that's exactly what we were doing!

⚜

And still, it wasn't over. We were all run down, operating on nothing but psychic fumes and the remains of Cowboy's stash. Cowboy, for his part, was proving himself to be completely inhuman. While the rest of us would slip off for an hour or two of sleep in the middle of the night, he just kept on going. He was always there, either at the side of the stage, restringing a guitar, or cranking up the volume on the PA system. Even New Years Day wasn't enough for him. "Let's keep it going through Bombay Brian's birthday!" he entreated us.

"When is that?" I said. "In May?"

"No, man, it's tomorrow, January 2! It should be a national holiday!"

And so, we played one more day. Brian even came up onstage and played a bass solo. And then we collapsed. We collapsed into a pile of broken parts. We collapsed into a sea of sludge. We collapsed into a mountain of goo. We'd played ten straight days and there was simply nothing left to do.

When I awoke a week later, everything had changed. The cocaine was gone and had been replaced by heroin. At first it was used simply to help balance the jittery high of the coke but then it became its own monster. Roberto was the first to indulge, his past history leading him down an all-too-familiar path. Neil was next, his days as an addict in England too easily rekindled. One by one we fell, like domino chips, but now we were chipping away at a much more dangerous pile of drugs. One of Roberto's songs fore-shadowed what was to come:

> *Trouble is my buddy*
> *Look out trouble*
> *Here I come*
> *Trouble's my buddy*
> *I know him like a brother.*
> *Look you straight in the eye*
> *Do a little shuffle from side to side*
> *See trouble, see trouble*
> *Sitting on, sitting on*
> *Sitting on my shoulder.*
> *You told me to chase what feels right*
> *And to run from the brainless side*
> *That's why trouble is my buddy*
> *Look out trouble*
> *Here I come*
> *Look out trouble*
> *Here I come*

The Music House, a large, airy, high-ceilinged edifice from Portuguese colonial times, now stood empty. It had been our refuge, a place to get away from the beach and the crowds, a place to practice and jam and create new material.

I'm not sure we even realized how unbelievably lucky we were. How many bands had unlimited practice time, a full set of equipment, beautiful surroundings and no day jobs to get in the way of pursuing their dreams? We were an international band on the fringes of a new kind of world music. Some of the musicians even had special gifts. Roberto had a golden voice and real charisma, and watching Neil blossom under the flickering lights of the stage was truly revelatory. The potential seemed truly limitless.

For the Anjuna Jam Band it all ended when Neil left for Rome with his Italian girlfriend, Nilda. It was to be a much-needed break from the pressures of playing month after month before an audience that expected something new each night. Everything fell apart when Neil was arrested for heroin possession and sentenced to six months in an Italian jail. I can only imagine the devastation wrought upon him as he went from the heights of fame in Goa to being just another junkie forced to kick drugs in a cold, unforgiving prison cell. He was eventually released to a halfway house, where a fellow inmate tried to steal his guitar. Neil's guitar was the one thing that offered him hope and a way out, but in the end even the guitar couldn't save him. A fight broke out, things escalated, and Neil was stabbed in the chest. He bled to death on the floor of the halfway house.

◦❦◦

Cowboy's legacy continued to grow. Stories emerged about where all that cocaine had come from. Legend had it that Cowboy had gone to Peru and convinced the military dictatorship that he was on the management team of the Grateful Dead. He claimed he was exploring the possibility of holding a rock festival in the Andes, and the government was so taken by the idea they flew him around in an army helicopter to scout out potential sites. The concert, of course, never happened, but the military somehow connected him with just the right coke dealer. It wouldn't surprise me if they flew him all the way to Goa.

On another occasion Cowboy convinced the management of the Hong Kong Sheraton that he was a member of Pink Floyd. Eager to make a good impression, they gave him a complimentary penthouse suite with everything included. What ensued was a week-long party for the ages. Then, several years later, there was the time he convinced a Polish princess living in exile in Canada that he was a member of the Greek royal family. He got her parents' blessing, raided the family jewels, and eloped with her to Mexico. They stopped off in San Francisco along the way and visited me in my cottage on Telegraph Hill. The Polish bride was still starry-eyed but I sensed some doubts creeping in about her quick-talking groom. I didn't have the heart to tell her.

My last brush with Cowboy came in a jarring phone call several years later:

"Good afternoon," came a gruff voice on the other end, "this is agent Malcolm Tooms of the Federal Bureau of Investigation."

"The FBI?" I said, feeling my knees, kidneys and bladder go weak. "*That* FBI?"

"Yeah, that one. We're looking into something you might be able to help us with. Do you know happen to know somebody named Theodoros Thanapolis?"

"Never heard of him," I said.

"Well, that's kinda strange. You see, we have his address book and your name and phone number are in it."

I actually had no idea who he was talking about, but his accusatory tone caught me off guard. I was already feeling guilty for a crime I didn't even commit. "Look, I'm sorry but I never heard of him."

"Hmm, well, like I said, that's kinda strange, you know? To have somebody's number—"

"Listen, the fact is I lived abroad for many years and met

a million people. Half of them didn't even use their real names. It could be anybody."

"Uh-huh, well, we have an arrest warrant out for Mr. Thanapolis for trafficking narcotics and since we were able to come into possession of some of his personal contact information, we thought we'd give you a call."

Narcotics? Cowboy! It had to be him! Who ever heard of a roadie named Theodoros Thanapolis?

"You'll call us if anything comes to mind?"

"Yeah, yeah, of course," I said, thinking about the first time Cowboy approached us on the side of the stage. He was a flim-flam man alright, but it turned out that separating the flim from the flam wasn't so easy after all. The guy had ten games going and not a single one of them was what it seemed to be.

⤫

But all of that was later. For now, the season in Goa was drawing to a close and we played one last gig. Roberto found his voice, Neil found his fingering, and the bass and drum found their rhythm. As the sun rose over the mountain, the sand came into view, then the ocean. I saw the ferry boat coming in from Bombay on its way to Panjim. I had a return ticket on that boat, set to depart in a couple of hours. I packed up my harmonicas, nodded my goodbyes and stepped off the stage as the band kept playing. Steve was taking a solo and a remarkably beautiful melody followed me right down the beach. It was the best I'd ever heard him play, a soulful, heartfelt, echoing plaint that carried over the palm trees, brushed against the sky, and floated off into the bright, fresh, rejuvenated morning. I turned back and saw him staring from the edge of the stage. The rest of the band was hidden by the trees and it was just Steve, standing there alone, a solitary figure holding a trumpet, playing a solo on a secluded Indian beach.

Chapter 26
Another Night in Benares

The train station in Benares was a great, hideous mess of confusion, even in the middle of the night. In addition to the usual thousands of passengers all fighting to get on a train, off a train, above, below or around a train, there were dozens of stretchers with the dying, the near dying and the already dead. They'd come from all over India to be cremated at the ghats along the Ganges and that's where I immediately went, to the Manikarnika Ghat, to pay my respects to the sadhus, the mourners and the bodies being burned on the funeral pyres. I'd been there several times before and always made it a point of returning to the same spot overlooking the river. There were fires burning up and down the banks and there was a quiet hush as people stood staring into the flames with a kind of disconnected reverence. Everyone was slightly out of their bodies, the dead whose spirits were rising into the ether, the monks who prayed for their safe passage, and the rest of us who existed at that moment in our own kind of nether-world, some undefined place between life, death and rebirth.

Benares was not a happy destination, not with the teems of mourners and a stream of tears, but it wasn't a sad place either. It was a spot to contemplate my place in the world, to consider my deeds and misdeeds, my steps and missteps, my attempts and failures. Staring into the river I thought of all the people I knew who'd died, many of them far too early. Looking back, the dates began to blur and the sequence of events became confused. Whether it was the fall of one year or the spring of another didn't much matter anymore, but Carmen was already dead, of that I was sure. That happened only a few months after she returned to Bali and died in a motorcycle crash. But what about Angus? Was that before he withered away in Kathmandu or after? And what about Devagiri? Was he still around or had he already overdosed on morphine on these very ghats?

I sat along the irregular stone steps, watching as the first rays of sunshine cast a flicker of light across the Ganges. A lone boat crossed to the center of the river, stopped to pour ashes from an urn into the current, then returned to the ghats. Several indistinct spires reflected against the surface of the rippling waves and then, as the sun peeked over the horizon, an ancient Shiva temple appeared at the edge of the water, half-submerged in the tide. More temples arose from the banks, dozens of them, as if awakening from the darkness. Someone blew a conch, someone else answered back, and the banks of the river came alive. Within moments there were hundreds of bathers washing in the river. My attention was drawn to an old woman who waded up from the water and sat along the banks, drying her hair in the sun. A girl massaged coconut oil into the woman's hair and ran a comb through her long tresses. The woman placed several kernels of rice on a banana leaf as an offering to Lord Shiva and set it next to the river. Within moments a bird swooped down, pecked a grain of rice, and flew off to a nest just above the temple.

I walked up along the steps and wandered through the twisting streets to the gold-encrusted domes of Kashi Vishwanath Temple. Inside the courtyard were a dozen shrines to Shiva and dozens more tridents, damrus and stone lingams. Several pilgrims knelt before an ancient bronze statue whose face had been rubbed smooth over the centuries by millions of people seeking a blessing. Nothing was left now but the vague outline of a head atop an indistinct body. I glanced around the courtyard to see a blind man holding a beggar's bowl, an old woman knitting together a wreath of marigolds, a boy rubbing red powder on his sister's forehead, a frail sadhu sitting in yogic position, a monk leading morning prayers, and a crippled child maneuvering on a skateboard propelled only by his hands. An Indian holy woman glanced up at me as I passed her outside the temple. Her eyes were clear and glistening, her lips relaxed in a placid smile. "Listen to the prayers," she said. "Watch the processions. Go to the river. Keep your heart open."

It was the best advice I'd ever received in all my years in Asia.

꿍

I headed down Chowk Godowlia Road, past the sari shops, tailors and bead merchants, and came upon Varanasi Lassis, which seemed like a good enough place to try out since I was, indeed, in Varanasi. To me it was still Benares, the ancient name of the city, even though it had recently been renamed in reference to the confluence of two rivers, the Varuna and the Asi, plus a third, invisible river that was said to flow either beneath the city, above the city, or in some still-undiscovered dimension.

The juice joint consisted of a counter, a table and a couple of mismatched chairs. I watched as the proprietor wiped a wet spot off the floor, then used the same rag to wipe down the table and dry some glasses. Anywhere else in the world he would've be closed down for health violations, but in Benares it would be considered exemplary behavior. "Sahib?" he said as I walked in. "A nice mango lassi?"

"With lots of ice, okay?" I said.

"Best ice in Varanasi," he responded. "On the double."

I loved the Indian sense of humor, even if I was never entirely sure that we were sharing the same joke. The proprietor scooped some yogurt into a blender, then added a few slices of freshly-cut mango and a squeeze of lemon. The machine was an ancient-looking thing with Russian lettering that reminded me of an old Hoover vacuum cleaner. He turned on the power switch and waited with a hopeful look. We were in luck. There was enough electricity that day not only to run the blender but also to power a slow-moving fan that periodically made a few revolutions, then paused intermittently as if to gather its resolve to go on. The fan actually seemed like a pretty good metaphor for India itself, except that it, too, was made in Russia.

The blender spun around as if it were grinding the Arctic Ice Shelf. After a terrible shaking and clamor, the contraption ground to a halt and the proprietor poured my lassi into a glass. "One mango lassi," he said.

Before he could wipe a little smudge off the rim of the glass with his all-purpose rag, I grabbed the lassi and drank it down in one gulp. "Good ice," I said, winking at him.

He winked back as I headed for the street, happy to have shared a little joke—if that was a joke—or at least a little wink—if that was a wink.

⤙❧⤚

Benares was famous throughout India for its fine silks and brocades. I decided to send a selection of pieces to my parents since their having something tangible to hold onto might convince them I was still alive. Purchasing the brocade was the easy part—it only took an entire morning of bargaining interrupted by complimentary cups of chai and Indian sweets that set my teeth to chatter—but when I asked for a box to ship the goods, we were back to the reality of doing business in India. Unlike most other big cities, Benares had no shipping agents so if I wanted to send something out of the country I'd have to brave the rough waters, high tides, and low-lying rocks of the Indian postal system.

The brocade shop, of course, had no boxes, nor did any of the other shops in the market, so it was necessary to go across town to the "box factory," which, of course, was closed. I returned several times before finding someone willing to make me a box since, of course, they had nothing actually in stock. The box walla eyeballed my pile of brocades, then went to a contraption that looked like something out of a Dickens workhouse. He turned this, switched that, maneuvered here, pushed there, and a mere forty minutes later produced a cardboard box that was of good size, good strength and had flaps that almost, but not quite, properly closed. No matter, it was close enough for my needs which, admittedly, weren't all that great. Next, I took a rickshaw to the Post Office where, after waiting in line for two hours, I discovered that all parcels being sent out of Benares had to be wrapped and stitched in cotton because, well, who knew why? It was a regulation from the days of the Silk Route and I wasn't about to question a system that had worked perfectly well since the Middle Ages. After all, if my parcel was going to go by camel caravan, it only made sense to let them have all the cotton they needed.

At the fabric market, a cotton walla unrolled several bolts of material so that I could inspect the various qualities; this, despite the fact that I only needed perhaps one square yard of cotton, the quality of which didn't matter to me in the least. After much arguing and bargaining I headed next for a tailor shop since, indeed, the material had to be sewn around the box. I found a box-sewing expert who examined the project as if he were fashioning Queen Elizabeth's coronation gown, then made a preliminary shell with his sewing machine and hand-stitched the whole thing together.

On day two I returned to the Post Office, waited two more hours in line, then was told that I needed special forms which had to be filled out in quintuplicate with a special ballpoint pen which the Post Office, of course, didn't have. I headed back to the market and found an "assundries" store which had exactly the kind of pen I wanted except that the ink had dried out. Not to worry, I went to another store, then another, and found a pen that worked. I took another rickshaw back to the Post Office, found a tiny space along an empty counter, and filled out the five forms as best I could. After waiting in line for two more hours, I discovered that the forms had to be *sewn* to the outside of the box which was so insane and impossible that I finally blew my stack. But not to worry, I was guided to a "specialist" in this art form who, in fact, had exactly the kind of needle necessary for such an operation. Unfortunately, he was out of thread, so I was led to another specialist in the thread business and he had exactly what I was looking for except for the fact that, when I returned to the needle walla, we discovered that the thread was too thick for the needle opening. But, once again, not to worry, because for only one rupee we could engage three other filament wallas to unravel the thread into three thinner strands. It was now official. I'd been transported into a Three Stooges episode in which I was the hapless dupe at the mercy of three madcap nincompoops. Alas, the thread was unraveled and a mere forty-five minutes later my forms were professionally sewn to the outer cotton shell of my handmade box. I was finally ready to face the long line again, which I was actually prepared to do and, in fact, would have done if only the Post Office weren't now closed for the day.

On day three, there was an unusual rush of customers so I stood in line for nearly three hours. Finally, sweat dripping from every pore of my body, I arrived at the Post Office window, where I was told they were out of all large denomination stamps and would have to affix row upon row of 25 paisa stamps and hopefully there'd be enough room on the box to fit them all. Plus, each stamp would have to be hand-cancelled to insure that no one along the way steamed them off to be resold, and, oh, they would need to seal the corners with special red sealing wax and encase the documents in plastic, and perhaps I'd like to engage someone for an excellent head massage or how about a professional ear cleaner should I need attention in that area—

"Would ten rupees placed between the second and third pages of the fourth and fifth copies help expedite things?" I asked.

"Well, that is very kind of you, sahib. But only if you wish."

"Believe me, I wish. I wish with all of my heart."

"Perhaps we could turn a few blind eyes and ensure that everything is tip-top and A-number-one. How would that be?"

"That would give me great pleasure," I said, slipping ten rupees under the window.

"Consider it done!" he said, pocketing the money with a sleight of hand that would've done Houdini proud. "First class service from here to there!"

"It's been good doing business with you."

"The pleasure is all yours. Now, about that ear cleaning..."

⤬

I awoke the next morning feeling sicker than I could ever remember. It could've been from the river, the temple, the lassi, the fan, the box factory, the rickshaw, the Post Office, the thread, the sealing wax, the stamps or, more likely, some toxic mix of all the above. I forced myself to Central Pharmacy and headed for a counter where a nervous-looking pharmacist was measuring out some pills. "I need some Vitamin C," I said.

He stared at me with squinty eyes and sweaty brows. "Are you feeling poorly?" he said with the kind of academic English reserved for those of the professional classes.

"I can barely move a muscle."

He looked at me for what I thought was a moment too long, then did some kind of hipster hand jive as if to indicate that everything was cool. I didn't quite catch the body language but I returned the gesture with a half-hearted wave which seemed to do the trick. The pharmacist came out from behind the counter and motioned for me to follow him. "Come this way," he said.

He led me to a door at the rear of the pharmacy, glanced around to make sure no one was looking, then led me inside. The room was stacked floor to ceiling with prescription pads, receipts and formularies. Along one wall was an ancient druggist's chest with dozens of tiny drawers. He motioned for me to sit down, then reached into his pocket for a key and unlocked one of the drawers. It all seemed more than a little odd.

"You... uh.... you have very good security," I said, wondering whatever possessed him to guard vitamins as if they were the gold of Fort Knox.

"One can never be too careful," he said. "So which of the *Vitamin C's* do you wish?"

"I didn't know you had more than one."

"Oh, yes, at the moment we are stocking codeine, cocaine, and cannabis."

"Uh, wait—"

"All are top quality, guaranteed."

"You're serious, aren't you?"

"If I might make a suggestion," he said, pulling out a small bottle with a sealed cap, "the cocaine has been our most popular product recently. It's from the Merck laboratories in

Switzerland and at only 80 rupees a gram, you really can't go wrong."

"I really appreciate the offer, but—"

"Yes, I see. If it is the codeine you want—"

"Listen to me. I feel sick as a dog. I want *Vitamin* C."

"You want *Vitamin* C?" he said, slamming the drawers shut. "Why didn't you tell me?"

"I did tell you."

"Westerners..." he muttered, as he led me out of the room, up the aisles, and back to the counter. He tossed me a bottle. "Two rupees."

"Thank you very much."

"Don't mention it."

"Don't worry, I won't."

"Not to anyone."

෯

Benares was one of the great cultural capitals of India and each spring it hosted a festival of the country's top musicians. When I arrived at Sankat Mochan temple, I was surprised at how informal the setting was. The dozen or so musicians, each of whom was legendary throughout all of India, mixed in with the audience and couldn't really be distinguished by their appearance or demeanor. There were no dressing rooms, no backstage areas, no cordoned off sections, and the stage, such as it was, was nothing more than a big rug.

The temple opened up onto a courtyard where a giant statue of Hanuman, the Monkey God, overlooked the surroundings. Outside, a large crowd huddled together under an ornate archway, hoping to get in. A sarod, tambura and tabla were playing an evening raga and the melody floated over the hall, building to a great crescendo, diminishing, then building again. The patterns kept repeating over and over, building, releasing, building, releasing, as constant and organic as a heartbeat. But then a singer took the stage and I was jarred out of my trancelike state. There was something so strange about his voice, so atonal and dissonant, that the beauty of the raga seemed lost amidst his bizarre vocal exercises.

For a musician in India to perform in public required such a level of artistry that few even dreamt of appearing at such an important festival. Musicians were known to sit at the foot of their masters for years on end before considering themselves worthy of even being called students. To be a musician was one of the highest callings in Hindu society and the study of classical Indian music and religion could not be separated. There was a time, it is said, when musicians knew the exact spiritual equivalent of every tone, that to play a raga was to experience the highest level of religious awareness.

In Europe, too, greater attention was once given to the meaning of tones. The devil's interval—the distance from the tonic to the flat five—was considered to be the sound of evil and to even play it in private was enough to be accused of witchcraft. While Indian musicians were well aware of the power of music to elicit negative emotions, they also knew the whole range of tones which could elicit feelings of love, honor and devotion. That's what we were listening to right now. Why, then, was this singer driving me half crazy? The voice, after all, was considered to be the highest instrument of all. In the voice existed every possible note and nuance.

I looked around at the audience. There were hundreds of people sitting on the floor and crowded along the walls. I noticed how they'd listen with rapt attention for only a few moments before somebody would casually strike up a conversation, call to a friend across the room, or just get up and leave. I couldn't even imagine insulting someone's performance like this, but I knew that the Indians actually had a great reverence for art. They simply didn't hold it separate from life and saw no need to treat it in some somber manner. To talk during a performance wasn't a sign of disrespect, it was a sign of comfort, joy and familiarity.

As I listened more, I began opening up to the vocals and appreciated the singer's wild runs through four octaves. The more he sang, the more I admired his melodic sense. When the raga hit a crescendo, his voice exploded into a series of notes which pushed up along my spine. I imagined I was on the roof of the giant temple, being buffeted by the wind, then falling into a great expanse where there was nothing but pure light and pure sound... falling... falling—

There was a commotion up near the stage. Someone made a sudden movement in the audience, the person next to him reacted nervously, a woman jumped to her feet, a whole row scattered and someone yelled, *"Naga!"* Within seconds, pandemonium broke out and everyone was pushing for the exits. The musicians kept playing for a while, but then they too stopped and backed away. For a moment, I thought we'd all be crushed in the onslaught, but then, just as quickly, a man called out and everyone turned to see him holding a piece of rope in his hands. There was some nervous laughter as everyone returned to their spots. It wasn't a snake, after all.

The tabla player counted in the rhythm, *"teen tal... dah, dah, tiki-tiki dah..."* and then the sarod and tambura joined in. A woman called to her husband, a few people pushed through the crowd, and someone began nibbling on a plate of pakoras. And then the singer reached back and unleashed a torrent of notes that filled the room, reverberated off the ceiling, and came flying right through the top of my skull. My mind was filled with visions of naked sadhus and burning bodies, but as the sounds burrowed deeper into my brain, the images blended into one long, deep tone, a tone that was so rich and full and all-encompassing that it reminded me of nothing so much as absolute, total silence.

The music hit a crescendo. The sarod and tabla traded solos, the tambura accented with a drone, and the singer improvised over the soaring melody. His voice galloped over the scales, exhibiting an astonishing range. What moments ago sounded completely atonal now exploded into a mesmerizing passage that sent the audience into ecstasy. People began to snap their fingers above their heads. Some danced in place. A few twirled around in complete abandon.

The raga ended to thunderous applause. A woman approached the singer and offered him a cup of chai. Someone passed him a plate of sweets. A little girl handed him a red rose. His face beamed with appreciation. I walked out of the temple grounds on a cushion of air. It seemed as though only an hour had passed, but it may have been an entire evening. I really had lost all sense of time. At that moment I could've been in any temple in any century along any body of water. I saw some smoke rising from the ghats, then noticed a stretcher being carried to the river by a stream of mourners. Their bodies blended into the black of night, then disappeared from view. A conch blew in the distance. A sadhu lit a chillum. I stepped over a cow sleeping along the path and made my way through the darkened alleyways. It was just another night in Benares. A night that would be repeated over and over into eternity. A night unlike any other.

Chapter 27

The Psychedelic Swami

I heard a tapping from the hallway that was so feeble I thought it might've been a cat brushing against the door or a slight rustle of wind. A few seconds later I heard the tapping again, but this time it was definitely the sound of somebody knocking out a syncopated rhythm reminiscent of a Gene Krupa drum solo. It was like a secret code that only those hip to the illustrious sounds of big band jazz could understand. It could've been Benny Goodman or Benny Berrigan, but that wasn't really likely in the hallway of a hidden apartment just off Durbar Square in Kathmandu. It could only be one person. I opened the door to find a little button of a man with a long white beard, coke bottle glasses, and a topi propped rakishly on his balding pate. "Namaste," I said. "Please come in."

"Yes, yes," he whispered, "but only for a moment." Shri Mahant Ganesh Giriji Maharaj entered with no small effort, one foot pushing the other until he arrived at his usual spot on a cushion in the center of the room. He sank into the well-worn grooves and might've disappeared between the folds were it not for his keeping his back so straight he actually posed a kind of towering figure, rare in a man not even five-feet tall.

"How was the class tonight?" I asked.

Ganesh Baba, as he was less formally known, slowly shook his head, as if wondering what was the point. "They are slow learners, if they learn anything at all. You Westerners, you come to dig the dust of our civilization and all you find is more dust. I'm trying to teach them Kriya Yoga and they are asking me how to chew their food. *'With your mouths,'* I tell them, *'with your mouths!'* And do you know what? They think I'm a genius of digestion!" Ganesh fell quiet, closing his eyes either in deep meditation or perhaps to catch a couple of winks. He looked tired, not unusual for a man in his late eighties who was still trolling around the streets well past sunset.

I went into the kitchen to put on some tea and let the old man relax a while. I was still getting used to the idea that my kitchen had a faucet and that water came out of it by simply turning a handle. I'd recently moved into the Rose Garden, a small compound of apartments surrounding, perhaps not surprisingly, a rose garden. It was my first time living in the city after several years in Swayambhu and I was feeling downright cosmopolitan. Running water, a toilet down the hall, and a whole host of shops and restaurants within walking distance. It's how I imagined Holland in the 1920s.

Ganesh had been coming around almost every night, either because the Rose Garden was on his way home or, more likely, because he had a special fondness for the Thai sticks I'd brought from Thailand hidden inside the speakers of my tape recorder. Bringing marijuana to Nepal might seem like bringing coals to Newcastle but Thai sticks were special and seemed worth getting arrested for—such was my state of mind—if anybody thought to look inside the speakers, that is, and thankfully no one had. There was something about electronic equipment that made customs agents shy away, like maybe it would them bring bad luck, cause sterility, or unleash a plague of short circuits and power outages.

I glanced into the main room to see if Ganesh was all right. He was unusually quiet and hardly seemed like the bête noir of the spiritual community, as he was known. He was more of a cuddly grandfather figure, what with his prodigious belly, his skintight orange pants and his pink kurta that reached almost to his knees. He wasn't really an imposing figure, at least not now, dozing away on the cushion like a cat entrenched in its favorite spot. It looked like a stiff wind could knock him over.

Ah, but years ago, as he always liked to tell me, things were not so. He'd grown up in Calcutta, the oldest of twelve children, the rest of whom were all girls. He'd been a brilliant student and had attended the finest universities. He was well-versed in physics, biology and psychology, and had studied under Einstein, Shrödinger and Jung when they came to colonial India to teach on sabbatical. The young Ganesh had a promising future in the sciences, but when his father died at an early age, he became head of the family and needed to raise a substantial dowry to marry off his eleven sisters. It was a daunting task which led to his quitting the university and opening a string of cinemas throughout Calcutta. It was, to be sure, a love-hate relationship. "I walked into one of my cinemas one day and thought I was in the bathroom," he said. "What a seedy enterprise!"

Ganesh became a successful businessman and was able to fulfill his promise to his family. Then, when he reached the age of fifty-five, he renounced all of his worldly possessions and became a holy man. This was in the tradition of ancient India, where it was common to experience life in all its mundane forms, then to seek the higher planes of consciousness. Ganesh donned the robes of a sanyassi and traveled from ashram to ashram in search of a spiritual awakening. In Benares he discovered bhang, ganja, charas, and a variety of sacred mushrooms that were to greatly alter his world view. He developed what he called a psychedelic awareness of the universe.

It was only natural that the first Western seekers who arrived in India would encounter Ganesh Baba, who spoke perfect English, was open to new experience, and was as funny as any performer on the comedy circuit. Over the years Ganesh turned on hundreds of young foreigners to the ways of India through his unique methods of teaching Kriya Yoga. They, in return, turned him on to LSD.

It was a match made in heaven. Ganesh Baba's brain was ripe for an awakening of neurons and synapses that lay long dormant and the result was an even more elevated state of consciousness. It was thus that he became known in India and abroad as the "psychedelic swami." As more Westerners flocked around to learn his techniques of yoga and listen to his spiritual ramblings, they were regaled by his profound, provocative and sometimes profane view of the world. Like Krishnamurti before him, the more he claimed to have no special knowledge, the larger his following became. He soon became surrounded by acolytes both Western and Indian and was accorded a respect given only to the highest gurus.

The whistling of the tea kettle brought Jonathan and Anouchka out of their room. They'd come up from Goa to check out the Himalayas for the first time and were sharing the apartment with me. "Baba's here," I said.

"Great, I haven't been abused all day," said Jonathan, who hadn't yet fully experienced the Ganesh Baba two-step. It was a dance of praise followed by a punch to the stomach, all to the benefit of our dense Western ways. Ganesh's reflections were meant to be taken with both a grain of salt and the seriousness of divine insight. Distinguishing the two wasn't always the easiest task.

"Don't worry. Ganesh only goes after those who can take

it," I said, recalling my own experiences receiving the bitter end of one of his barbs.

"That's right, it's just a little push-pull," said Anouchka, swirling her hands around in a gesture that indicated both profound understanding and complete confusion at the same time. What she meant was anyone's guess, but we nodded in agreement. Anouchka had a German-French-Czech accent that left much to the imagination. I'm not sure if she actually had a native language or a native country or even a real passport. It was more like she'd descended from some multinational department store in the sky. There was a little of this, a little of that, and a pinch of paprika thrown in to keep us on our toes. Who knew what she was thinking?

We went into the main room and sat in a semicircle around the cushion. There was something about Ganesh that always led to semicircles, like it was only natural that we form a kind of amphitheatre around a stage from which he could expound. "Here's your chai," I said, placing the cup next to Baba.

He looked more tired than before. I figured he'd have a quick cup of tea and we'd get him home somehow or other. Baba looked up at me with half-closed eyes and mumbled something I couldn't quite understand. "Mmmmmph... mmmmphhhh."

"What's that, Baba?"

"Why don't you... roll up... a nice big fat one," he said, forcing out the words with such effort I began to wonder if he'd make it through the night.

"Okay, Baba, whatever you want," I said.

"This is a good thing for such a man?" whispered Anouchka as I reached over for my bag of Thai sticks. "Who knows which way his heart beats?"

"A guy his age will take a heartbeat anyway he can get it," said Jonathan, handing me the rolling papers.

I rolled up a Ganesh Baba Special—short, fat and hazardous,

just like him—and handed it to him to light. *"Bom, Shiva,"* he said as he took a long drag from the tightly packed joint. Before he even exhaled, Ganesh began to transform right before our eyes. His cheeks got pinker, his eyebrows rose like little tents, the corners of his mouth began to twitter, and his eyes darted around in delight. "Ha!" he snorted. "Ha! Ha! Ha!"

"Feeling better are you, Baba?" said Anouchka.

"I'm ready to dance, my dear... did you bring your bala-laika?"

Anouchka recoiled in a push-pull of alarm. "Does he think I am Russian?" she whispered to Jonathan.

"I don't know," Jonathan whispered back. "Are you?" Even though they'd been married five years, I don't think Jonathan actually knew where Anouchka was from or how old she was. I think he preferred it that way.

"Baba?" I said, pointing to the joint burning down in Ganesh's fingers. This was entirely predictable as he invariably forgot it was there. "Would you like to pass that on?"

"We Naga babas don't bother with petty formalities," he said, staring at the long ash ready to drop on his pants.

"I know that, but if you'd just pass it on, we'll get it back to you in no time."

Ganesh wasn't listening. He was already off on a dissertation that might lead anywhere. "We are the oldest monks in the world," he laughed. "No one can compare with us in our phoniness! We will outshout you all the time. We are not ordinary monks but hipster monks. I am the hippopoto-master!"

Ganesh Baba was a legendary teller of tales short and tall, some of which were true, some of which were false, and most of which fell into that broad raconteur's limbo where all that mattered was that they were entertaining. It was a stream of conscious oration held together by a thread that was constantly unraveling but refused to completely break.

If there was one consistent theme, it was the necessity of keeping one's back straight. Whether experimenting with drugs, attempting esoteric meditation practices, or shooting craps on the sidewalk, the back must be kept straight. At least once a night, Ganesh would shoot me a disapproving glance. "You are slouching again!" he'd intone. "If you want to be a psychedelic, you must keep your back straight. Otherwise everything will cave in on you. My own guru said to me: *'Sit with your back straight until you drop dead. Then you will be sitting in my lap and I will be sitting in the lap of God.'* I believe him and I am still going that way."

"What is this thing exactly, to be a psychedelic?" said Anouchka.

"It's to experience the higher realms not seen by others. Yoga can help get you there. Maybe meditation. Me, I prefer a nice hit of acid."

"You are suggesting I take LSD?"

"I'm not suggesting it, I'm *demanding* it!" he said with a roar of laughter. "Listen to me. There are certain rules you must follow. First: *Beware of the non-psychedelic.*"

"The *non*-psychedelic?" said Anouchka.

"Correct! Life is short, why waste it on mundane foofaraw? Rule two: *Once a psychedelic always a psychedelic.*"

"I knew something changed the first time I tripped," said Jonathan. "I've been doomed to a life of wonder ever since."

"And here is the third and most important Ganeshian principle: *A non-psychedelic can never enlighten a psychedelic.*"

"Of course!" said Anouchka. "All of those teachers we had were barking up the wrong chimney!"

Ganesh mulled it over a moment, then exploded again in laughter. "People who have not felt God do not know how cool is his laugh," he said in between gasps of air. "Ha! Ha! Ha!" He then rolled to his side and laughed until he began coughing. "Chai! Bring me chai!" he sputtered between coughs.

"The cup's right next to you," I said.

He took a sip, then spit it out. "You bring me cold chai?" he screamed. "Is this the respect you show me?"

"Baba, it was hot when I brought it—"

"Bring me hot chai, I tell you!" Ganesh paused a moment for dramatic effect, then leaned forward with his hands in prayer position. "*Dear God, if there is a God, please help me, if you can help me.*"

"So, Baba," said Jonathan, hoping to engage the old man in conversation, "on our way up from Goa, Anouchka and I stopped off to see Rajneesh—"

"Did he charge you?"

"Um, I don't know, we might've donated five rupees—"

"*What?*" said Baba, narrowing his eyes. "If you have to pay five rupees to see Rajneesh, then you have to pay five rupees to see my doo-doo!"

"Will that be five rupees each," said Jonathan, "or can we get a group rate?"

"The history of India is a continuous stream of high hoax. Wise men don't love wise men, wise men love fools. And you are such divine fools."

We all laughed uncomfortably.

"A fool laughs three times," he said. "The first time when others are laughing. The second time when they understand the joke. The third time when they wonder why they laughed when they didn't understand the joke." Ganesh Baba was like a boxer, jabbing and feinting, then putting his arms around you when the round ended. "Ha! Ha! Ha! I love all of you so much. You know that, don't you?"

"Of course, Baba."

"Then why don't you roll up another fat one before we all fall asleep on your floor? And bring your guitar! I want to dance!"

"Right away, Baba, right away."

"Ha! Ha-ha-ha!" he said, shaking with laughter. "Ha! Ha! Ha!"

❦

Jonathan, Anouchka and I walked along the Bagmati River to the outskirts of Kathmandu. It was one of my favorite places in the valley, a spot far from the crowds of the city but close enough to still be in the shadow of the pagoda-shaped temples and centuries-old stupas. The path alongside the river was irregular, with stone slabs in some places, dirt in others, and little pools of water in others still. In a civilization dating back thousands of years this seemed like a particularly ancient area, with ruins of forgotten villages interspersed amongst remnants of temples so old their derivations could no longer be identified with certainty. No one knew if they were Hindu, Buddhist, or perhaps some animist precursor.

We passed a towering banyan tree whose dozen trunks wound around one another and spiraled into the sky. In the upper branches of the tree hundreds of giant bats hung upside down, their winged bodies swinging in the breeze as if being rocked to sleep in a cradle. Far off in the distance was a whoosh of birds migrating farther north ahead of the coming monsoon. From somewhere in a patch of rhododendrons came the shriek of an owl and a rustling of leaves. We walked a little further and came upon a tiny alcove built into the ruins of a long-abandoned temple. Sitting on a rough slab of concrete was an old sadhu whom I'd seen every time I passed this way. He sat in classic yoga position and stared out at the holy river which meandered through the mountains on its way to the plains of India, where it would feed into the Ganges. There was nothing particularly notable about this spot along the river. It was no more beautiful than any number of other sites, the temple was no more impressive than older ruins, and the sadhu was no more remarkable than many others I'd met. Still, there was something about the place, maybe its very ordinariness, that made it so special.

"Do you ever get used to being here?" asked Jonathan.

"No, never," I said.

"I mean, how do you explain this to anybody?"

"You don't."

We sat near the sadhu, who began chanting a prayer under his breath:

Om sarva mangal manglaye
Shivay sarvaarth sadhike,
Sharanye trayambake gauri
Narayaani namostu te.

As we stared into the river, something in the slow-flowing waters called out for silence and contemplation. What any of us were doing in Nepal at that moment was completely beyond sense and sensibility. Part of me felt I'd reached a particular destination, a place to step off the wheel and give in to something greater around me. Another part felt this was just one of many stops along my own meandering river that might just as easily lead to a cave in the mountains, a dune in the desert, or a stage on the beach. The river drifted along the banks, seeping between the rocks, rolling over some boulders, picking up speed as the current pulled it along. Every inch along the way there was a new twist, a new angle, a new story waiting to be told.

❧

I hadn't been to Swayambhu for a while and walked across the rickety swing bridge, through the rice paddies, around the army barracks, and onto the tiny main street of the village to see that things were quieter now and pretty much back to normal. The Karmapa was long gone, the Tibetan pilgrims were a distant memory, and the carpet weavers were back in business. Kids were playing in the street and several dozen people were lined up outside the local shop waiting for the daily delivery of buffalo milk. As always, the van would be two hours late and six bottles short.

As I reminisced about my several years living on Kimdol Hill, a young girl approached with a cautious smile. *"Tashi deleg,"* she said in Tibetan.

"Tashi deleg," I replied, wondering what she might want. She just stood there a moment, either not knowing what to say or how to say it. Finally, she held out her hand for me to take a look. I saw a thick scar that ran from her forefinger right down to her palm. When she flexed her fingers to show me that she had full movement, I realized she was the girl who'd almost severed her finger with a shears several years earlier. She'd been part of the group that had camped out near my house waiting for the Karmapa's arrival. "Good! Good!" I said, clasping her hand.

She beamed at me with a smile that spread across her round, flat face. "Good! Good!" she repeated as she waved good-bye and headed up the street. I noticed that she had a schoolbook in her other hand and wondered if she'd come all the way back over the mountains to pursue her education. I thought back to the day that Delia and I took her to the hospital in a taxi and felt gratified to know we'd actually done something useful. It was the least we could do to help repay the generosity of the Nepalis and Tibetans.

༺ঔৡ༻

On my birthday a friend invited me to the Yak & Yeti Restaurant, there being a rare reservation available. To call the Yak & Yeti an anomaly doesn't do justice to just how spectacularly out of place this five star restaurant was in one of the world's most backward countries. It was located in an old Rana palace that had been refurbished to its previous grandeur by Boris Lisanevich, a Russian ballet dancer who'd fled the Russian revolution, was exiled in Paris, and eventually arrived in Nepal upon invitation of newly restored King Tribhuvan. Boris brought exquisite Russian cooking to a ruling class that probably couldn't distinguish Chicken Kiev from Chicken Vindaloo, but no matter, with its plush velvet walls and mirrored columns, the Yak & Yeti was truly fit for a king.

I felt out of place the instant we arrived, my freshly washed pajama pants and silk vest standing out among the suits and ties. Still, I was quite unprepared for the sight of a half-dozen American secret servicemen who descended upon the dining room a few moments later as if in search of a royal assassin. I only hoped it wasn't me they were after, since I hadn't paid my taxes for the previous eight years. What, did they want twenty-two percent of my wages from playing that night in Tokyo? Was America that hard up?

The crew-cut servicemen fanned out across the room, looking under tables, beneath seat cushions, inside flower vases and behind paintings. It all seemed just a bit odd, even in Nepal, where the odd was normal, the bizarre was typical, and the unthinkable entirely ordinary. It had been so many years since I'd seen pants this pressed and shoes that polished that just looking at them made me want to confess to something. Okay, I admit it. I was one of those rioters back in college who sat in against the Dow Chemical recruiters who were trying to hire graduates to help them make napalm. Remember when they ordered us to disperse? I didn't.

I sank down in my seat, trying to avoid eye contact and trying to ignore the fact that the place was being searched as if we were dining in Hitler's bunker. It made me long for the Tibetan chai shop in Swayambhu, where the worst I could expect was to contract hepatitis, not risk arrest. Moments later, I felt a shadow over the table and the smell of fine cologne. "How's the borscht?" came a stentorian voice.

I glanced up to see a man of about seventy with thick black glasses and a ruddy complexion. He was smiling at me with the kind of forced friendliness of a politician seeking votes. It took me a moment to put the face, the hair, and the posture together, but then the pieces of the puzzle coalesced into a giant cartoon balloon that radiated above me like a float at the Macy's Thanksgiving Parade. It was Nelson Rockefeller, the former Governor of New York, the former Vice President of the United States, and one of the world's richest men. What he was doing here was anyone's guess. Maybe he was buying the country as an anniversary present for his wife. Maybe he was arming the military against the ever-present danger of invasion by Bhutanese monks. Maybe he wanted to drill for oil beneath Mt. Everest.

I thought how perfect it would be if right here in Kathmandu, at the Yak & Yeti Restaurant, over a bowl of Russian borscht, Nelson Rockefeller were to renounce everything. The mansions, the banks, the trust funds, the mistress, the yacht, the fleet of limousines, the summer home, the winter home, the nursing home, the home on the range, the investment portfolio, the stock options, the club memberships, the bomb shelter, the tax shelter, the bonds, liens, securities, foreign accounts, savings accounts, checking accounts and retirement accounts. Right here and right now he tosses it all away to become a wandering sadhu. I could already see the headlines of the New York Times:

NELSON ROCKEFELLER RENOUNCES ALL
WILL WANDER ASIA WITH DHOTI AND BEGGAR'S BOWL

I was snapped out of my reverie by Rockefeller coughing nervously as he awaited my response. "The borscht is good," I finally said. "It could maybe use a dash of paprika." He nodded to me and glanced at the woman I was dining with. She was so thin that when she lifted a spoon to her mouth, it seemed like an extension of her arm. The spoon and her wrist were just about the same thickness. It looked as if the soup was drinking her.

"Maybe I'll go with the blinis," he said.

"Yeah, that's probably a good idea," I said. After all, if this was to be his last meal before setting out on the path of infinite self-awareness, he should definitely have the specialty of the house to remember it by.

⚮

I headed down Asan Tole toward Indra Chowk and the White Machindranath Temple. It was my favorite temple in Kathmandu and was held in special reverence by both Hindus and Buddhists. The thousand-year-old shrine had been rebuilt over the years but it felt older than most of the neighboring stupas, and on this particular evening it felt truly timeless. Inside, the statue of Karunamaya, freshly painted with a white face and an almost comical grin, was wrapped in garlands of marigolds. The statue exuded a welcoming grace as it gazed out across the temple grounds.

It was very late at night and I was the only person in the temple. I didn't normally visit temples at these hours, but this was not a normal night. It was my last night in Kathmandu and I didn't know if I'd ever be back again.

There was a profound quiet inside the temple, so much so that my thoughts felt sharper than usual, as if they were being projected along the walls of the courtyard. I could see myself arriving some five years earlier, still tanned and confident from Africa, and falling almost immediately into a kind of supernatural spell in which every step seemed propelled by destiny. One place led to another, one person to another, one book to another, and even if I had no idea where it was all taking me, it felt as if I were being pushed along by something just slightly out of my own making.

As I glanced around the walls of the temple I saw a parade of all the people I'd met. There were poets and musicians and dancers who'd thrown themselves into an unknown adventure that some wouldn't survive. Was it worth it?

Who knew? If I'd been looking for some answer, I still hadn't found it. If I'd been seeking a direction for the rest of my life, it was still elusive. For all I knew, it had all been a glorious waste of time. But even if it was, I knew I wouldn't trade a moment of it for anything.

I glanced around the temple one last time and paid my final respects to Karunamaya. "Catch you on the flip side," I said with all due irreverence. Under his painted white face, I could almost see him rolling his eyes.

Outside, the street was completely deserted. There wasn't much to keep people awake at night in Kathmandu and I could hear my flip-flops echoing off the cobblestones. I walked toward Durbar Square, then turned up the twisting road that led to the Rose Garden. Along the way I passed Kasthamandap Temple, the legendary stupa that had been built from the wood of a single tree and had given the city its name.

"Chillum, baba?" came a call from somewhere on the steps. I glanced over to see a solitary sadhu sitting in the shadows of the pagoda roof. It had been years since I'd smoked with the babas at the temples, but it occurred to me that I shouldn't let this opportunity escape me, not tonight of all nights.

"Namaste, baba," I said as I approached the Shiva sadhu, who sat erect next to a small fire, a metal trident stuck into the ground. It was hard to clearly see his face beneath the ashes and the three orange stripes across his forehead, but I guessed he was about my age. The moment I sat down, he took a healthy-sized piece of charas from the cloth bag strung over his shoulder and mixed it in his palm with equal parts ganja and tobacco. He then funneled it into his clay chillum, touched it to his forehead in a blessing, and leaned to the side for me to light it. I took three matches, struck them against the cardboard box, and held them over the top of the pipe. "Bom, Shiva," I intoned as he lit the chillum.

We passed the pipe back and forth, then settled in to watch the fire. *"Kathmandu, pandrah din,"* he said, letting me know that he'd been in Kathmandu for fifteen days already. *"Varanasi, chhakka saptaah,"* he continued. Six weeks in Varanasi. He was an Indian sadhu on a pilgrimage to the holy spots of the subcontinent, and he told me how much he liked it in Patna, how hot it was in Calcutta, and how he enjoyed bathing in the Ganges. In a way, he was like any other traveler recounting his adventures.

I thought back to when I first arrived in India, when I spoke not a word of Hindi, and how I'd listen to the sadhus speaking to me with what I was sure was some kind of arcane wisdom. If only I could understand their message, I thought, surely I would attain some higher state of being. Now, years later, my Hindi was still extremely primitive but I could at least comprehend the basics of what was being said. Sitting here with this sadhu, I finally understood what had eluded me all those years. It was two guys shooting the breeze about the weather, chanting to Shiva, and relating stories of the great gurus of days past. It was somehow both reassuring and absurd, this crazy mix of knowledge and desire that we shared.

"Kathmandu, panch saal," I finally said, telling him I'd been in Kathmandu for five years, which wasn't exactly true, but when you added Goa and Benares into the mix... ah, it was all too complicated—

"Panch saal?" said the sadhu, looking at me with great deference. I was suddenly an elder in the community of wanderers, a man of experience and respect. He waited for me to go on, certain that I had some wisdom I might share with him to help him along his path.

"Yes, well," I said in English, "Kathmandu is one hell of a town."

He stared at me a long moment, not understanding a word, but then nodded in deep appreciation for my sage advice. Who knows? Maybe it was sagacious. Maybe he'd derive some hidden meaning from my observation that would someday alter his life. I truly hoped so.

"Jai, baba," I said as I took a last toke off the chillum, wished him a long life, and headed back to the Rose Garden. The sun would soon be up and I needed to get to the airport. It was time to leave Nepal.

Chapter 28

Mohini's Dance

So here we are, at the succulent garden in Golden Gate Park of all places, Mohini is all dolled up with a ceremonial wedding sari and all the attendant regalia—the nose ring, the hennaed palms, the ankle bracelets—and Tobias is equally done up in silk pajama pants, brocade kurta and even a touch of koal around his eyes to give him an even more crazed look of adoration, and then there's me, standing here with some piece of tattered embroidery that Mohini grabbed off the living room sofa as an afterthought, but I have to play the part as best I can because, are you ready, I'm the *best man,* that's right, I'm the best man at my own wedding, given that Tobias and I are, of course, the same person, okay, fine, just so long as I don't have to spend the wedding night with them, no, that's one twisted delight I'll happily forgo, let them go down any path they want, ridiculous as it may be, but this is not only stretching the bounds of marital propriety, it's stretching the laws of physics as well, but fine, I've done everything I could do, the warnings have been delivered, the cold water has been thrown on their effervescent bliss, and the bubble has been burst, but here we are anyway, right back where it all began—if only Mohini understood the irony of her marriage vows taking place at the very spot of Tobias's reincarnation!—and now here we go, the big Hindu wedding, what a joke, where are the elephants, the tigers, the ten thousand relatives and the out-of-tune brass band, no, Mohini says none of that matters, all that matters is the dance, it's a dance of devotion, a dance of everlasting love, a dance of eternal obedience— *just follow everything I do, Tobias*—sure, why not, he's been dancing to her tune since the moment they met, it only makes sense that they formalize it, so here we go, she strikes a pose, one hand along her cheek, the other parallel to the ground and Tobias follows her movements gesture for gesture, the hand, the arm, even the suggestive mudras she flashes his way, okay, I admit it, it *is* kind of cute, these two foolish lovers performing a mating dance to the setting sun, even the animals of the forest duck behind the bushes and slip beneath the water as if embarrassed by the seductive display, yes, this is what it's all about, holy matrimony, a union of the souls, Tobias and Mohini will take on the trials and tribulations of modern life together, they'll wander the dark paths of a troubled world illuminated by their internal light, and now Mohini lifts a leg and twirls in a circle, her toes pointed out with a delicate grace, rising, rising, as if pointing to the heavens, and Tobias follows her move for move, she holds her hip and he holds his, she touches her knee and he touches his, she taps her shoulder and he taps his, she raises her arm and he raises his, she twirls her hand and he twirls his, she touches her head and he touches his, and with this innocuous gesture, this innocent, inconsequential, meaningless movement of the hand, Tobias instantaneously reduces himself into a pile of ashes—*whaaaaaaat?*—it's not even a big pile, it's just a little smoking mound, that's all that's left of him, the Hindu legend has been fulfilled, and I look at Mohini and she seems quite pleased with herself—*did you really think I was about to marry a literary device?*—poor Tobias, smoldering away right next to a patch of aeonium, crassula and sedum, it's an ignoble end, this life of ours, ignoble and idiotic—*and what a pity, he was such a good lover, too*—oh, God, listen to her, and now, as I stare into the diminishing mound of ashes, I see images of ancestral figures beginning to escape into the ether, then stone carvings and lotus blossoms, and now Tobias's memories themselves are pulled from their roots and arise as if by a magician's hand, the reflections are floating by all mixed up and out of order, the sulfur pits of northern Honshu, the Styrofoam snow of Southampton, the raging bulls of Anjuna Beach, the cocaine on David Bowie's hand, the knife in Alejandro's palm, the wave of Carmen's wrist, and then, just like that, it all dissipates—*poof!*—the birds return to the trees, the fish are restored to the pond, the turtles revisit the rocks, and everything is exactly as it was, order is restored, gravity is re-engaged, the compass is reset, and all that's left is Mohini and me, I feel her eyes upon me, it's that enchanting look, that seductive stare—*so, what are you doing now?*—oh, God, tell me she's kidding—*because it's getting late and I'm getting hungry*—she can't be serious—*and I know this great little Indian restaurant*—at which moment a flock of birds flies off into the sunset—*"kee-yur-kee-yur,"* intones a red-shouldered hawk, *"chep-chep-chep,"* trumpets a yellow-rumped warbler, *"coo-coo-ca-choo,"* chants a black-bearded ringo starrbird—and as the final embers of Tobias's ashes scatter to the wind, Mohini raises her foot and the hundred tiny bells of her ankle bracelet chime in the breeze, it's a beautiful sound, something from a forgotten time when every tone of the Indian scale was known to have a specific intent, I feel pulled by the music and an almost uncontrollable desire to follow wherever it might lead, Mohini saunters up the path and I head for the Bamboo Pond, it's dark now and I can barely see a thing, oh,

God, what am I doing here, there's no Tobias to talk to, no stories to share, it's just me—*dear Universe, if there is a Universe, please help me, if you can help me*—and I search the pond for a clue, something that might guide me, and finally I see a little glimmer in the ripple of a wave, it's the reflection of a woman in the window of an apartment, she's looking out onto the street as if waiting for somebody, she has creamy skin and hair that reaches just to her shoulders, the waves radiate toward the shore and the building begins to shimmer, everything's in motion, it's hard to tell what's up and what's down, the windows move into one another, the roof droops and touches the garden, the fire escapes dance side to side, everything's alive, flowers are sprouting out of doorways, fish are swimming through living rooms, birds are flying across the bedroom walls, and I know I have a decision to make—*should I stay or should I go?*—I feel the push and pull of the past and the present as Mohini glances out the window one last time and draws the curtain closed on the bedroom, the apartment, and the reflection in the pond.